The Handbook for Scout Masters

Scout Masters

The Original 1914 Edition

Originally published in 1914 under the supervision of the Editorial Board Representing the National Council of the Boy Scouts of America.

First Skyhorse Publishing edition, 2020.

Skyhorse Publishing books may be purchased in bulk at special discounts for sales promotion, corporate gifts, fund-raising, or educational purposes. Special editions can also be created to specifications. For details, contact the Special Sales Department, Skyhorse Publishing, 307 West 36th Street, 11th Floor, New York, NY 10018 or info@ skyhorsepublishing.com.

Skyhorse® and Skyhorse Publishing® are registered trademarks of Skyhorse Publishing, Inc.®, a Delaware corporation. Visit our website at www. skyhorsepublishing.com.

10 9 8 7 6 5 4 3 2 1

Cover design by Kai Texel

Library of Congress Control Number: 2019954896

Print ISBN: 978-1-5107-5861-2
Ebook ISBN: 978-1-5107-5862-9

Printed in China

The Handbook for Scout Masters

The Original 1914 Edition

The Boy Scouts of America

Skyhorse Publishing

The Handbook for Scout Masters

The Boy Scouts of America

INTRODUCTION

In the early summer of 1911 we sent out our Boys' Handbook, which was most kindly received. Boys in all parts of the country have found the information of great value. Its use, however, disclosed the need of a supplemental book, the primary purpose of which should be to consider the principles and methods of Boys Work and Scouting, and to show Scout Masters how to use the material in the Boys' Handbook. This need was emphasized by the constant calls for information which came from all parts of the country to the office at National Headquarters.

In response to these calls this book was prepared and some thousand of copies in proof form were sent to Scout Masters and others, asking for candid criticism and suggestions as to how it could be made more useful. The response to this request showed a great deal of interest on the part of those who were actually engaged in Scouting, and many of the suggestions have been embodied in the book, which is now sent out in permanent form. It goes into the hands of the Scout Masters with the sincere hope that it will help them in maintaining the interest of their troops and in directing their activities along right lines. As in the Handbook for Boys, so in this book, we have placed the boy in the midst, and have tried to keep his interests in the forefront; for we realize that our purpose in this Boy Scout Movement is not to exploit methods, nor to glorify movements, nor to honor Scout Masters, but to lead boys into useful lives.

An examination of this book will show how we have tried to accomplish this purpose. In order that the Scout Masters might be intelligently informed concerning the movement of which they are so important a part, the National Organization is described; various suggestions are made for the purpose of promoting an effective local organization, and to bring about uniformity the scout requirements set forth in the Handbook are here elaborated so that they may be applied intelligently in the same manner in all places.

As a great many requests came in from Scout Masters

for advice as to how the meetings of their troop should be conducted, we have tried to meet them by our chapter on programs. These programs are intended to carry the troop progressively through the year, with indoor and outdoor activities. They are intended as suggestions and need not be followed in the order in which they are printed.

We are glad to have this opportunity of expressing our appreciation of the splendid services rendered by a host of friends in the preparation of the book; many of their suggestions have been incorporated in these pages. But we are especially anxious to acknowledge our indebtedness to Mr. John L. Alexander, formerly of our staff, Dr. Paul C. Philips, Dr. J. C. Elsom, Prof. Irving E. Vining, Mr. Samuel A. Moffat, Mr. Ormond E. Loomis, and Mr. George H. Merritt.

The task undertaken by the Boy Scouts of America is not an easy one. The appeal is made to so many different kinds of boys, and so much of our effort must necessarily be experimental, that we crave the indulgence and coöperation of the men, Scout Masters and others, who are working with us in our endeavor to help the boys of America into more purposeful lives and better citizenship.

THE BOY SCOUTS OF AMERICA.
William D. Murray,
George D. Pratt,
Frank Presbrey,
Editorial Board.

CONTENTS

CHAPTER I

ORGANIZATION

Origin of the Boy Scouts of America.

In the beginning of 1910 the idea of introducing the Boy Scout Movement along lines similar to those of the English Boy Scouts, which had been organized in 1907 and developed. under the personal supervision of Lieutenant-General Sir Robert S. S. Baden-Powell, was first proposed by Mr. W. D. Boyce of Chicago. Prior to this time a number of troops had been started in various parts of the country by men who had been impressed with the possibilities of the scheme, through reading Lieutenant-General Sir Robert Baden-Powell's English handbook, " Scouting for Boys." It is significant that Mr. Boyce's interest was occasioned because of an actual service rendered him in true Scout spirit by a London Boy Scout, who because of his obligation to do a good turn daily and the rule against the acceptance of tips, greatly astonished and impressed Mr. Boyce. After the conference with Sir Robert Baden-Powell he secured the coöperation of friends in Washington, D. C., and proceeded to incorporate an organization of the Boy Scouts of America under the laws of the District of Columbia. This was effectively accomplished on February 8th, 1910. Headquarters for the Boy Scouts of America were temporarily established at 124 East 28th Street, with the coöperation of representatives from a number of National organizations having headquarters in New York City.

Growth and Development.

Simultaneously with this effort, other organizations established National Headquarters for themselves. Happily, however, before the middle of July, 1910, all of these organizations with the exception of the American Boy Scouts merged with the Boy Scouts of America. It was largely through the efforts of Mr. Edgar M. Robinson that the different organizations were brought together. From the very beginning he saw the possibilities of the Scout movement; his wide experience in boys' work enabled him' to give wise counsel in his endeavor to have the movement inaugurated under satisfactory conditions.   The continuance of the American Boy Scouts in the field proved to be a source of embarrassment and greatly retarded the proper development of the movement in this country.   Furthermore it was one of the important factors in causing a misunderstanding as to the true aims and purposes of the movement because so much emphasis was placed by the American Boy Scouts upon military drill and training.

Through the influence of Adjutant-General Verbeck, one of the National Scout Commissioners, the National Scouts disbanded early in the year.

The National Council.

Early in the summer of 1910, it was deemed wise to secure for the movement a more representative and substantial backing. A conference was called of representatives from all existing organizations who might be interested in the development of this new organization. As a result of this meeting, at which thirty different existing organizations were represented, a committee on permanent Organization was appointed. This committee consisted of Ernest Thompson Seton, Chairman; Lee F. Hanmer, Secretary; George D. Pratt, Treasurer; Dr. Luther H. Gulick, Jacob A. Riis, Edgar M. Robinson, Colin H. Livingstone, Daniel Carter Beard, Adjutant-General William Verbeck and Col. Peter S. Bomus. As a result of the deliberations of this committee a working plan of the present organization was developed. This puts the administration of the Boy Scouts of America as an association in the hands of a National Council working through an Executive Board. This National Council is composed of representative and prominent men who are selected for their positions by Local Councils throughout the country. Each member pays an annual membership fee of at least five dollars a year. The officers of this National Council are an Honorary President, two Honorary Vice-Presidents, a President, five Vice-Presidents and a Treasurer. There are also a National Scout Commissioner and a Chief Scout who are honorary members of all standing committees.

Fortunately, about this time, the infant organization was honored by a visit from Lieutenant-General Sir Robert

S. S. Baden-Powell. A dinner was arranged at the Waldorf Astoria in New York City. The presence of the General and the publicity gained did much to focus the attention of the American people on the organization as the real organization of the Boy Scout movement in this country.

Early Definite Accomplishments.

The demand for information from all parts of the country compelled the hasty production of a mass of literature giving an outline of the movement. Six bulletins were written and a revised edition of the English handbook for boys hastily prepared under the direction of Mr. Ernest Thompson Seton. The organization will ever be under obligation to Mr. Seton for his unremitting zeal and effort to produce this book and for his willingness to send it out in an uncompleted form in order to meet the insistent requests from the field.

President Taft cordially consented to serve as Honorary President of the organization and Col. Theodore Roosevelt as Honorary Vice-President. Col. Theodore Roosevelt and Honorable Gifford Pinchot have become more closely identified with the movement by accepting membership on the chief scout staff, Colonel Roosevelt as Chief Scout Citizen and Mr. Pinchot as Chief Scout Woodsman. Other men of national reputation accepted membership on the National Council. An unusual group of efficient men consented to serve as members of the Executive Board. They not only gave freely of their money but generously gave much time at this important period in the development of the Movement.

Beginning January 1st, 1911, permanent headquarters were secured in the Fifth Avenue Building and an executive officer was employed. The first meeting of the National Council was held February 14th and 15th at Washington, D. C. The members assembled in the East Room of the White House and were addressed by President Taft. In connection with the meeting of the National Council, there was a conference of Scout Masters and Scout Commissioners.

The Executive Board and Its Duties.

At each annual meeting the National Council elects an Executive Board of eighteen members, who have immediate charge of all the business of the organization. This Board, having also legislative powers, makes its own rules, grants charters to Local Councils and credentials to Scout Commissioners and Scout Masters, copyrights badges, insignia, and other scout designs, arranges for their manufacture and distribution, selects designs for uniforms and scout equipment, and appoints an executive officer or Chief Scout Executive and such other officers and employees as may seem desirable.

National Headquarters.

These latter officers and employees have charge of the bulk of the national business of the organization and the routine work of the National Headquarters. They hold their positions at the pleasure of the Executive Board.

The Chief Scout and His Staff.

Also upon the recommendation of the Executive Board, the National Council elects a Chief Scout, who is the honorary head of the organization. He appoints and is the active director of his own staff, made up of experts on the different phases of Scouting. This staff consists of the Chief Scout offices of Surgeon, Woodman, Stalker, Camp Master, Citizen, Director of Health, Director of Athletics and Director of Chivalry. These officers are appointed with the approval of the Executive Board, and are specifically charged with the development of the Scout programs.

The National Scout Commissioner and Staff.

The National Scout Commissioner is the head of a staff of official representatives of the various national organizations engaged in work with boys and also interested in the Scout program. The Commissioner and his staff adapt the activities to the needs of the groups represented, and work for the development of a high grade of leadership in boys' work.

The Community and the Local Council.

The promotion of the Boy Scout Movement is essentially a community enterprise. It is the community's opportunity to reach the boy with corrective influences for character-building and good citizenship. To give the work proper direction, a governing committee, known as the Local Council, is needed in each community where Scouting is developed. Like the National Council these are composed of men who are seeking for the boys of the community the very best things possible, and who are representative of all community interests. The Local Council, through Scouting, makes a valuable asset of the boy; it makes him coöperative in promoting the interest of the community and places a value on the minority years of his citizenship life; it is proof of the community's interest in the healthful, normal, mental and moral development of its boys.

Organization Policies

In proceeding with the organization of Local Councils, the committee should observe closely the following policies outlined by the National Council:

1. The boundaries of a town, city or county council shall be determined by the boundaries adopted by such town, city or county for political purposes.

2. Any village or town just outside of or adjoining a city having a Local Council may affiliate with such Local Council by making application to the National Council to do so.

3. Charters for county councils are granted with the understanding that such councils have no jurisdiction over any city council already organized within the county and further that the right is reserved by the National Council to grant separate charters to any other city within the county when in its judgment it is for the best interest of the Scout movement to do so.

4. The National Council reserves the right to authorize the establishment of provisional Local Councils for territories larger than one county, such Councils to be recognized as provisional and temporary in character; and that any county, town or city within such provisional area may have the privilege of withdrawing from this temporary organization upon the approval of the National Council.

5. It is the conviction of the National Council that any federation of Local Councils and the formation of district organizations at this time would not be for the best interests of the Scout movement, and that it would be unwise at the present time to authorize the formation of state organizations in any part of the country.

Methods of Organization of Local Councils.

In order to understand thoroughly the duties and activities of the Local Council, it is needful to know how such a council is organized. A small group of six or seven men who believe in the scout idea and wish to start the movement in their community, should meet as a " Committee of Organization," to take such steps as are necessary to awaken an interest in the movement, and bring about the regular organization of a Local Council. Details of the plan to be pursued should be carefully considered, and the work divided among the men present. In proceeding to organize a Local Council, the following steps must be emphasized: —

The Publicity Campaign.

First — The necessity for a community-wide publicity campaign in an effort to inform the public generally about the Scout Movement is all-important. This may be accomplished through the medium of the local newspapers, by personal interviews and, by public addresses. Newspaper articles may be written, outlining the general scope of the Boy Scout Movement, stating its aim and objects, and its relation to other institutions; also showing the opportunity it presents a community to interest boys in character-building activities and make them an asset in city life. It should be clearly stated in newspapers and interviews that the Boy Scout Movement is not antagonistic to any civic enterprise, but rather seeks to coöperate with all other good movements in the interest of the boy. The Movement is wholly *non-sectarian* and plans to work with every sect and creed alike; it is *non-military,* and seeks to promote Peace Scouting, and to develop educational character-building for good citizenship. It is wholly *non-partisan.* It cannot favor one interest against another and cannot countenance interference on any debatable questions, whether social, religious or political. It seeks to make the boy a more useful and appreciative son to his parents or to those to whom he owes his home comforts, a more diligent and obedient student in his school life, a more valuable aid to the community in promoting its material progress and protection, and a more efficient and better prepared young man in development for future citizenship and the pleasures and hardships of mature existence.

Coöperation with Other Interests.

By personal interviews, the committee on organization should seek to enlist the interest and coöperation of the principals and superintendents of public and private schools, representatives of churches, Sunday Schools, boys' clubs (both denominational and undenominational) directors of playground associations, settlement houses, etc., and wherever possible, should endeavor to present the work by addresses in churches, schools, city clubs, or other organizations interested in the welfare of boys. Suggestive material for newspaper articles and lantern slides for illustrated lectures are always gladly furnished by National Headquarters.

Membership of Representative Citizens.

Second — A selected list of representative citizens should be interviewed to obtain their consent to serve as members of the Local Council. All different creeds and sects should be recognized and all organizations dealing and working with boy-life should be represented. In case any such organization or institution forms a troop to carry out the Boy Scout program and uses the name of the Boy Scouts of America, such organization should be invited to designate an adult representative other than the Scout Master to serve as a member of the Local Council. Such an organization should be in honor bound to have its troop and Scout Master conform to the regulations made by the Local and National Councils. The following is a list of some of the sources from which to select members of the Local Council: — civic authorities, boys' clubs, charity associations, juvenile courts, public schools, Sunday Schools, church clubs, men's brotherhoods, Young Men's Hebrew Associations, Young Men's Catholic Associations, Young Men's Christian Associations, playground associations, boys' brigades, social workers' clubs, medical societies, settlement houses, business and professional men, the Press, the police forces, fire departments, military organizations, and public and private institutions for boys.

Size of the Council.

The number of men composing the Local Council should be determined by the size of the community. In a small town there should be at least ten members; larger com-

munities may have from twenty-five to one hundred and
fifty or more.

A Constitution.

The committee on organization should further be prepared to submit to the newly organized Council a Constitution and By-Laws for their approval. It is deemed advisable that the following Constitution be adopted without
alteration; the By-Laws, however, should be changed to
meet local requirements. As a suggestion the following
Constitution is herewith submitted : —

SUGGESTED CONSTITUTION AND BY-LAWS
For a Local Council of
THE BOY SCOUTS OF AMERICA.

ARTICLE I.— NAME.

The name of this organization shall be the ....
Council of the Boy Scouts of America.

ARTICLE II.— OBJECT.

The object of the organization shall be to promote the
general welfare of the Boy Scout Movement within the territory specified in the charter granted under the direction
and with the coöperation of the National Council of the
Boy Scouts of America.

ARTICLE III.— MEMBERSHIP.

This Council shall be composed of .... members,
representing the civic, business, educational, philanthropi-
cal, religious, and other interests of the territory as specified.

ARTICLE IV.— OFFICERS AND ELECTIONS.

Section 1. The officers of the Council shall consist of
a President, one or more Vice-Presidents, Secretary, Treasurer, and Scout Commissioner.

Section 2. The regular election shall be held at the
annual meeting to be held some time during the month of
October in each calendar year, and all officers shall serve
until the next annual election or until their successors shall
have been elected.

Section 3. Any vacancies occurring in the membership of the Local Council or among the offices thereof may be filled temporarily by the Executive Committee, but shall only be filled permanently by action of the Council.

Article V.— Meetings.

Section 1. The Council shall hold at least two stated meetings in each calendar year on the third Tuesday of .... and ...., and the meeting in .... shall be the annual meeting of the organization.

Section 2. Due notice of all regular meetings shall be sent to all members of the Council.

Section 3. Special meetings of the Council may be called by the President upon his own authority and shall be called by the President and Secretary upon petition of any five members of the Council, providing that notice in writing be given each member not less than two calendar days before such meeting.

Section 4. A quorum shall be as specified in the By-Laws.

Article VI.— Committees.

Section 1. The standing committees shall be an Executive Committee, a Finance Committee, a Nominating Committee, and a Court of Honor.

Section 2. The Executive Committee shall consist of the officers of the Council, who shall serve respectively as chairman, vice-chairman, and secretary of the Committee, together with such other members elected at the regular annual election.

The duties of the Executive Committee shall be as follows : —

(a) To pass upon the qualifications of Scout Masters and Assistant Scout Masters on recommendation of the proper authorities in charge of local troops.

(b) To register troops, patrols, and scouts.

(c) To pass upon recommendations of the Court of Honor to the National Council for the award of badges and other honors.

(d) To recommend ways and means of giving instruction in Scoutcraft to Scout Masters.

Section 3. The Finance Committee shall consist of such members as may be appointed by the President.

Section 4. The Nominating Committee shall consist of three members selected by the Executive Board not later than one month before the Annual Meeting.

Section 5. The Court of Honor shall consist of at least three members appointed by the President with the approval of the Executive Committee.

It shall be the duty of the Court of Honor: —

(a)   To conduct examinations for the various merit badges and such other Scout tests as may be prescribed in the By-Laws.

(b)   To investigate and recommend all claims for honor medals or other special awards.

(c)   To pass upon appeals made from Scout Masters' decisions.

ARTICLE VII.— REPRESENTATION ON NATIONAL COUNCIL.

(The article covering this subject should be framed to fit conditions in each case. One representative on the National Council is allowed to each Local Council where there are five or more Scout Masters, with one additional member for each 1,000 enrolled Scouts.)

ARTICLE VIII.— DUES.

Each member of the Local Council shall pay annually the sum of $—— as dues, $1 of which shall be transmitted to the Treasurer of the National Council for the work of the national organization with the understanding that each member will receive a yearly subscription to the semi-monthly bulletin, *Scouting* and the official magazine, *Boys' Life*.

ARTICLE IX.— AMENDMENTS.

This constitution having been adopted in accordance with the charter granted by the National Council may be amended upon motion of the representative of the Local Council at any of the regular meetings of the National Council.

Public Meeting for Plans of Organization.

Third — A public meeting should be arranged for at which the entire plan of organization should be submitted. This meeting should be for adults only. Sufficient notice should be given through the daily papers in order that everyone, who is at all interested in the scout work, may be able to attend and take part. Wherever necessary, special notices should be sent by mail. Greatest care should be exercised both in choosing the date and in the proper selection of a meeting place. The time of the meeting should not conflict with anything else of general interest to the public; and the meeting place ought to be centrally located in order to be available to all parts of the community alike, and should be wholly non-partisan in order not to give cause for prejudice to any class at this very important stage in the development of the work.

Need for a Clear Conception of Purposes and Results

In planning the program of this meeting, everything should be done with a view to giving the people of the community a clear conception of the aims of the Movement and its unusual possibilities for good among boys, so as to enlist their friendship and secure their sympathetic support. The chairman of the meeting should be one of the most representative men available in the community, but preferably not connected with the militia. Military men have greatly aided the Movement with their support, but it is essential because the character of the Movement is Peace Scouting, to have men as officers in the Council who are not connected with the military, so that the ideas of peaceful scouting activity which we seek to promote, may find greater favor and more hearty support in the minds of the general public. Such men are usually very busy, but our greatest American citizens are none too busy to give such service to the boys of their communities, if they can be assured that by serving in this capacity, they will assist in forwarding this work among the boys. Arrangements should be made well in advance to secure an inspiring speaker to give an address on the Boy Scout Movement, which will lead up to the need of a Local Council. It is essential that the speaker be well versed in the principles and methods of the organization, so as to be able to answer questions on this subject. Such a man may be obtained from some adjacent city in which scout work has already been organized or the National Headquarters may be able to assist in securing a speaker. Whenever it is possible the

National Headquarters will always be glad to lend such aid.

Purpose of the Meeting.

One of the local men, preferably a member of the " Committee on Organization," should outline the purpose of the meeting and state fully what steps have been taken to start and develop a scout organization. The nominations of the Committee on Organization for the membership of the Council and its officers should be given, and opportunity extended to those present to submit additional nominations.

Officers of the Local Council and Their Duties.

The officers of the Local Council are a President, from one to five Vice-Presidents, a Secretary, a Treasurer, an Executive Committee of five or more, a Court of Honor of five, and a Scout Commissioner. The duties of the President, Vice-Presidents, Secretary, and Treasurer are the same as those of similar officers in other organizations. The Executive Committee should consist of these officers and as many more business men as may be necessary for the proper promotion of local affairs. The Court of Honor of a Local Council passes upon the examinations of Scouts for Merit Badges and reports upon such cases through the Scout Commissioner to the National Council. It investigates all cases of life-saving and presents affidavits to the National Court of Honor for the award of Honor Medals. It also acts as a final court to pass judgment on appeals from opinions and decisions of Scout Masters and their Assistants.

The Local Council Charter.

At the earliest date, after the organization of a Local Council and the selection of a Scout Commissioner, application should be made to National Headquarters for a local charter and for the official appointment of the Scout Commissioner. In making this application, a complete list of officers and members of the Local Council should be submitted together with a statement showing what business and religious interests each member represents in the community. All requests for charters should be submitted on a regular application blank which will be supplied by the National Council upon request. Charters when granted are issued for one year and must be renewed annually thereafter.

There are two general classes of Local Councils, based upon the development of the Scout work in the community.

Two Classes of Local Councils

Local Councils are divided into two classes — First and Second Class.

A First Class Council maintains an office and provides the services of one or more employed officials to give all of their time to the promotion of Scout work in that district.

Councils of the Second Class are those organized in communities where the work is not sufficiently developed to make necessary the employment of a Scout Executive to give all of his time to the work.

Each Local Council having five or more registered troops is entitled to elect one representative to the National Council and an additional member for every one thousand boys enrolled as Scouts.

Local Councils shall transmit annually to the National Council a sum equal to at least twenty-five cents for each enrolled Scout as provided for in the membership plan, and a registration fee equal to one dollar for each member of the Local Council and other Scout officials. Such registration fee will entitle each member of the Local Council and other Scout officials to receive the semi-monthly bulletin *Scouting* and the official magazine *Boys' Life*.

National Council.

The National Council is made up of representatives of the Local Councils and such others as are elected in accordance with the articles of incorporation and the Constitution and By-Laws and includes representatives of the various agencies and organizations definitely interested in work for boys, the president and ex-presidents of the United States, the governors of the various states and other men distinguished for achievement in boys' work or public service.

Each member of the National Council pays an annual membership fee of at least five dollars.

Scout Movement direction and act as the local authority on all Scoutcraft matters. In almost every community there is some man who has had considerable experience in out-of-door life, whose natural qualifications for leadership would commend him for the position of Scout Commissioner.

Scout Executives.

The Scout program has proven practical as a civic enterprise, because, where properly organized, every phase of boy life is being reached by its activities. It is adapting itself not only to the wealthy boys of the community, but to the boys of the slums, to the news-boys and foreign boys alike. It can be successfully introduced and promoted without the expenditure of a large sum of money for equipment and running expenses. A budget of $2000 or more a year will enable any city to set up an effective organization and employ a Scout Executive. It will be seen at once that the cost is infinitesimal compared with the possibilities for good citizenship which the Movement offers.

The Scout Masters, for the most part, are volunteer workers, and when they give one evening a week, with perhaps a Saturday afternoon in addition, to the boys in their care, they cannot be expected to do much original work in the preparation for Scout meetings. They want to feel that there is someone who knows Scoutcraft better than they, to whom they can go for advice and help. If this advice and help is not forthcoming without a great deal of effort on their part, they are likely to become discouraged and give up their scout work. Therefore, while the Scout Commissioner is usually a volunteer worker, it is essential that he should be able to give considerable time to the work, so that it shall have proper supervision. When a Local Council has secured the services of a capable and efficient man to serve as a Scout Commissioner, he should make proper application to National Headquarters for his official commission. Application blanks will be mailed upon request.

The Scout Commissioner and His Duties.

The duties of the Scout Commissioner, who acts as local authority on Scoutcraft and directs the work of the Scout Masters in his community, are really fourfold. He is first of all an executive in his relation to the Local Council. Secondly he acts as the representative of the National

Headquarters. In this official capacity he must investigate all applications for Scout Masters' Certificates, seeing that these are issued only to men of good character whose influence will be uplifting; and he must safeguard the sale of the official badges and uniforms so that only boys who have passed the various Scout examinations receive them. Thirdly, as a leader of Scout Masters he organizes and presides at the Scout Masters' Council, which should be composed of the officers of the Local Council and the Scout Masters in the community; plans Scout Masters' meetings; takes the initiative in the promotion and development of new work; outlines courses of instruction for Scout Masters and their patrol leaders; arranges for summer schools for Scout Masters; plan inter-troop meets, games, camps, and in general assists the Scout Masters in putting all the work of the community on a uniform basis. Lastly, the Scout Commissioner acts as an organizer, introducing the scout work in unorganized districts under his jurisdiction, and otherwise continuing the general policy of promotion of the scout work as outlined by the "Committee on Organization," namely, in keeping up the interest of the public through newspaper articles.

The Scout Executive.

The Scout Executive is the employed officer of the Local Council who devotes his entire time to carrying out the program for Scouting as outlined by the Executive Committee. His duties in the field are defined by the Executive Committee, and he is responsible to the Scout Commissioner for carrying out such activities as may be delegated to him. He should be a man of high ideals and a zealous worker with boys; the employment of such a man has been found absolutely necessary in the larger cities of the country, in order to carry on the work of the district with efficiency and despatch. In some localities, on account of local conditions, the offices of Commissioner and Scout Executive are combined by the vote of the Local Council.

The Scout Master — His Duties and Responsibilities.

The officer of the organization in immediate charge of the boys is the Scout Master. He must be at least twenty-one years of age, and is usually chosen because of good moral character and interest in the development of boys. He should be genuine in his own life, have the natural ability to lead, and should command the boys' respect and obedience. He need not be an expert on Scoutcraft, but he should at least by personal study and effort seek to keep himself enough in advance of the boys to be prepared on the different topics of study as they are considered in the program; moreover, a good Scout Master will easily progress through his mature comprehension of the work and by his own initiative, and will discover experts to aid him in the various activities. As a leader of the troop, the Scout Master is responsible for its meetings, outings, and general program; he supervises the work of patrol leaders and prepares the members of the troop to take their various scout examinations. He is the representative of the Local Council in charge of a troop, and is responsible to the Council in carrying out the Scout program as outlined in the official "Handbook for Boys," and for the use of badges, uniforms, and other Scout equipment; but his independence and initiative in his manner of carrying on his work is not to be questioned. It is essential that he consult with the Local Council or Scout Commissioner on every important question that may affect the movement, either locally or nationally.

The Method of Obtaining a Scout Master's Commission.

A man may apply for commission as Scout Master by filling in properly a blank form similar to that of the Scout Commissioner. This, duly made out, is filed with the Secretary of the Local Council. It is then the duty of the Secretary to bring the application before the Executive Committee of the Local Council for its approval, and, having secured such approval, to send the application to the National Headquarters with a request that a certificate of commission be granted. Where there is no Local Council established, the applicant for the Scout Master's commission should send the application blank direct to National Headquarters. Then upon proper investigation as to character and reputation of the applicant, the application is passed upon by the Executive Board of the National Council. Blank applications will be mailed at once upon request.

Scout Masters' commissions are granted for a probationary period of six months, during which time the Scout Master has an opportunity to satisfy himself as to his personal qualifications for the work and demonstrate to the Local Council his ability as a leader of boys. At the expiration of this period the commission may be continued in force for the balance of the year, and thereafter renewed annually upon the recommendation of the Local Council on condition that the Scout Master has kept up an active interest in the work, and has provided the Local Council with such regular reports as may be required.

Assistant Scout Masters.

When the Scout Master cannot give all the time he would like to in the direction of scout work with his troop, and especially where the membership is large and the boys are anxious to meet oftener than the Scout Master can attend, assistance can be secured through the appointment of Assistant Scout Masters. In such case, these Assistants must be at least eighteen years of age, of good moral character, and acceptable to the Scout Master and Local Council. It is the Assistant Scout Master's duty to take the place of the Scout Master in the latter's absence, and to carry out the program under his suggestions and direction. Often young men are appointed to such position after they have reached the age of eighteen and have already been First Class Scouts; the step up from one rank to the other is a natural promotion for the energetic and efficient First Class Scout. The Assistant Scout Master fills out an application for commission on a blank very similar in form to that for Scout Masters, and the procedure of application, consideration by the National Executive Board, and appointment by official certificate is the same.

Local Troop Committee.

The organization of a Troop Committee is as important as the selection of a Scout Master. The applicant for the Scout Master's commission is required to organize a Troop Committee, consisting of three or five representative men of the community, preferably members of the organization with which the troop is connected, to supervise the work of the troop. This Committee should endorse the application of the Scout Master and agree to coöperate with him in carrying out the Scout program should a commission be granted.

The formation of such a committee is of great value in securing permanency to the work. It will be found of great assistance to the Scout Master in determining policies and otherwise advising and aiding him with the work of the troop.

The assurance that three men are to work with the Scout Master throughout the year will add greatly to the success of the work of the troop. It will give added confidence to the parents of the boys and reassure the National Council that the Scout program is being carried out in accordance with the official handbook, thus assuring to the boys the full benefits and pleasure which the Scout program makes possible.

In the event of his resignation as Scout Master, this Troop Committee takes charge of all troop property and directs the work of the troop until such time as they may be able to secure a permanent Scout Master.

Each Troop Committee is entitled to elect one representative to the Local Council.

Troops and Patrols.

The Boy Scouts, themselves, are organized into troops and their subdivisions, the patrols. A patrol consists of eight boys, one of whom becomes the patrol leader, and another the assistant patrol leader. A troop consists of three or more patrols, but preferably three, as that seems to be the most efficient for working purposes, and a Scout Master can do a great deal better work with a small group of boys than with a large one. It is one of the emphatic rules of the National Organization that boys under the age of twelve years must not be enrolled.

Each Boy Scout pays an annual membership fee of twenty-five cents.

Collection of Dues.

Each troop pays annually to the National Council as a registration and membership fee a sum equivalent to twenty-five cents for each boy and Assistant Scout Master enrolled. The minimum registration of a troop is three dollars. However, when there are less than twelve boys enrolled, additional boys may be registered at any time within one year from the date of registration to complete the full quota of twelve boys without the payment of additional dues. If there are more than twelve boys, twenty-five cents additional to the three dollars must be paid for each boy to be enrolled.

Where there is a Local Council this registration is transmitted through the officials of the Council — otherwise it is sent direct to the National Headquarters of the Boy Scouts of America, 200 Fifth Avenue, New York City. Blanks are provided for this purpose.

From the troop registration fee, one dollar and a quarter is set aside at National Headquarters each year to pay for the registration and certificate of the Scout Master and for one year's subscription to the semi-monthly bulletin *Scouting* and the official magazine *Boys' Life*. The balance of the fund is used to pay for the registration and certificates for members of the troop and for the expenses of the National Organization. It is recommended that the members of the troop as individuals or collectively earn the money with which to pay their registration fee.

Additional Names.

Blanks are provided for the registration of additional boys who join the troop at any time after the troop has been officially registered. Twenty-five cents per boy is paid for each unless twelve boys were not registered with the original registration.

Troop Affiliations.

Patrols and troops are usually organized in connection with a Sunday School, boys' club, playground, public school, settlement house, or other local institution. In this case the meeting place is furnished by the organization introducing the Scout work. Under special circumstances and where it is impossible to make use of existing institutions, troops are sometimes organized independently among the boys of the neighborhood. In such case, the first duty of the prospective Scout Master is to secure a club room or meeting place where regular weekly meetings can be held. Better results, however, are generally secured when troops are connected with some well-established institution.

Preliminary Troop Meeting.

When arranging a preliminary meeting for the organization of a troop, publicity should be avoided, as otherwise there will probably be more applicants than can be well managed at the preliminary meetings. It is always best to start with a few boys, preferably a patrol, and develop gradually in size and efficiency. A Scout Master should never begin with more boys than can easily be handled and given the first lessons in Scouting. At this first meeting it will usually be found that a goodly proportion of the boys already know something about Scouting, and therefore they should understand that a troop is to be organized because of their personal interest in the Scouting work. They should be put at ease, and their interest and enthusiasm should be encouraged and developed as much as possible. The method of developing the organization should always be natural rather than artificial. Starting with the knowledge already possessed by the boys and their awakened enthusiasm as a basis upon which to build up the Scout work, the Scout Master should proceed naturally in succeeding meetings to enlarge their interest, so as to include the many other things connected with Scouting.

How to Start.

At the first meeting, after furnishing the boys with application blanks to be filled in and signed by their parents, it is best to arrange for a definite date of meeting for the purpose of definitely organizing patrols. In a number of places it has proved successful to adjourn this second meeting long enough to allow sufficient time for the training of leaders, who will assist with the organization at the next meeting. Suppose there are twenty-four boys at this first meeting. As soon as practicable six of these boys should be selected as leaders and assistants and organized as a Scout Patrol. Then the training of these boys in the Scout principles should be begun at once, preparing them for the Tenderfoot Requirements. When they have successfully passed the examination, the first regular meeting should be called and the whole troop organized into patrols. In this way the twenty-four boys may be formed into three patrols of eight boys each with a trained patrol leader and assistant patrol leader in charge of each. The fact that these leaders have passed the Tenderfoot requirement will give them prestige among the other boys. The leaders should be given real responsibility: they should feel that their special task is to teach, influence, and lead the boys of their patrol. In assigning the boys to the patrols it is advisable to group boys as near the same age as possible, taking into consideration the natural instincts of the boys and their desire for association with one another. This is often a more important factor than age.

Troop Meetings.

It is desirable that troop meetings be held at least twice a month,— for instance, the first and third Fridays of the month. On the intervening Friday nights, the patrols could meet separately either at Scout headquarters or at a Scout's home, and one afternoon, preferably on a Saturday, be set aside for outdoor Scouting. It is important that the evening meetings should be held on a night that will suit the convenience of most of the boys, and at the same time will not interfere with their regular school work. The Scout Master should be present at these meetings, or, when absent, be represented by a competent Assistant Scout Master. It is dangerous to have Scout meetings without the presence of an efficient adult. It is essential that these meetings be held regularly. Scout meetings should be conducted with order and decorum. The boys should be taught the value of parliamentary law in all of their proceedings. There should be a special method adopted for opening and closing all sessions. Minutes of every meeting should be kept, so that proper reports may be submitted from time to time to the Local Council. Every meeting should have its purpose, so that it may be conducted with profit to the boys.

It is desirable not to take up too much time with instruction. If talks are to be given on First Aid, Signaling, Woodcraft, or any other subject, these talks should not continue longer than fifteen minutes. The rest of the time should be taken up with Scout games or with a social program. A right proportion of reality and romance is essential.

The " Daily Good Turn."

From the very beginning the importance of the " Daily Good Turn " and the principles of the Scout law should be emphasized. A newly organized troop is apt to be impressed with the pleasurable features of Scouting, and to believe that its chief aim is to have a good time. The boy must be led to realize that much more is expected of a Scout than any other boy in the community, and that he should make himself useful as far as a boy may do so. He should know that there is lots of hard work to be done, and that the harder the work, the more good it will do him and the greater the fun.

The Patrol Leader.

The patrol leader is one of the members of a patrol, and may be selected either by appointment by the Scout Master or elected by the patrol. It is his duty to aid the Scout Master with the work of the patrol, in keeping patrol records of the individual members or in performing such other duties as the Scout Master may require. He is responsible for the discipline of his patrol to the Scout Master, who is his superior officer. In carrying out his work, the patrol leader may have as an assistant one of the other members of his patrol.

The Scout Scribe.

Troop records giving details of the progress of the boys enrolled are invaluable to the Local and National Organizations. A complete set of records should therefore be kept by every troop. Inasmuch as the Scout Master himself may not be able to give the time required in the preparation of data of this kind, it is important that one of the members of the troop be chosen as Scout Scribe or Troop Secretary. Any member elected to such a position may feel proud of the honor conferred upon him by being appointed as the reporter of his troop. At the same time the service he renders will relieve the Scout Master of considerable work and be the means of developing and training one of the members of the troop in business efficiency. This position is of equal importance with that of Patrol Leader or any other officer.

The Scout.

Any boy 12 years of age or over is eligible to become a Scout. He should make application to the Scout Commissioner, who will place him in a troop in the neighborhood in which he lives, or will assist him in organizing a troop among the boys of his neighborhood. The only requirements are that he knows: —

1. The Scout law, sign, salute and significance of the badge.
2. The composition and history of the national flag and the customary form of respect due to it.
3. Tie four out of the following knots: — Square, reef, sheet bend, bow-line, fishermen's, sheep-shank, halter, clove hitch, timber hitch, or two half hitches.

The Scout is also required to take the Scout oath.

Things to Remember.

There are several things with which every Scout Master should be familiar in organizing a new troop, namely the official words of caution sent out to each Scout Master through the medium of books, bulletins, and Scout papers from the National Headquarters. These five cautionary measures follow: —

Start Efficiently.

1. In organizing, begin on a small scale. Do not undertake a greater task than can easily be done with credit. It is better to begin Scouting with a few older boys, giving them careful training in the principles of the movement, so that they in turn may render some assistance in promoting the work among other boys.

Keep Correct Age-limit.

2. Do no enroll boys *under twelve years* of age. They do not stick and will only lessen the interest of the older members who really need what the Scout work can give them. Scouting is a comprehensive plan of activities to enlist and enlarge the interest and to help the development particularly of the adolescent boys; and boys under twelve are generally too young to understand seriously the principles of Scouting or be materially helped by the movement.

Build Strong Impression of Scout Principles.

3. Do not fail to impress upon the boys the importance of the Scout Oath, Scout Laws, and the requirements for the various degrees. While there is some danger in making the examination so hard as to discourage the class of boys who need the work most, yet you must guard against any tendency to make the tests too easy.

Be Original in Meetings.

4. Do not undertake at the beginning to give the boys everything there is in Scoutcraft. Work out your own plan with the boys from time to time, carefully avoiding a stereotyped form of meeting at each session, and always reserving something of interest for the next meeting.

Urge Ideal of Peace Scouting.

5. The primary object of the Boy Scouts of America is not military, but Peace Scouting and educational character-building for good citizenship.

The Scout Masters' School.

In every community where two or more troops have been organized it is advisable that a Scout Masters' Council be formed and that bi-weekly or monthly conferences be held for the discussions of local problems under the direction of the Scout Commissioner. In some cities, schools for Scout Masters have been successfully conducted. Here the Scout Master learns of plans that have met with success in other troops, and gains helpful suggestions about problems that confront him in the conduct of his own work. National Headquarters will be glad to furnish suggestions forth e promotion of such courses or render whatever help may be needed for the solution of local problems.

In the larger cities of the country, leadership training for Scout Masters is provided by means of small district and neighborhood conferences as a more effective method of training the individual Scout Master, in preference to the larger Scout Masters' meetings, which include all the Scout Masters within the city.

National Anniversary Week.

The week beginning with the eighth day of February has been set apart as Anniversary Week of the Boy Scouts of America. During this week a special program is arranged for the purpose of bringing to the attention of the community the aim and scope of the Scout Movement throughout the United States and other countries.

In presenting the Nation-wide aspect of the work, emphasis is placed upon the possibilities of the Movement in developing the idea of the brotherhood of man and in proving a positive factor in the promotion of universal peace.

During the week a special troop meeting is held at which

Scouts are given an opportunity to do one great " Good Turn " for boys who are not Scouts, by making a troop contribution for Boy Scout work in unorganized sections of the country. This contribution usually consists of the regularly weekly dues of the patrol or troop. A special program is furnished each year by the National Council.

CHAPTER II

SCOUT REQUIREMENTS

Test Requirements.

Hardly a day passes but that one or more Scouts write to National Headquarters asking for additional information about some one of the requirements for the Tenderfoot, Second Class or First Class Scout tests. All the requirements for the different Scout ranks are fully outlined on pages 29–32 of the "Handbook for Boys."

Tenderfoot Requirements.

In discussing this subject, however, it should be understood that no deviation from the requirements for these degrees as set forth in the Handbook will be permitted. During the past four years, numerous requests for exceptions have been considered by the Committee on Requirements, but no case has been presented that has warranted the establishment of so serious a precedent. It is very important that the standard of requirements be maintained and that boys in all parts of the country be required to pass the same set of tests in order to be enrolled as Second Class or First Class Scouts. In fact, the Scout badge should give assurance that the boy wearing it is capable of doing the things that are the measure of a Scout. Even if excused by the Scout Master from passing one of the required tests a Scout would feel that he was sailing under false colors if forced to confess his inability to do that particular thing. Even if the requirement seems hard, persistent effort and the exercise of a little patience should enable one boy to meet the requirements as well as any other boy. It should always be kept in mind that what has been accomplished by one can usually be accomplished by another fellow if he but *wills* to do it.

Very frequently some Scout who finds it hard to learn to swim appeals to his Scout Master to write to the National Headquarters for a substitute. This is wrong. Every Scout, every boy for that matter, should know how to swim. Swimming is conceded to be the most graceful of all physical exercises and furnishes a better all-round development than any other sport. Besides being a personal safeguard, it prepares the Scout for service in saving the lives of others. There is no good reason why a boy should be excused from meeting so necessary a requirement, except possibly the fact that he is physically unfit. Even then it would be far better for a boy to enlist the care of a competent physician to help him regain his health to meet this requirement before he undertakes to complete the examination for his First Class badge.

The Tenderfoot.

The requirements for the Tenderfoot degree are for the purpose of giving the newly elected Scout a clear idea of the principles of the movement which he is joining. In reality the Tenderfoot is not a Scout at all. He is only a "green-horn" who has taken out his first papers, and is placed upon probation to become familiar with the laws that govern Scouts everywhere and to put into practice in daily life principles that will enable him to become resourceful, self-reliant, and of service to others.

Age Limit.

This statement prefaces the requirements for the Tenderfoot degree, "To become a Scout a boy must be at least twelve years of age." This does not mean that a boy be "in his twelfth year" but that he has actually passed his twelfth birthday. The requirements of the Scout Movement are such that only the older boys are capable of properly understanding them. The hikes and endurance tests are too severe for younger boys. The two classes of boys care for entirely different sports and activities and it is not fair to the older boys of the patrol to be handicapped by youngsters who cannot keep up with the requirements. The underlying principle of Scouting is the development of community interest among boys. Community interest awakens with adolescence. There is as little toleration for the younger boy by older boys as there is among men for the youth of eighteen or nineteen. In fact, it is quite generally true that the older boy will not associate with boys whom he considers "mere kids." It would be, therefore, unfair to the organization to limit its effectiveness in dealing with adolescent problems, by seeking to enroll boys under twelve years of age.

The Scout Master is placed upon his honor not to violate this fundamental requirement. The age limit, therefore, has been fixed at twelve as the youngest age at which a boy may join a patrol of Scouts. During the period of organization of the Scout Movement in this country some boys under twelve were admitted to patrols and are now of Tenderfoot rank. It would not be fair to ask them to withdraw, but it is only right that they should not become Second Class Scouts until they have reached their twelfth birthday. In the future, however, no boy under twelve will be allowed to join the organization. This is one of the hard and fast rules that Scout Masters are asked to live up to and in fairness to others no one should ask that an exception be made. Junior Scout clubs will not be officially recognized.

Knowing the Scout Oath and Law.

The first requirement for the Tenderfoot is that he know the Scout law, sign, salute and the significance of the badge. These are fully explained on pages 26 to 29 of the "Handbook for Boys." The question is often asked in what sense the Scout should know these things. Should he memorize word for word so as to be able to repeat each law and the interpretation of it, or should he be able to give the meaning of each law as he understands it? It is not the purpose that a boy be able to repeat these laws as he would poetry, but that he may so firmly fix in his heart and mind that a Scout is trustworthy, courteous, clean, etc., that these may become part of his daily thought and life. It is better for a boy to learn every word of these laws and to repeat them daily until his habits of living become firmly set than to allow any Tenderfoot (having learned them for that purpose only) to take his test and thereafter to forget all about them. Similarly the Scout Oath is an obligation that should not be taken lightly by the Tenderfoot, who should never have to confess that he has forgotten the three planks. The various parts of the badge, the trefoil, the eagle, the scroll and the knot are constant reminders of his obligation as a Scout, and he should be able to explain their significance.

Composition and History of the Flag.

The second requirement is that he know the composition and history of the National Flag and the customary forms of respect due to it. Every American boy, whether a Scout or not, should take an oath of allegiance to the American Flag. Every Boy Scout is required to pledge himself to do his duty "to God and his country," and in this connection the oath to the Flag, given on page 377 of the Handbook for Boys, should be taken. The following brief history has been prepared to meet this requirement. It is merely suggestive and should only be used as a basis for further knowledge of the National Flag. The customary forms of respect are suggested by the Sons of the Revolution, State of New York.

THE STARS AND STRIPES

History fails to inform us who first suggested the idea for the composition of the National Flag. Some writers claim that the design was suggested by George Washington's coat of arms, while others say that the stripes were taken from the thirteen stripes in the banner of the Philadelphia Troop of Light Horse. The story, however, most generally accepted, is that the first flag was planned and made in 1776 by Betsy Ross, who kept an upholstery shop on Arch Street, Philadelphia, and that this, a year later, was adopted by Congress. The special committee appointed to design a national flag consisted of George Washington,

Robert Morris, and Col. George Ross, uncle of the late husband of Betsy Ross. The star that the committee decided upon had six points, but Mrs. Ross advised the five-pointed star, which has ever since been used in the United States flag. The flag thus designed was colored by a local artist, and from this colored copy Betsy Ross made the first American flag.

The first time that the new flag of the United States was carried in battle was at Fort Stanwix, named Fort Schuyler, where Rome, New York, now stands. The first salute ever given " Old Glory " by a foreign power, was when the *Ranger,* commanded by Captain Paul Jones, entered a French harbor in 1778 and received a salute from the harbor forts. When Washington was in command at Cambridge, in January, 1776, the flag used by him consisted of a banner of thirteen red and white stripes with the British Union Jack in the upper left-hand corner. This was known as the great union flag. For a period of seventy years preceding the War of the Revolution the flag generally used by the American colonies was made up of the red cross of Saint George, representing England, and a white cross, which represented Scotland. This was known as the Union Flag. During the first two years of the Revolutionary War all kinds of battle flags were carried on land and sea. These were of various designs and their emblems represented local sentiment. Every Colony and almost every section had its special flag. One of the most famous of these was a yellow flag with the emblem of a rattlesnake and the motto, " Do not tread on me," underneath it. Also two trees are closely associated with the history of the flag, the pine and the elm. One of these was a reproduction of an old elm which stood on the corner of what is now Washington and Essex Streets, Boston. This was known as the " liberty " tree and was the scene of many patriotic meetings. On November 3rd, 1773, the citizens of Boston gathered under this tree to consider resolutions protesting against the Stamp Act. This resolution being ignored, resulted in the famous Boston Tea Party, December 6th, 1773. The pine tree also appeared on the silver coins of the Massachusetts colonies as early as 1650.

The official history of our flag begins on June 14, 1777, when the American Congress adopted the following resolution proposed by John Adams:

Resolved: That the flag of the thirteen United States be thirteen stripes, alternate red and white: that the Union be thirteen stars, white on a blue field, representing a new constellation.

" We take," said Washington, " the star from Heaven, the red from our mother country, separating it by white stripes, thus showing that we have separated from her, and the white stripes shall go down to posterity representing liberty."

In designing the flag there was much discussion as to the arrangement of the stars in the field of blue. It was thought at one time that a new stripe as well as a new star should be added for each new State admitted to the Union. Indeed, in 1794, Congress passed an act to the effect that on and after May 1, 1795, " the flag of the United States be fifteen stripes, alternate red and white; and that the union be fifteen stars, white in a field of blue. These additional stars and stripes were for the States of Vermont and Kentucky.

The impracticability of adding a stripe for each State was apparent as other States began to be admitted. Moreover, the flag of fifteen stripes, it was thought, did not properly represent the Union; therefore, on April 4, 1818, after a period of twenty-one years in which the flag of fifteen stripes had been used, Congress passed an act which finally fixed the general flag of our country, which reads as follows:

An Act to Establish the Flag of the United States.

Sec. 1. Be it enacted, etc. That from and after the fourth day of July next, the flag of the United States be thirteen horizontal stripes, alternate red and white; that the union have twenty stars, white in a blue field.

Sec. 2. Be it further enacted, that, on the admission of every new state into the union, one star be added to the union of the flag; and that such addition shall take effect on the fourth day of July succeeding such admission.

Respect Due to the Flag.

The customary forms of respect due the flag are:

1. It should not be hoisted before sunrise nor allowed to remain up after sunset.

2. At " retreat," sunset, civilian spectators should stand at attention and give the military salute.

3. When the national colors are passing on parade or review, the spectators should, if walking, halt, and if sitting, rise and stand at attention and uncover.

4. When the flag is flown at half staff as a sign of

mourning it should be hoisted to full staff at the conclusion of the funeral. In placing the flag at half mast, it should first be hoisted to the top of the staff and then lowered to

SALUTE TO THE FLAG

position. Preliminary to lowering from half staff it should first be raised to top.

5. On Memorial Day, May 30th, the flag should fly at half mast from sunrise until noon, and full staff from noon to sunset.

Knowledge of Knot-Tying.

The third requirement is not at all difficult. If the Scout will secure a piece of rope two or three feet long and sit down with the Handbook before him he will find it very easy to follow the instructions for making any of the required knots given on pages 72–75. Rope is much better for knot-tying practice than either string or cord. Having met these requirements he takes the Scout oath, is enrolled as a Tenderfoot and is entitled to wear the Tenderfoot badge.

Second Class Scout Requirements.

Passing from the requirements for a Tenderfoot to the set of tests outlined for a Second Class Scout, the aim and purpose of the work changes materially. Up to this point attention has been paid only to the uninitiated — the Tenderfoot in fact as well as in name, who knowing nothing of the life of a Scout or the things required of a Scout, has been seeking initiation into the mysteries of the craft. But having imbibed the spirit of Scouting and having put into practice in daily life the Scout Law, the candidate is prepared to take the second step in his development along scout lines. He acknowledges his limitations and lack of knowledge and confesses his need of further training so that he may the better " Be Prepared " for further service to others. The second class requirements, therefore, are so arranged, as to meet this need. By means of them it is hoped to cultivate in boys, habits of observation, resourcefulness, thrift, and ability to adapt one's self to conditions.

If it were necessary to warn the prospective Tenderfoot against obtaining merely a superficial knowledge of the Tenderfoot requirements, it is doubly important to remind him of the necessity of thoroughly mastering the requirements of the Second Class Scout. It is only by daily exercise that habits become our servants and subconsciously serve us in times of need.

Tenderfoot Service.

Test No. 1 calls for at least one month's service as a Tenderfoot. This does not mean one month from the time of application for membership in the patrol, but that from the time the Scout took the oath of a Tenderfoot and was invested with the badge of that degree, he has for at least one month put into practice in daily life the scout ideals.

First Aid.

Test No. 2 calls for a knowledge of Elementary First Aid and Bandaging. It is not the purpose of the Scout Movement to develop a lot of amateur doctors, but to give Scouts sufficient information on the subject of First Aid to enable them to act quickly in cases of emergency. They should be able at any opportunity to give sufficient help to prevent the patient receiving any further harm in cases of fractures, fits, etc.

In the case of a serious accident, the first thing to do is to send for the nearest doctor. If the nature of the injury is known, the messenger should be informed so that the doctor may come prepared to deal with the case. In many instances the most that can be done, until the doctor arrives, is to relieve the patient by placing something under his head, unbuttoning his clothes and keeping back the crowd so that he may have sufficient air. In case of a fracture, if it is necessary to remove the patient, care should be taken to adjust the splints so that no further damage can be done.

Detailed instruction in a number of these requirements is given so clearly in the "Handbook for Boys" that without reproducing the information here, it will be enough to refer by page number to the Handbook in such cases.

(a) General directions for first aid to injured, p. 285.
(b) Treatment for fainting, p. 294.
(c) Shock, p. 286.
(d) Fractures, pp. 286–289.
(e) Bruises and sprains, p. 289.
(f) Injuries in which the skin is broken, pp. 289–290.
(g) Burns and scalds, p. 297.
(h) Demonstration of methods of carrying injured, pp. 301–303.

Elementary Signaling.

Test No. 3 calls for a knowledge of Elementary Signaling. Nothing further can be added to what the Boys' Handbook gives under this subject. The rememberable American Morse and International Morse Codes are excellent helps to the beginner in learning the alphabets.

(a) Semaphore, pp. 237–238.
(b) American Morse, p. 239.
(c) International Morse, p. 239.

The International Morse, known also as the Continental and General Service Code is the official Scout Code. It is used in wireless telegraphy, commercially and in the Government service.

The American Morse is employed by commercial telegraph lines and by land lines only. It is interesting and stimulating to the mind, after the alphabet is once learned, to try the different methods by which signals may be exchanged.

The semaphore, because of its quicker results at close range, may also be learned, but not to the exclusion of the International Morse.

Elementary signaling means a knowledge of the theory of signaling, how to hold the flag or torch, the letters of the alphabet, the numerals, and the meaning of conventional signals. In other words a Second Class Scout should be able to send a message with the assistance of some-one to call the letters to him from a code card, and to read a message when the letters are sent slowly.

In reading it is important that the Scout keep his attention fixed on the distant stations. There should be at least two Scouts on each station, one to read or send the message and one to record or call off.

One of the best methods of practising signaling for Second-Class requirements is to have the troop count off by fours, then the odd numbers step two or three paces to the front and all face half right to follow the best versed Scout, who acts as guide and is placed three paces in front.

The patrol can now wave the alphabet in unison, as called for, letter by letter or by rotation; this makes a very pretty sight for exhibition if it is well done. With a larger number distance can be taken towards the front, each No. 1 — 2 — 3 — 4 Scouts stepping off together at two-pace intervals.

Night signaling should also be tried, using an old broom or bunch of oiled rags for a torch, or an ordinary hand lantern. In either case a foot light must be employed as a point of reference to the motions. The lantern is more conveniently swung out upward to the right of the foot-light for a dot, to the left for a dash, and raised vertically for a " front " or three.

To use a stationary light, a lantern or Baldwin lamp, the hat or a piece of paper may be passed back and forth in front of the light. A shutter of two or more pieces worked with a spring or rubber band to close it and a button or key lever to open it, is much better and is easily constructed. Use a short flash for a dot and a long, steady flash for a dash.

Tracking.

Test No. 4 calls for the ability to track half a mile in twenty-five minutes, or, if in town, to describe satisfactorily the contents of one store window out of four observed for one minute each. The chapter on Trailing in the Boys' Handbook furnishes excellent information on tracking.

For the purpose of this test a trail may be previously laid by the Scout Master or Examining Committee covering at least half a mile. The candidate for examination may then be started out over that trail and allowed to follow up its devious windings until he arrives at the other end. Care should be taken to see that he is able to keep to the trail for the entire distance and to make the distance in the time required. As this test is given to develop the power of observation, the game called " Shop Window Out-Doors in Town " is usually played in cities where it is not always convenient to follow the tracking requirements.

On grassland or in the woods, where actual tracks cannot be readily seen, or in the winter when the ground is frozen without a snow covering, the Scout Master may lay out a trail with corn, beans, or small bits of paper. The method employed by the Scouts of Pioneer times of indicating a trail by breaking a leafy twig in the direction followed, leaving it hanging to the branch, will help to train the Tenderfoot in noting all signs. Small chalk marks may also be made on rocks and tree trunks. The greatest care, however, should be taken not to injure plants or to deface the woods with unsightly signs or litter.

Much valuable information can be obtained from examining tracks. It is important that the Scout learn to read them correctly. He should tell at a glance whether a man was walking or running or whether a horse was walking, trotting, cantering, or galloping. In following a horse's tracks, note the difference between the impressions made by the hind and the fore feet. Tracks of different horses vary. Tracks of some horses may even seem different when the horse is being held in or being given free rein.

Impressions of a horse's feet are usually seen in pairs; and the impressions of the hind feet are smaller than those of the fore feet. An eminent authority on tracking gives the following valuable information: "When a horse is walking, the impressions made are separate and there is a distance of 2½ feet between the toe of the one fore foot and the heel of the other fore foot. When trotting the impressions are touching each other and the distance between the fore feet is about 4½ feet. When galloping the impressions are much deeper and much farther apart. With the average-sized horse the distance between the fore feet is over 10 feet."

In making observations the following points should be noted:

1. Whether all tracks run in the same direction, and what the approximate compass direction is.

2. Whether there is any indication of the number of men or horses that have formed the tracks.

3. Whether the tracks are quite recent and if all are of the same period. (Of course atmospheric conditions must be taken into account as tracks will be affected by rain, heavy dew or dry winds.)

4. Whether the whole party was moving at a uniform rate.

5. Whether the tracks of any wheeled vehicle are visible, and if so, whether heavy or light.

6. In what formation the party was moving.

7. Whether any side tracks leave the main trail at any point.

8. Whether any halting places are visible.

9. Whether any camping places are visible.

Scouts should practice this method of observation and after noting these points and others, write their own story of just what occurred. To improve his power of tracking every Scout should take constant opportunities to follow up tracks of different kinds on the ground, drawing inferences from them and, whenever possible, verifying any conclusions he may have drawn.

Scout's Pace.

Test No. 5 calls for the ability to go a mile in twelve minutes at Scout's pace. Scout's pace is fifty steps running and fifty steps walking. It is a method of travel which permits of endurance when covering a long distance. To pass the test it should be noted that the mile is to be traversed in twelve minutes. This is not a record for the distance because it can be easily accomplished by almost any Scout in eight minutes. The boy who does it in less than twelve minutes fails equally with the boys who take fifteen minutes to do it. The object of this test is to prac-

A TROOP PRACTICING SCOUT'S PACE

tice Scout's pace until a Scout knows that whenever he keeps up that given pace for twelve minutes he has covered exactly one mile. Or on the other hand, a Scout should know that whenever he has covered one mile at that given pace, he has taken just exactly twelve minutes to do it. It is a measure of distance and time rather than a record for the mile.

Use of Knife and Hatchet.

Test No. 6 prescribes the proper use of knife and hatchet, which are about the most useful implements of a backwoodsman. In fact a good camper, hunter or mountaineer would be lost without them. The manner in which a camper handles his knife or ax is a sure sign whether he knows anything about woodcraft or not. It is only the unskilled and untrained who brandish an open knife or carelessly handle unsheathed axes; experienced men are always extremely careful in their use. These two tools should be carried not as playthings but for serious work whenever they are required. Owing to the great danger of injury by the indiscriminate use of the Scout ax before the boys have received proper instruction, many troops permit the Scout ax to be carried by the Patrol Leader only and the rest of the Scouts are permitted to add the ax to their equipment after they have passed this requirement and have become Second Class Scouts. It is important that the following advice about the proper use of the knife and hatchet be noted.

1.   They should be properly taken care of and never used upon objects that will dull or break them.

2.   They should be handled in such a way as not to injure the user or any person nearby.

3.   They should never be used to strip the bark off birch, beech or madrone trees or to disfigure other people's property by cutting initials thereon.

4.   The correct methods of handling the knife and hatchet should be learned by each Scout at his earliest opportunity. The same also applies to the ax.

When Using the Knife.

1.   Whittle away from you, *not* toward you.

2.   Don't drive a knife into a stick by hammering on the back of it, and don't use the handle as a hammer.

3.   Beware of wood with nails in it.

4.   Keep the knife blade out of the fire.

5.   Keep the blades clean; boil or scald the blades before cutting food.

6.   Don't use the blade as a screw-driver, or to pry things open with.

7.   Don't carry an open knife in your hand.

8.   Don't lay it on the ground when not using it, or keep it in a wet place.

9.   Know how to sharpen the blades properly.

A knife, if kept in good condition, is the most valuable and important personal tool.

When Using the Ax.

1.   Never chop in such a position that the ax will cut you if it slips.

2.   Never chop through wood on a hard surface.

3.   Never chop pine or hemlock knots with a sharp ax.

4.   If you carry an ax on your shoulder, always have the edge outward from your neck. Otherwise you might stumble and be killed.

5.   Always muzzle the ax in traveling.

How to Cut a Log and Fell a Tree.

The wood fibres running lengthwise form what is known as the grain of the wood, and this must be taken into consideration in splitting or cutting. Thus the line from R to K in illustration A, is the grain and the direction of least resistance, while from M to E is across the grain and the direction of the greatest resistance. This being the case, the angle A1—C1, which is a little less than 45 degrees, is the direction of least possible resistance when cutting across the grain of the log, and should be applied in all cross cuts, from the smallest branch to the largest log.

Notch No. 1 in the figure shows how to chop through a log that cannot be moved. It is made by alternating cuts from A1 to C1 and B1 to C1 until the notch is cut through, unless the latter is so wide that the chips at D do not fly out of their own accord, when an extra cut must be made parallel to B1—C1 or to A1—C1, midway between A1 and B1, as the notch deepens. This extra cut should not go deeper than the point where the chips release themselves from A1 to B1.

Notch No. 2 is used when the log can be rolled over, by cutting to the center of the log in the same manner as in the first case, then turning the log and chopping from the other side, keeping in mind the one great principle in wood chopping, that a true woodsman never cuts from more than two sides.

Notches No. 3 and 4 illustrate the proper method of felling trees. To cause a tree to fall in a desired direction, cut a notch A3—C3—B3 low down on the side on which it is to fall, by repeated cuts, first from A3 to C3 and then from B3 to C3, with your cut B3—C3 on a downward angle (as in B5 in figure C, which shows the notch as the ax enters) until well past the heart-wood of the tree, when Notch No. 4 is cut in a like manner on the opposite side, and well above Notch No. 3, until the tree falls.

Never chop from more than two sides, no matter how tempting it may be to give the standing part a few cuts between the notches. It would be far from good woodcraft, and might affect dangerously the fall of the tree. When the latter is down, trim the branches from the top, and the limbs will not interfere with your work.

An expert axman can chop with either the right hand or the left hand. When he is chopping left handed, the

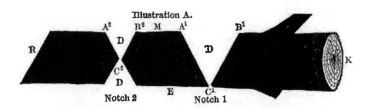

Illustration A.

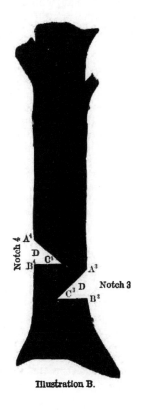

Notch 4

Notch 3

Illustration B.

Illustration C.

right hand is at the haft and the left hand slides and vice versa.

Fire-Making.

Test No. 7 calls for the ability to lay and light a fire in the open using not more than two matches. The beginner usually makes the mistake of trying to start with too large a fire. First be careful to clear away any dry leaves or grass; neglect to do this may cause an awkward fire. Then collect sufficient wood and with a hatchet or knife cut a large enough quantity into fine shavings that will easily catch fire. It is best to leave the shavings on the stick, and prop them up against another stick to let the air under it; the fire may easily be killed by laying the bunch of shavings flat on the ground, with no air space under them. When the first small quantity is thoroughly ablaze, continue to add more fuel until it is safe to put on the large pieces of wood. A fire should not be lighted in a hollow where there is absolutely no wind as a fair draught is needed to fan it. When the fire has been thoroughly started, place some logs at the back, that is, at the side opposite to which the wind is coming. Gradually logs may be placed at the sides thereby forming a little channel for the bed of the fire in which the draught may have a clear sweep. In very wet or stormy weather the fire may be started with small chips taken from the center of a log of wood. These can be placed in a tin can or water pail until the fire has been obtained. In lighting the Scout fire with two matches, the use of paper is prohibited.

Cooking.

Test No. 8 calls for the ability to cook a quarter of a pound of meat and two potatoes without the aid of ordinary kitchen utensils. This means of course that the cooking must be accomplished in the open upon a fire built with two matches, and under conditions that usually obtain while camping in the woods. While the requirements as stated in the Boys' Handbook do not prohibit the use of the mess kit, the Scout should be able to pass this test without the aid of any utensils whatever other than those furnished by Nature.

Chops, steak, ham or other meats can be satisfactorily broiled over hardwood or heavy bark coals by using one or more split sticks, and may be cooked upon a thin slab stone

wiped clean and placed over a flaming fire. As for potatoes, the Scout usually throws them into the fire, from
which they later emerge with a small edible core surrounded by a thick layer of charcoal. The proper method
of roasting potatoes is to embed them in a ball of moist clay,
when this can be obtained, or else to dig a hole directly in
front of the fire, into which a layer of glowing coals is
raked; and the potatoes are placed upon this, covered with
another layer of coals, and the pit is then filled up with earth
and tramped firm. They may also be sliced very thin and
fried upon the flat stone, if it is firm and not porous in
texture so as to absorb too much grease.

The Dollar Bank-Deposit.

Test No. 9 prescribes that the Scout earn and deposit one
dollar in a public bank. There are several important
things to be noted regarding this requirement. First, the
purpose of it all is to cultivate the habit of thrift. It is not
sufficient that a Scout may have earned more than one dollar in times past before he became a Second Class Scout
and is credited with a bank account, but it is necessary
that from the time of his initiation as a Tenderfoot he
has earned one dollar which he has deposited to his credit
as a Scout. But it would be far better if the Scout without stopping here pledged himself to make this dollar the
basis of a bank account which he hopes to develop during
his lifetime. It is certainly contrary to the spirit of the
requirement for any boy to earn and deposit a dollar in
the bank and then withdraw it as soon as the test has been
passed.

The Sixteen Points of the Compass.

Test No. 10 calls for the knowledge of the sixteen principal points of the compass. In order to facilitate the gain-
ing of that knowledge describe a complete circle on the
ground. Take the position at the center in the hub. The
point directly ahead may be marked North; the point directly at the back will be South; the direction to the right
will be East; and the position of the left hand, or a straight
line through from the East will be West. This divides the
circle into four equal parts of 90 degrees each. These are
the four primary points of the compass. If a line were
drawn directly between the North and East and continued

through the hub of the circle it would bisect the South and West. The point midway between the North and East is called N. E. and the point between the South and the West is called S. W. Another line drawn between the North and West through the center would be known as N. W. and the S. E. respectively. This then gives the eight principal points of the compass, but the task is to secure sixteen. These are at once obtained by drawing lines between the N. and N. E., between E. and N. E., between E. and S. E., S and S. E., etc. These lines if continued across the circle or directly through the hub to the other side will give the full sixteen points. The line between N. and N. E. is known as N. N. E. The line between E. and N. E. is known as E. N. E., and so on around the circle. The Scout will easily learn these points by this method, and a few practical demonstrations.

Every Scout should also learn how to find the points of the compass by means of his watch and the sun, as described in Chapter II of the Boys' Handbook.

Requirements for First Class Scouts.

Turning from the discussion of Second Class Scout requirements to the consideration of those for First Class Scouts, it is to be noted that as the Scout works higher in rank, there is more and more need of standardizing requirement details. A consideration of First Class Scout requirements presents many new points for discussion.

Purpose of First Class Scout Requirements.

The first Class Scout tests are intended to teach the boy his obligation as an individual in the community so that he may properly coöperate with others for the public welfare and render public service wherever it is needed. This ability to coöperate with others in doing the little things will enable a Scout later on to assume his position one day as a leader. The ultimate aim of every Scout should be leadership.

Occasionally boys who are sixteen or seventeen years old write to the National Office asking if they must give up scout work after they have reached their eighteenth birthday, or if they may continue in the movement as First Class Scouts. While the age at which a boy may join the movement is fixed at twelve years there is no stated age at which he must resign as a Scout. If he has been properly trained as a Tenderfoot, Second Class and First Class Scout, it seems reasonable to suppose that by the time he has reached his eighteenth birthday he will have acquired such a thorough knowledge of Scoutcraft that he will be prepared to take his place as an Assistant Scout Master, to continue for others the training which he has found helpful to himself. The movement is depending upon the Scouts now in training to assume leadership as Assistant Scout Masters and Scout Masters for the boys who succeed them.

Several of the First Class Scout requirements are merely a continuation of the course of instruction given Second Class Scouts. Very little further can be said about these requirements. Practice alone is needed to qualify in passing these tests. This is particularly true of signaling, first aid work and cooking. In some cases where the Handbook gives detailed information about the requirement, it is thought best to simply refer to the page without repeating such information.

Swimming.

1. " Swim fifty yards."

Inasmuch as a Scout should be prepared to care for himself under all circumstances and be capable of rendering service to others when in danger it would seem almost of first importance that he know how to swim. The Scout camp presents a wonderful opportunity to learn the art. Many times it is possible for the Scout Master to make arrangements for his boys to use a pool in some local club house during the winter. Unfortunately there are some troops so situated that provisions for swimming are very limited. But, this requirement is considered so valuable to the individual boy that even though he is capable of passing every other test it is advisable that he learn to swim before becoming a First Class Scout. To pass the test it is necessary that the boy be able to swim by whatever stroke he has learned a distance of fifty yards without assistance from anyone and without holding on to any object or touching bottom during the distance.

Two Dollars in the Bank.

2. " Earn and deposit at least two dollars in a public bank."

If the Scout has followed instructions regarding the earning of one dollar for his Second Class Scout test, it is safe to assume that he will add to that amount another dollar and thus begin a savings account. The requirement is not intended to mean that he should have two dollars in addition to the one already deposited for Second Class Scout tests, but only that he add another dollar to the first one in the bank. If, however, he has withdrawn his deposit he should by all means earn two dollars more to meet the requirement. But the Scout should not stop here; he should make this deposit the basis for the savings of a lifetime.

Signaling.

3. " Send and receive a message by semaphore or International Morse code alphabet, sixteen letters per minute."

Practice alone is needed. The difficult part of this requirement is not in the sending, but in receiving the message. It is not sufficient that once in a while the Scout may have the luck to take a message at the rate of sixteen letters per minute; the test should be a longer message of fifty or one hundred words which will demonstrate the ability to take down this message at the required average. He must also know the conventional signals, uses of numerals, etc., so that if called upon in an emergency, he could send a message and be sure to get it through. Such emergencies may arise in the shape of great calamities, such as floods or inundations.

The Big Hike.

4. " Make a round trip alone (or with another Scout) to a point at least seven miles away (fourteen miles in all), going on foot or rowing a boat, and write a satisfactory account of the trip and things observed."

By all means a route should be selected that takes the Scout into the woods, over mountains or through uninhabited territory where he may be alone with the great outdoors. Anyone can take a walk through crowded towns or city streets but the inspiration once felt by the brave-hearted Scout who has gone out into the virgin forest is an experience to be highly coveted.

The purpose of this requirement is to test one's ability in observation, and to prove how dependable the Scout is in giving the account of his experience. Speed is of no importance. In fact the more leisurely the trip is made the better able the Scout will be to tell all the things encountered on the journey and describe all of the details of the route traveled. If two Scouts travel together it would be interesting for both to keep independent reports of the things observed. At the end of the journey it will be surprising to see the number of things which one observed that the other did not see and vice versa. Moreover, if the Scout travels this route a second time he might be astonished at the number of things observed on the second trip that was overlooked the first time. The ability to note details will prove invaluable throughout life. Such trips as these should be taken frequently.

First Aid.

5. "Advanced First Aid."

The manual is perfectly clear on this subject and should be followed in meeting these requirements.*

(a) Know the methods for panic prevention, p. 279.
(b) What to do in case of fire and ice, pp. 279–282.
(c) Electric Accidents, p. 282.
(d) Gas Accidents, p. 283.
(e) How to help in case of runaway horse, p. 284.
(f) Mad dog, p. 285.
(g) Snake bite, p. 291.
(h) Treatment for dislocations, p. 291.
(i) Unconsciousness, p. 289.
(j) Poisoning, p. 294.
(k) Fainting, p. 294.
(l) Apoplexy, p. 294.
(m) Sunstroke, pp. 294–295.
(n) Heat exhaustion, p. 295.
(o) Freezing, p. 295.
(p) Know treatment for sunburn, p. 295.
(q) Ivy Poisoning, p. 298.
(r) Bites and stings, p. 298.
(s) Nosebleed, p. 298.
(t) Earache, p. 299.

(u) Toothache, pp. 299–300.
(v) Inflammation or grit in eye, p. 300.
(w) Cramps or stomach-ache, p. 300.
(x) Chills, p. 301.
(y) Demonstrate artificial respiration, pp. 310–311.

Cooking.

6. " Prepare and cook satisfactorily, in the open, without regular kitchen utensils two of the following articles as may be directed : — eggs, bacon, hunter's stew, fish, fowl, game, pancakes, hoecake, biscuit, hard tack or a twist baked on a stick; explain to another boy the methods followed."

Do not overlook the words " as may be directed." It is not intended that the Scout should choose *any* two articles. In that case every Scout in the country would be living on bacon and eggs. A Scout should know how to cook everything mentioned in the list. He may be directed by the Examining Committee to cook a hunter's stew and a twist baked on a stick. In the chapter on Campcraft in the Handbook cooking recipes are given for eggs, bacon, fish and pancakes, pp. 172–173. The recipes for the other dishes are given herewith : —

Hunter's Stew : — To make a hunter's stew, chop the meat into small chunks about an inch or one and one-half inches square. Then scrape and chop up any vegetables that are easily obtained,— potatoes, turnips, carrots, onions, etc.; and put them into the mess kit, adding clean water, or soup, till the mess kit is half full.   Mix some flour, salt and pepper together and rub the meat well into the mixture, then place this in the mess kit or kettle, seeing that there is just sufficient water to cover the food,— and no more. The stew should be ready after simmering for about an hour and a quarter.

To cook a fowl : — In preparing a fowl or bird of some description it is unnecessary to remove the feathers. After removing the entrails and cleaning the inside, plaster the fowl over with a mixture of clay, earth, ashes, etc., and place it in the middle of the fire. When sufficiently cooked knock off the coating of clay, and the feathers will come away with it, leaving the chicken or bird deliciously ready for the eating.

Rabbit Stew : — A rabbit (cottontail, jack rabbit, or

hare) is a form of food that is likely to come in the way of a Scout, so every boy should know how to cook one. Having removed the skin and cleaned the inside, cut the rabbit into pieces and place in the mess kit with sufficient water to cover it, adding pepper and salt and sliced onion. Stew gently for about an hour, and when done thicken with about a tablespoon of flour.

Hoecake: — Make a thick batter by mixing warm (not scalding) water or milk with one pint of corn meal, and mix in with this a small teaspoonful of salt and a tablespoonful of melted lard. To cook hoecake properly, the frying pan should be perfectly clean and smooth inside. If it is not, too much grease will be required in cooking. Scrape it after each panful is cooked, and then only occasional greasing will be required. Greasing is best done with a clean rag containing butter. Spread a thin batter in the pan with a spoon so that the cake will be very thin; disturb it as little as possible and when the cake is firm on one side turn it and cook on the other.

Biscuit: — (See Kephart's "Camp Cookery" and also Kephart's "Book of Camping and Woodcraft," pp. 118–119.) Just as good biscuits or johnnycake can be baked before a log fire in the woods as in a kitchen range. Bread making is a chemical process. Follow directions, pay close attention to details as a chemist does, from building the fire to testing the loaf with a sliver. It requires experience or a special knack to *guess* quantities, but none at all to measure them. In general, biscuit or other small cakes should be baked quickly by a rapid or ardent heat; large loaves require a slower, more even heat, so that the outside will not harden until the inside is nearly done. For a dozen biscuits use: —

> 1½ pints flour.
> 1½ heaping teaspoonfuls baking powder.
> ½ heaping teaspoonful salt.
> 1 heaping tablespoon cold grease.
> ½ pint cold water.

The amount of water varies according to the quality of flour. Too much water makes the dough sticky and prolongs the baking. Baking powders vary in strength; the directions on the can should be followed in each case.

Mix thoroughly with a big spoon or wooden paddle, first

the baking powder with the flour and then the salt. Rub into this the cold grease (which may be lard, cold pork fat or drippings) until there are no lumps left and no grease adhering to bottom of the pan. This is a little tedious, but it doesn't pay to shirk it; complete stirring is necessary for success. Then stir in the water and work it with the spoon until the result is rather a stiff dough. Squeeze or mold the dough as little as possible; because the gas that makes the biscuit light is already forming and

BAKING "TWIST" ON A STICK

should not be pressed out. Do not use the fingers in molding; it makes biscuit "sad." Flop the mass of dough to one side of the pan, dust flour on bottom of the pan, flop dough back over it, and dust flour on top of the loaf. Now rub some flour over the bread board, flour the hands, and gently lift the loaf on the board. Flour the bottle or bit of peeled sapling which is to be used as a rolling pin, and also the edges of the can or can cover to be used as biscuit cutter. Gently roll the loaf to three-quarters of an inch in thickness. Stamp out the biscuits and lay them in the pan. Roll out the culls or leftover pieces of dough and make biscuits of them too. Bake until the front row turns brown; reverse the pan and continue until the rear row is similarly done. Ten to fifteen minutes is required in a closed oven, and somewhat longer over the camp-fire or camp earth or stone oven.

" Twist " baked on a stick: — Work the dough, prepared as for biscuit, into a ribbon two inches wide. Get a club of sweet green wood (birch, sassafras, poplar or maple) about two feet long and three inches thick, peel the large end, and sharpen the other and stick it into the ground, leaning toward fire. When the sap simmers wind the dough spirally around the peeled end. Turn occasionally while baking. Several sticks can be baking at once. Bread enough for one man's meal can be quickly baked in this way on a peeled stick as thick as a broomstick, holding it over fire and turning it from time to time.

The applicant for First Class Scout rank should be familiar enough with these recipes to be able to take another Second Class Scout out and teach him how to cook any or all of these articles.

Map Reading.

7. " Read a map correctly and draw from field notes made on the spot an intelligible rough sketch map, indicating by their proper marks important buildings, roads, trolleys, main landmarks, principal elevations, etc. Point out a compass direction without the help of a compass."

To read a map correctly the first thing necessary is to make note of the scale used. By the term *scale* is meant the proportion which a certain distance between any two objects on the map bears to the country it represents. The scale may be represented by —" ten inches to a mile " which means that a road which is ten inches long on the map is a mile long in reality. After getting the scale distance properly in mind, locate the north point or direction. In some maps true north is indicated by a star, while an arrow shows the magnetic north point. In all U. S. Coast and Geodetic Survey maps the left and right sides of the map from bottom to top run true north. It is necessary when reading a map to ascertain if one point is visible from another point. To do so intelligently requires an understanding of contours and contour lines. The height of one contour above another is known as the Vertical Interval. This is always expressed in a certain number of feet, and the foot distance per interval is usually stated at the bottom of the map.

In drawing a rough sketch map, clearness of perception is the chief requisite, and nothing should be put in that is

DRAWING A SKETCH MAP

unnecessary for the full understanding of the sketch. As each i n d i v i d u a l would most likely have a different way of showing the various things in the map, such as houses, roads, trees, etc., certain " conventional signs " are generally used for such purposes. These can be secured by addressing the Army War College, Washington, D. C., or usually by application to the office of a surveyor or abstractor. A few such signs are shown in the following illustrations:

In d r a w i n g a rough sketch map, the following principal points should be noted:—

Margin:— Leave a margin of at least an inch all around the sketch.

Scale:— Always state the graphical scale of the map.

Direction:— Remember that the map will be practically useless unless the north point is shown to indicate direction.

Roads:— A road is drawn with continuous lines when it is closed by a fence, hedge, ditch or other obstacle of any kind; and with dotted lines when unclosed or bounded by open fields or woodland. Every road must have "from" printed to the left of it on the margin of the sketch, and "to" at the right of it.

Railways: — A railway is shown by continuous lines with cross bars. The words "single" or "double" should be written along it, as the case may be.

Woods: — Indicate the nature of the woodlands, whether chestnut, pine, oak, etc., and also whether they are passable or not.

Cultivation: — State the nature of the crops or condition of the fields,— as barley, wheat, corn, alfalfa, etc., and fallow land, pasturage, irrigated, rocky, etc.

Bridges: — Always indicate the material of which bridges are composed as wood, stone, brick, steel, etc.

Rivers: — Write the name along their courses and indicate the direction of the stream by an arrow.

Towns and Cities: — Locate properly the approximate position of towns, villages and cities on the map, by a dark spot, or circle. Large cities are often marked by a number of closely drawn parallel lines with perpendicular intersections.

Lettering: — Names of towns, villages, and rivers should be in block letters.

For Conventional Signs see pp. 54-57.

Use of the Ax — Handicraft.

8. "Use properly an ax for felling or trimming light timber; or produce an article of carpentry or cabinet-making or metal work made by himself. Explain the method followed."

The first part of this requirement was fully described in the discussion of Test 6 of the Second Class Scout tests. A word of caution should be inserted here however. Scouts should not fell trees except under the direction of their Scout Master who will always see that permission is granted by the proper authorities before this is done. A Scout should always respect property rights and avoid violating any of the State forestry regulations.

The ability to produce an article of carpentry or metal work comes only from practical experience in handicraft work. This should be taken up under the personal instruction of some teacher provided or recommended by the Scout Master — some expert craftsman who is willing to give the boys all the knowledge he can.

Conventional Signs Used in Field Sketching.

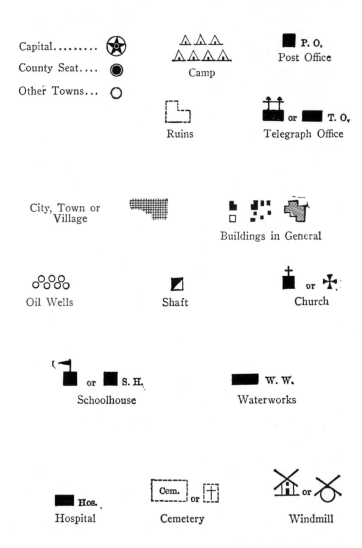

Capital......... ⊕

County Seat.... ◉

Other Towns... ○

Camp

P. O.
Post Office

Ruins

or T. O.
Telegraph Office

City, Town or Village

Buildings in General

Oil Wells

Shaft

Church

or S. H.
Schoolhouse

W. W.
Waterworks

Hos.
Hospital

Cem. or
Cemetery

or
Windmill

CONVENTIONAL SIGNS (*Continued*)

FENCES.   BOUNDARIES.   ROADS.

Stone

National, State or
Province Line

Wagon Road (good)

Hedge

County Line

Footpath or Trail

Barbed   **Smooth**

Wire

City, Village, or
Borough Line

Fence of any kind
(or board fence)

Wagon Road
(unfenced)

RAILROADS.

Railroad Station of
any kind

Double track

Electric Power Trans-
mission Line

Tunnel

TELEGRAPH LINES

Symbol (modified below)

Along Road

Along Trail

Along road
(Small-scale maps)

CONVENTIONAL SIGNS (*Continued*)

BRIDGES

General Symbol

Drawbridges (on large-scale charts, leave channel open)

Truss (W. Wood; S. Steel)

Foot

Suspension

Arch

Pontoon

Ferries

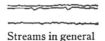
Streams in general

Falls and Rapids

Levee

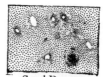
Lake or Pool in General with or without tint, waterlining, etc.)

Spring

Sand Dunes

CONVENTIONAL SIGNS (*Continued*)

Grassland in general

Tall Tropical Grass

Cultivated fields in general

Cotton

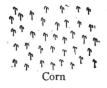

Corn

Orchard

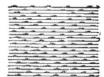

Marsh in general
(or Fresh Marsh)

Tidal Flats of any kind

Woods of any kind
(or Broad-Leaved Trees)

Pine
(or Narrow-leaved Trees)

Distance Judging.

9. "Judge distance, size, number, height and weight within twenty-five per cent."

Read carefully the material contained on page 64 of the official Handbook on the subject of measuring distances. Every Scout should know to an inch what is his usual pace when walking and running. Judging short distances should be practiced first, and then the lengths gradually extended. Begin by judging objects twenty yards away; then increase the distance ten yards at a time until any space a hundred yards in length or so can be estimated. It must be remembered that the distance is judged from the eye to the object without taking into account the contour of the intervening ground. The following points should be consistently kept in mind and studied in judging distances: —

The range of objects is usually overestimated:

1. When kneeling or lying.
2. When the background and the object are of a similar color.
3. On broken ground.
4. In avenues, long streets, or ravines.
5. When the object is in the shade.
6. In mist or failing light, or when heat is rising from the ground.
7. When the object is only partly seen.

Points to be noted. The range of objects is usually under-estimated:—

1. When the sun is behind the observer.
2. When the atmosphere is clear.
3. When the background and the object are of different colors.
4. When the ground is level or covered with snow.
5. When looking over water or a deep chasm.
6. When looking upward or downward.

It is further worth noting that:—

At 50 yards the mouth and eyes of a man can be clearly seen.

At 100 yards the eyes appear as points.

At 200 yards buttons and any bright ornament can be seen.

At 300 yards the face can be seen.

At 400 yards the movement of legs can be seen.

At 500 yards the color of clothes can be seen.
Scouts should practice constantly such games as

(a) Quick Sight, p. 330,
(b) Shop Window (Outdoors in Town), p. 341,
(c) Kim's Game, p. 343,
(d) Morgan's Game, p. 343,
(e) Far Sight, or Spot the Rabbit, p. 331,

in order to become expert in estimating numbers. Handling solids will improve the ability to tell at a glance the comparative weights of different objects. Only practice and comparisons will develop ability to make accurate judgments.

Nature Observation.

10. "Describe fully from observation ten species of trees or plants, including poison ivy, by their bark, leaves,

A SCOUT PATROL STUDYING THE TREES

flowers, fruit or scent; or six species of wild birds by their plumage, notes, tracks, or habits; or six species of native wild animals by their form, color, call, tracks or habits; find the North Star and name and describe at least three constellations of stars."

Chapter II of the Handbook was written with the express purpose of enabling the boy to learn something of trees and plants, wild birds, and animal life. This chapter should be studied carefully. Further information on these subjects can be secured at any public library, or from encyclopedias, etc. The best way to become familiar with trees and birds is to go into the woods with an instructor and have him point out typical life-types of trees and bird life. Such knowledge is first hand and most easily remembered. It will not be possible for most of the Scouts to observe the habits of wild animals in their native haunts, but many boys may some time visit a Zoölogical Garden in some large city and learn something of the animals there. Close observation of any form of outdoor life will prove of great interest to the observer, and create in him a desire for a more thorough knowledge of the great Outdoors.

Poison Oak and Poison Ivy.

Every Scout should be able to recognize instantly the one or both of these plants growing in his part of the country. Poison ivy is distinguished from the harmless Virginia creeper or woodbine, which it resembles, superficially, by having three instead of five leaflets, glossy on the upper surface. The berry-like fruits are grayish-white instead of bluish-black. Poison oak or poison sumac, which is still more dangerous, resembles the harmless staghorn sumac, but its leaflets are also glossy, and its fruit gray instead of red.

Star Constellations.

Almost every boy is familiar with the Big Dipper. Many boys can even point out the Little Dipper and other constellations. When these have once been pointed out to a Scout he will never forget them.

The North Star or Polaris is the bright star in the handle of the Little Dipper. It may be located by continuing the line in the outer side of the bowl of the Big Dipper about five times its own length.

While the outline of the Little Dipper is not always clear, the North Star and the two outer stars on the bowl of the Little Dipper are usually bright. These two outer stars are known as the " Guardians of the Pole."

On the opposite side of the pole star from the Big Dipper at about the same distance will be found a bright constellation known as " Cassiopeia's Chair." It is formed by six stars, five of which are bright enough to be seen on any clear night. These five take the shape of an irregular " W." The location of this constellation is to be noted.

The most wonderful combination of stars in the heavens is known as " Orion." There are several brilliant stars in this constellation.

The Real Test in Scouting — Assimilation of Scout Principles.

11. " Furnish satisfactory evidence that he has put into practice in his daily life the principles of the Scout oath and law."

After all, Scouting does not consist in the wearing of a khaki uniform decorated with badges of various degrees. Unless the Scout has caught the spirit of the early Pioneers, the Frontier Scouts or the Knights of old, and has thereby become trustworthy, loyal, helpful, friendly, courteous, kind, obedient, cheerful, thrifty, brave, clean and reverent, he has certainly failed in meeting the requirements necessary to become a First Class Scout. It is not even sufficient that the Scout be satisfied with himself along these lines. This requirement is intended to furnish evidence as to what other people think of him. The parents at home, the teachers at school, and other associates should give evidence that the Scout can be counted on more than the ordinary boy who is not a Scout. This is the kind of evidence that the Scout Master is asked to obtain before passing the applicant in the First Class requirements.

Training Others.

12. " Enlist a boy trained by himself in the requirements of a Tenderfoot."

Here is the first opportunity to be of real service to another. Thousands of boys are awaiting an opportunity to become Scouts, but owing to the great scarcity of Scout Masters and the need of trained Scouts who can give real assistance in training others in Scoutcraft, these boys are deprived of the privilege of joining a troop and becoming a member of the Boy Scouts of America. When the Scout is ready to pass his final test and finds some boy who wants to become a Scout he should give him sufficient instruction to enable him to pass the Tenderfoot requirements. If for some good reason he cannot join the same troop the first rank applicant should help to find some man in his neighborhood who will be willing to start a new troop of Scouts and become its Scout Master.

Scout Work is Progressive.

In all of the Scout work the advancement of the Scouts from rank to rank should be encouraged as much as possible. It is essential to keep the interest of the boys aroused, if there is to be continued success in the work from month to month, and the program of new activities and new interests provided by the different Scout ranks has been originated and developed to meet this need of a graduated interest-series. The whole work is progressive and the whole Scouting idea has been so mapped out and developed that the boy of twelve or thirteen starting as a Tenderfoot should find new interests to attract and more complex and different things to accomplish as he advances, that will keep him busy throughout his whole period of Scouting days, and build him gradually and surely along efficient lines for the preparedness of his future manhood and citizenship. The Scout Master should endeavor to keep the interest from lagging by carrying out the general programs of Scouting, originate such new work as his geographical environment might suggest or seem to warrant, keep in touch with his fellow Scout Masters in his district or State, and join with them in any sort of inter-troop contest or district work that will lend virile action or arouse more interest, and encourage his boys to keep moving in their work from one class rank to the next, and so attain the goal of all Scouts, entire preparedness and full efficiency by qualifying as an Eagle Scout.

Scout Advancement.

As indicated by the Scout Class Requirements given in the Handbook pp. 29–32, there are three main divisions of progress. First the Scout attains the rank of Tenderfoot. After one month's service he may become a Second Class Scout, providing he has shown preparation necessary to pass the standard tests. After that as soon as he is sufficiently prepared in the next rank requirements, he may become a First Class Scout. The way is now open for qualification for merit badges, in which the Scout makes practical application of his general knowledge gained in Scoutcraft practice, and gains a greater efficiency and development along particular pathways of knowledge.

Merit Badges.

The examination for these badges should be given by the Court of Honor of the Local Council. This examination must not be given any boy who is not qualified as a First-Class Scout. After the boy has passed the examination, the Local Council may secure the Merit Badge for him by presenting the facts to the National Council. These badges are intended to stimulate the boy's interest in the life about him and are given for general knowledge. The wearing of these badges does not signify that a Scout is qualified to make his living by the knowledge gained in securing the award.

In any case where through lack of knowledge or experience, the Court of Honor representative giving the examination is unfamiliar with the Merit Badge Requirements, he should obtain the aid of an expert on the subject whose signature should appear with that of the Court of Honor member on the recommendation sent to National Headquarters.

When the applicant for the merit badge has appeared before the Court of Honor and passed the examination on the subject as set forth in the official Handbook, the application blank is submitted by the Court of Honor of the Local Council with recommendations to the Court of Honor of the National Council. A monthly meeting of the National Court of Honor is held at National Headquarters when all applications received from various Local Councils throughout the country are considered and finally passed upon or rejected by them.

In communities where there are but one or two troops of Scouts and where a Local Council has not been organized, Scout Masters are advised to organize a Local Committee of representative men, including the superintendent or principal of schools, to pass upon these various qualifications. Application blanks for merit badges properly certified by this Committee will be recognized by the National Court of Honor.

The way is also open to attain the higher ranks open to all prepared Scouts, with badges indicating the steady advance toward a greater and greater efficiency and more complete development. So passing from the first grade as a Life Scout, the possessor of five merit badges, the Scout will through persistence and training become also a Star

Scout, and in the end the Eagle Scout. By this time the boy should be reaching maturity both mentally and physically, and having attained the highest Scout rank is quite prepared to cope with all problems of his future.

This progressive plan of development should give to the Scout all that is necessary to keep him interested and busy during his five or six years of Scout service. There are certain things which have been planned for the younger boys and certain other attainments for the older boy, and with the large amount of time given to general Scoutcraft practice, there should be plenty to do for every boy before he has attained his rank as an Eagle Scout and has reached the coöperative period of his life in young manhood. The boy should not be hurried or pushed on from one grade to another, as he will gain best development by slow assimilation of details and gradual development, but on the other hand the Scout Master should guard against lack of action or loss of interest. Stagnation of the onward impulse anywhere along the line is usually indicative of something wrong, either with the methods of the Scout Master, with the appeal of the developing Scout work, or with the general program of procedure of Scouting. Steps should at once be taken in such case to clear up the situation, revive the interest and progress, and invigorate the desires of the boys with the spirit of advancement.

Examinations for Scout Tests.

Special care should be exercised to guard against too rapid advancement by scouts, so as to insure thoroughness in their work.

The members of the local courts of honor and others who may be duly appointed to conduct examinations should keep in mind that the lists of questions as set forth for the various tests are merely an outline of the scope of the examination to be given and do not restrict the examination to the lists. In no case, however, is the court of honor or other examiner authorized to omit any of the points covered by the list, or accept as an equivalent any examination which does not include each of the questions as set forth in this handbook.

It should further be remembered that the purpose of these examinations is not to secure mere technical compliance with the requirements, but rather to ascertain the scout's general knowledge of the subject covered as a result of his own application and study. *Practical knowledge* rather than *book knowledge* is desired.

A Scout should be prepared at any time to submit to an examination reviewing the work for which he has previously received badges. Every examination given for advanced work should include questions of review covering previous tests taken by the applicant. He should also be required to show that he knows and has put into practice the scout oath and law.

Tenderfoot.

Tenderfoot scout tests are given by the Scout Master of the troop in all communities whether there is a local council or not. This does not, however, relieve the local council of the responsibility of maintaining standards.

Second Class.

In communities where there is a local council, second-class scout tests should be given by the Scout Commissioner personally, whenever practicable, or by a deputy designated by him.

First Class.

In communities where there is a local council, first-class scout tests, whenever practicable, should be conducted by the court of honor, or under the personal supervision of the Scout Commissioner or by a deputy designated by him.

In all other communities where local councils have not been organized the examination for second-class and first-class scout tests should be given by the Scout Master of the troop with the cooperation of the troop committee, or by a special committee representing the court of honor which has been selected to conduct examinations for merit badges.

PART I.— WRITTEN.

1. Give date of your becoming a Tenderfoot.
2. Describe how to apply and bandage a splint to a broken bone in the forearm.
3. What is a compound fracture?
4. What is a triangular bandage and what is its use?
5. Describe how to apply a tourniquet to upper arm.
   (a) When vein is cut.
   (b) When artery is cut.
6. When is a stimulant administered to a person who is bleeding badly, and what is given?
7. Describe how a roller bandage is used.
8. How did you earn $1.00 and in what bank is it deposited?

9. Draw a diagram showing the sixteen points of the compass and name each.
   (a) Give degrees of the North, South, East and West points.
10. Give six rules for: —
   (a) Proper use of the knife and ax.
11. Name the twelve points of the Scout Law.

PART II.— ORAL OR BY DEMONSTRATION.

1. Describe treatment for: — Fainting, Shock, Fracture, Bruises, Sprains, Injuries in which the skin is broken, Burns, Scalds.
2. Signal the following by the method or code you have learned: —
   (a) Be Prepared.
   (b) He is absent from Camp.
   (c) Now is the time for all good people to come to the aid of the party.
   (d) Absent.
3. Deliver a message at the distance of one mile at Scout's pace in 12 minutes.
4. Satisfy the examiner that you can lay and light a fire without paper, using only two matches.
5. Upon the fire just lighted cook two potatoes and a quarter of a pound of beef. (Use of ordinary kitchen utensils is not allowed, but mess kit permitted.)

Suggested Methods of Marking for Use in Inter-Patrol Contests.

As inter-patrol competitions are held during the year in the city from which these suggestions come, the examination papers, as above, are marked as follows: —

(1) Scouts passing with a percentage of from 85 to 100 will be awarded an " H," which means that the Scout has passed with honor, and his patrol will be credited with 25 points.

(2) Scouts passing with an average of from 70 to 85 per cent. will be given a " C," which shows creditable work, and his patrol will be awarded 15 points.

(3) Scouts passing with a percentage of from 60 to 70 will be given a " P," which means he has been successful and passed the examination. This patrol will be awarded 5 points.

(4) Any Scout receiving a percentage of between 50 and 60 will be marked with an "F," which means that he has failed to meet the standard of requirements. However, he will be allowed to take the next regular examination given by the Court of Honor.

(5) Any Scout failing to receive a percentage of at least 50 will be marked "FF" and his patrol will have to forfeit 10 points. He will not be allowed to take the next examination, but may take anyone succeeding that.

The Investiture Ceremony.

No certain form of investiture of Scouts in their different ranks has been followed, but the question of simplicity or impressiveness of such ceremony has been left largely to the individual tastes and originality of the Scout Masters. Some prefer to have the ceremony as simple as it may be, while others find best results in incorporating fraternity ceremonies to create interest, give a strong impression, and provide added dignity. As a matter of fact the boy at Scout age is impressed with ceremonial just because he is, and likes to be counted as, one of the gang or troop, and some form of ceremonial certainly lends a greater meaning and stronger feeling in the attainment of any social achievement. It is best however to guard against complexity of such ceremonial lest the boy become wearied with its make-believe formalism and lose respect for the underlying principles. The first ceremony, too, should be simple and pointed, as for the Tenderfoot, and as the Scout advances in rank new symbolistic ceremonies should be added to the investitures to produce a stronger impression of the achievements' worth and give a greater dignity to the importance of the rank.

In the chapter on "Programs for Scout Masters," which by suggestions carries a troop onward from its first organization to First Class Scout rank, investiture ceremonies are suggested as parts of regular programs. In some cities or districts such ceremonial is sometimes standardized by the Scout Commissioner for the use of all troops in his community, but while the wording and thought varies according to the locality and initiative of the Scout Leader, the general outline of investiture must remain very much the same. One of the best forms in actual use for the Tenderfoot Scout rank is herewith suggested: Form the troop into a horseshoe formation with the Scout Master and his Assistant in the gap. The Tenderfoot with his patrol leader stands just inside of the circle and opposite to the Scout Master. The Assistant Scout Master holds the staff and hat of the candidate. When ordered by the Scout Master to come forward the Patrol Leader brings the Tenderfoot to the center. The Scout Master then asks: "Do you know what your honor is?"

Tenderfoot replies: "Yes, it means that I can be trusted to be truthful and honest" (or words to that effect).

Scout Master: "Can I trust you on your honor to do your duty to your God and country and to obey the Scout law? To help other people at all times? To keep yourself physically strong, mentally awake and morally straight?"

The Tenderfoot then salutes, as do the whole troop while he repeats the Scout Oath:—"On my honor I will do my best:—

(1)   To do my duty to God and my country, and obey the Scout Law.

(2)   To help other people at all times.

(3)   To keep myself physically strong, mentally awake and morally straight."

The Scout Master replies: "I trust you will keep these promises. You are now one of the great brotherhood of Scouts."

The Assistant Scout Master then puts on his hat and gives him his staff, decorates him with the Tenderfoot badge and greets him with the grip or Boy Scout Handshake for the Tenderfoot. In case there is no Assistant Scout Master, the senior patrol leader will have charge of the staff and hat, and the Scout Master decorates him with the badge and greets him with the handshake of the Tenderfoot. The new Scout then faces about and salutes the troop. The troop then present staves, the Scout Master gives the word to the troop "Right by twos, march," whereupon the new Scout takes his place in his patrol, and the troop shoulder staves and march once around the room or square and then disband on the order and take seats.

Chapter III

PRINCIPLES AND METHODS

Changes in Scout Oath, Scout Law and Requirements.

In a review of the official English handbooks of Scouting it will be noticed that considerable change has been made in the Scout Oath, Scout Law and Scout Requirements to adapt them to American conditions. The laws have been increased from nine to twelve. The Scout Oath has been modified and the Scout Requirements changed to make them more representative of American life. All these changes have been made in order to more effectually help the American boy.

Reasons for Changes.

The attitude of the Scout authorities in making the changes has been that of open mindedness. Suggestions from all over the country were asked for, received and given careful attention, the one thing in mind being to get the Scout Oath, Scout Law and Scout Requirements as simple as possible for the normal boy. Much consideration was given to the suggested substitute for the term Scout Oath. It was agreed that the word promise was not strong enough to grasp the imagination of the boys; that the word pledge has been given a distinct temperance content, and that the word vow had too much of a religious significance. Therefore, the word oath was kept after due deliberation, it being thoroughly understood that the Scout Oath was not in any way like the oath taken in a formal court of law, but that it was more on the order of the knightly oath of the Middle Ages, where the knight pledged his word of honor to reverence his king as his conscience, and his conscience as his king. It is indeed a pledge of fidelity by knights of a newer era for the building of a better and more social chivalry.

The Third Section of the Scout Oath.

It will be noticed that the Scout Oath has undergone considerable change. The third section of the Scout Oath has been incorporated with the first section of the new, and a third section has been added, namely: "To keep myself physically strong, mentally awake, and morally straight." It is desired by this latter section of the Oath to keep before the boy the fact that it is his business to keep himself strong, to get for himself an education for life, and at the same time to keep himself clean in his resolutions, to himself, and to others, and to his Creator. The desire underlying the change was to sum up all the cardinal things to be brought to the boys' attention in the Scout Oath.

Aim of the Scout Law.

The Scout Law is intended to inculcate those ideas which should underlie the life of each boy. The aim is to get the boy to understand the value of his honor, to be trustworthy, loyal, helpful, friendly, courteous, kind, obedient, cheerful, thrifty, brave, clean and reverent. Laws 10, 11 and 12 have been added to the original number because it was thought that these things had been touched on in the Scout Oath but had been omitted in the Scout Law. Besides this, several additions and emendations have been made to the original nine, and General Baden-Powell, the author of the original law, has commended the changes and additions.

The Spirit of the Scout Law.

It will not be to the interests of the Scout Master to teach the Scout Oath and Law to the Scout without living up to the spirit of these himself. To-day we teach more by example than by precept, and the life of the Scout Master will be the most potent teaching that the boy can receive. In every activity the Scout Master should impress upon the boy that it is his business to manifest the spirit of the law and that he should not allow himself to be side-tracked from doing his duty as set forth in the Scout Law.

Laxity Versus Discipline and the Scout Law.

The Scout Master should not be anxious to discipline the boy. There will be many little lapses on the part of the boy because the boy is not mature and is not possessed of a developed mind. In fact the Scout Master will make some of these lapses himself if he is not careful. The Scout

Master should not be petty in his discipline but should stand on the high plane of honor in everything. On the other hand he should be careful not to be lax, and the Boy Scout should understand that when he has said a thing, he means it. Liberal and cautious in his judgment, but firm in his attitude when once his judgment has been made, should be the rule of the Scout Master in matters of discipline, if he has not come to the point where he can trust the boys to make their own laws and judge their own offenses. A form of punishment which has worked out well in other boys' organizations has been to delay the examination of the boy for advanced work because of his offense to a later time, thus depriving the boy of the pleasure he had anticipated.

Law 3 and the Home.

Law 3 has been broadened so that it covers the home. One of the essential things that the Scout Master should do is to coöperate with the home in matters of parental authority and obedience. The requirement that he shall share the home duties is intended to give the Scout the intimate touch and contact with those of the home circle which he ought to have.[1]

Law 10 and Courage.

Law 10 seeks to encourage the boy to be the possessor of moral courage, to face danger in spite of fear and to stand up for the right in spite of the coaxings of his friends or the jeers of his enemies; and, when he has been defeated, never to feel broken, but to be ready again for another onslaught and a possible victory. This law recognizes that it is right to fight if there is necessity.

Law 11 and Cleanliness.

Law 11 recognizes the idea of environment and urges the boy to choose his companions rightly, knowing that the life of his companions very largely molds the life of the growing boy. Law 11 considers cleanliness and deals with the opposition to tobacco, cigarette smoking, liquor and profanity, but covers a great deal more in its scope.

Law 12 and Reverence.

Law 12 directs the attention of the boy to the idea of reverence. It holds his religious duties as an ideal worthy

[1] An interesting booklet on Home Training has been written by William A. McKeever of the Kansas State Agricultural College, Manhattan, Kansas.

of being worked for, and urges upon him the duty and responsibility of respecting the convictions of every other man in the matters of tradition, custom and religion. Should he think he has more light on these matters than the man next him, he should be the more generous and liberal because of that fact.

Spread of the Scouting Idea.

The idea of Scouting is no longer a national or provincial thing. Like the sun, it has penetrated to all the corners of the earth and now it holds twenty-six countries, including the English Colonies, in the bonds of its brotherhood. Starting with the ideas of a few Americans, as they have been worked out in various American boy organizations, they have been adopted and organized by Lieutenant General Sir Robert Baden-Powell, and have gone forth from him to circle the globe and draw the boys of the world into the great brotherhood of boyhood and peace. Other boy organizations have had a national scope,— the Boy Scout Movement is international and world wide in its influence.

General Characteristics of the Adolescent Age.

The interests of the adolescent boy are general and not specialized between the twelfth and eighteenth year. The boy gets his impressions of the community objectively, in addition to increasing his knowledge of the external world through his acquaintanceship with its phenomena. The Universe and the Community are extensive and many sided. The step also between twelve and eighteen years is short. The boy's contact with these, then, must be rapid and general. The Scouting activities afford such contact.

Scouting as an Auxiliary to the Home, School and Church.

There are three institutions that should mold the life of the boy,— the Home, School and Church. Nothing should interfere with the functions of these, and the place of any auxiliary organization should be supplementary in its nature and educational in character. The Scout Idea takes the non-supervised, leisure time of boys and fills it with recreation, — educational activity. It teaches him facts about nature and citizenship and how to get the most out of life. It leaves parental and School and Church ties stronger because of non-interference. It is primarily educational, leading the boy by degrees to a rounded symmetrical development.

Scouting Provides Occupation for the Leisure Hours.

The preventative work of the Boy Scouts of America cannot be tabulated in statistical form but beyond question it is its largest achievement. You can sum up the whole philosophy of reaching and holding boys for all that is noble and right in one word,— pre-occupation. The fathers and mothers do not fear for their boys when they are busy in school, at the factory or in the office. The time to be alarmed in their behalf is in connection with the un-accounted-for evenings, the half-holidays, the time between the closing of school and supper. To these hours we may trace the formation of most of the life habits which mean the undoing of the best of our boys. The Boy Scouts of America in providing helpful and character-building occupation for these hours is therefore rendering a service of inestimable importance.

The Call of Service and Citizenship.

The call of the Community is service. This constitutes Patriotism to State and Country. The cry of the adolescent boy is Service. This means that citizenship, in its formation, begins with the twelve-year-old boy. The Scout Idea recognizes the voice of Adolescence, and in this, his thought and life challenges the developing boy to seek new expression in a " Good turn done daily " to someone.

The Appeal of Scouting.

In brief Scouting appeals to boys because it affords them activities suited to their years in a complete symmetrical way. These activities do not interfere with the home, school or church, are primarily educational, and urge the Service Spirit in adolescent boyhood.

Scouting means a great deal more than merely outdoor activity. It touches all the interests of the boy life and besides giving an occupation in woodlore activities such as being able to find a direction in the woods without a compass, to discover the latitude by the stars, to know the birds, fish, reptiles, insects, butterflies, rocks, pebbles, flowers, ferns, grasses, fungi, trees and wild animals, gives him practical instruction in how to camp out, to canoe, to sail a boat, to take care of his health, to appreciate the spirit of the past with its gentle manners and rich achievements, to render first aid in case of fire and water accidents, to play games with the spirit of fair play, and to compete in athletic contests with a sterling regard for his own and his competitor's honor, and finally how to achieve citizenship — to know the things that enter into the making of a citizen, to understand how to be a citizen — *to know, to be, and to do*.

Qualifications of the Scout Master.

The qualifications of a good Scout Master may be divided into three classes; fundamental, essential and secondary. The fundamental qualities which the Scout Master must have to make him an acceptable worker with boys are "*horse sense*" and the *judicial capacity*. No man can expect to lead boys for any great length of time who fails to have a keen appreciation of the perspective of things. There is an everlasting fitness which the boy looks for in the man and nothing steals the boy's confidence from his leader more than the lack of ability on the part of the man to size up things in a common-sense manner and to deal with them without fuss or feathers. He must also avoid anything that looks like favoritism or partiality. He is given the oversight of twenty-four boys for a definite reason. One boy would often gain his point with his Scout Master were it not for the presence of the other twenty-three. The Scout Master must not give way to the boy's desire against the boy's good, and must never become unduly emotional in dealing with his Scouts. In other words he must be judicial in his attitude as he works with the boys.

Given these fundamental characters of common sense and judicial capacity, he must have the three essential qualifications of every leader of boys. He must be possessed of a *good character* because the movement in which he works is a moral movement and aims to build up character as well as citizenship. He must also have the *ability to gain the respect of boys*. No weak, vacillating, inert, back-boneless creature may ever aspire to the leadership of a group of boys. There must be in him that quality which will appeal to the boy's respect and which will compel them to follow him. The Scout Master must also, as an essential qualification, have *executive ability for leadership*. He does not need to be an expert in Scoutcraft but he must have a deep interest in boys, be genuine in his own life, and have the ability to lead and command the boys' respect and obedience. The good Scout Master because of his executive ability will discover experts for the various activities such as woodcraft, signalling, camping, canoeing, hiking, tracking, first aid, and life saving. He will also be able to find men who will gladly give the boys interesting talks on the principles of chivalry and citizenship.

To be a really successful leader, a Scout Master must also have four secondary characteristics. He must not be like a ship without a rudder at sea, and no matter what he does with his boys, he *must always have a definite aim in mind.* He ought to know what he is driving at, what he is aiming for. Not only this but he should *have a well-defined plan,* having clearly in mind the stages through which he will bring to pass his aim. In doing this he must have a great stock of patience and be *possessed of a mighty desire to invest himself and his time.* No Scout Master can hope to do very lasting work with any group of boys who is sparing of himself or grudges his own leisure time to the work. Above all the Scout Master must remember that he is not dealing with a physical boy only, but that *the boy is physical, mental, moral and social in his make-up.*

The Scout Master who has these fundamental, essential and secondary qualifications stands a fair chance of doing the most acceptable kind of work with a troop of Scouts.

The Need of Study.

To keep properly in advance of the boys in his troop, the Scout Master will need to be a student. He cannot hope in these days of numerous books to lead his boys in the discovery of new things if he is not determined to do a good deal of reading. A Scout Master, where possible, should attend a course of lectures concerning Scouting to get a knowledge and insight into the subjects which are covered by the movement. He should do a great deal of reading along the lines of Scouting besides attending lectures on outdoor activities.

The Scout Master and the Father.

The Scout Master should by no means try to become a father to the boy. The responsibility and duties of parents must not for one moment devolve upon him. The following editorial from a New York evening newspaper puts this idea in a very clear manner and it should be given careful consideration by every Scout Master.

" It takes time to point a boy right. The great merchant

can touch a desk bell to give orders for a steamship or a draft of a million dollars. But the merchant's young son, age fourteen, cannot be touched off in that way. The lad has just begun to move out among other boys. They do a world of talking, these young chaps. The father must watch that talk, and he can, if he will take the time.

Influence of the Father.

The older man has every advantage for he is looked up to and beloved. It is not so much the 'don'ts' as the 'do's' that constitute his power. He can inspire with high resolve. He can narrate his own victories over sore trials and fiery tests of his integrity. He can draw the sting of poisonous suggestions, moral disheartenings and malice which his child has been cherishing in his young heart. But this means time, and time may be money. Yet no money can buy the sort of instruction, nor put a price on it. The coin is struck in the soul. It is the costliest barter, the very exchange of the soul.

Boys who go right have invariably had a world of time spent on them in this way. Boys go wrong because the father would not take the time from the market. In after years the same parent will take vastly more time to try, in tears of sorrow, to straighten out that boy."

The Scout Master and the Home.

The Scout Master can do his best work when working in conjunction with the home. It is a good plan to visit the father and mother of the boy before the boy is enrolled in the patrol, explaining to them just what Scouting means and what is to be gained by it. It is also a pretty good thing occasionally to drop in to see the father and mother of the boy, telling them how the Scout is getting along, giving them a hint here and there how to apply the Scout Law and Oath in the home. The meetings of the troop and patrol should never be secret in that parents and friends are debarred from them. An invitation extended to the parents through the boy himself to attend a meeting of the patrol or troop will also afford a valuable means of contact with the home and parents.

The Scout Master and the School.

The Scout Master must keep in mind that it is his business to work in coöperation with all of the forces that are trying to help the boy to live rightly in his community. The work of the Public School must continue to go on without a break if the ideals of our American citizenship are to be maintained, and it is the business of the Scout Master to give his support, encouragement and coöperation for the carrying out of the idea for which the school stands. The public school seeks to give the boy the necessary education towards his earning a livelihood, and the business of Scouting is to supplement this training by recreational education in the form of outdoor life, scout activities and training in courtesy and citizenship. The Scout Master then is doing his best work when he so plans his Scouting that it will fit into the school or employed life of the boy.

It frequently happens that active and ambitious boys are so eager to make progress through the different Scout ranks that their school work suffers in consequence. When this happens, the Scout Master is usually blamed by parents and teachers, although he may have planned the required work with great care; so as not to make a heavy demand upon the boy's time. The best way to restrain an over-ambitious Scout is to make him understand that examinations for promotion will be held after a certain specified period, and that rapid work will be a hindrance, rather than a help. In troops which have adopted the merit system, it is an excellent plan to allow a credit of a certain number of points per month for a general average of high percentage in school, thus placing a premium on scholarship.

The Scout Master and Religion.

No Scout Master should think for one moment that the moral life of the boy depends entirely on him. The religious life of the community was in existence long before Scouting was ever thought of. The Scout Master by his own life should be an example to the boy and he should never under any circumstances seek to supplant the influence of the church, Sunday school or religious organization in the mind of the boy.

Coöperation.

Recognizing the fact that the boy is physical, social, mental and moral, he should bend every effort to work with all of the organizations and institutions in the community for the boy's best development. He should also seek the sympathy, coöperation and approval of the community's religious teachers.

Scouting is Recreational.

The Scout Master should always keep in mind the fact that Scouting is recreational education. It is not the education of the schoolroom and should never be formal. An informal group of boys gathered around a Scout Master on a plot of grass, in a clump of trees, by the side of a brook, or lying lazily before a warmth-giving log fire affords a setting in which a Scout Master can give the best instruction to the boys.

Worth of the Story.

The method employed should be the story-method instead of academic instruction. It is much easier to impress upon the boy-mind the necessity of fitness and endurance and the habits that make these by telling a story of a football game that was won by the physical prowess of some player, than it is to tell him of the principles which should enter into his life to make him strong. The telling of the story will leave a vivid impression upon the mind of the boy, and the impression will stay with him when the incident and the lesson that was to be taught are forgotten. To be a successful teacher of life's lessons, to make a boy a strong and a good citizen, depends very largely upon the way in which the information is imparted. The great speakers to boys always use the story-telling method of omitting a moral at the conclusion by wrapping the lesson and moral within the story itself. A well-told story often has more influence through suggestion than any amount of direct advice.

The Spirit of Scouting and the Spirit of the Scout Master.

The Spirit of the Scout Master must be the spirit of Scouting itself. There is hardly any use of a Scout Master trying to teach the principles of the Scout Oath and Scout Law, if he is not living them himself. The spirit of the Scout Oath and Law must permeate his own life before he can hope to make an impression on the boy. The boy is a hater of shams, and once he sees through a man who is trying to teach him something that he himself is not, nothing on earth can make the boy do other than despise the man. This means that a Scout Master must always be on his mettle, that he will have to keep himself " physically strong, mentally awake and morally straight " if he is to lead his boys; and that he will have to " help other people at all times," as well as displaying in his own life the principles that underlie chivalry. It means that he will have to do always his " duty to God and his country," and " to obey the Scout Law." It further means that he himself will have to be trustworthy, loyal, helpful, courteous, kind, obedient, cheerful, thrifty, brave, clean and reverent, and if the Scout Master does his best to carry out these principles in his own life, as a great teacher of old once said, others shall see him and shall follow. There then will be no difficulty with Scout Masters handling their boys and the Scout Master and the boy will develop together, and together find success in Scouting.

Principles of Boy-Work.

Several well-defined and exceedingly clear principles of action underlie the successful handling of groups of boys : —

First, there must be a clear plan well thought out, progressive in its stages with an aim for each stage. In other words no man need try to work with a group of boys unless he knows what he wants to do, not only in outline but in detail. He must have these details in mind and so well worked out in his thought, knowing exactly what comes next and just what is to be added to that which he has already accomplished, as to be master of the situation at all times and to be the recognized leader. Not only this, but the boys must feel that he really knows what he is driving at in everything that he attempts.

Secondly, before the leader of a group of boys tries to do anything with the group, if he is to be successful, it is necessary for him to make a frank outlined statement of his plan. That is to say, he should tell the boys what the game is and how it is to be played, getting their approval, and agreement to get in on the deal. He can explain this to all of the boys at one time or singly to each boy. There is no question but that he will succeed best if he should go over the matter first with each individual boy personally, finding out the individual impressions, and also having discussion before the group or patrol unit. This being done the boys know the plan, the leader knows what he is working towards, and the leader and the boys are partners in the work.

In this way the right idea of Scouting will be given to the boys and they will understand just what it means. Too often groups of boys are brought together and the aim is so hazy in the leader's mind that all the boys can possibly see in the scheme is a " good time." No Scout Master who fails to hold up before the boys a clear, comprehensive statement of Scouting that the boy can understand, can ever hope to see his boys do anything else but look for fun and mischief in everything they do. Such a patrol or troop cannot last very long because the Scout Master will very soon be asking himself if the thing that he is attempting is worth the trouble to which he is going.

Application of Self-Government.

Thirdly, the best way to have boys accomplish things is to allow them to do the things. Many a leader of boys thinks out a plan, gives it to a group of boys and then thinks that the boys are themselves doing it, whereas he is only trying to use the boys as his instrument. The most effectual way of getting boys to do things themselves is to let them do as much as they can and will do under adequate supervision. Lead by suggestion, so that unconsciously the boys follow your advice and dictation, giving them the benefit of their decisions and impulses. Pure self-government in which the boys are entirely the dictators of their policies and activities can not be thought of, because such a course is so generally fatal to successful development. But self-government fostered and dealt with through suggestion by the adult mind is just what is needed, and should always be encouraged.

The Scout Master as a Real Leader.

Fourth, in letting the boys run their own affairs in this way, the Scout Master must become a real leader. A real leader never stalks in front, nor gives orders openly. The generals of to-day fight their battles and win them twenty-five miles in the rear of the firing line. So it is with the Scout Master. He must be the power behind the throne, rather than the throne itself. He must be as a conscience — to hold the boys back just a little when they go too fast and to push just a little when they are going too slow. The Scout Master must recognize himself to be the impetus, not the goal. The solution of each problem that comes before

a patrol or troop should not only be considered by the
whole group, but should be solved by the boys whenever
such action will not interfere with the best interests of the
group and the movement. The important thing for the
Scout Master to remember in these matters is that his
fundamental objective is good citizenship and that the
method of practical American citizenship is the majority
rule. But this boy majority rule should, of course, be tem-
pered by governing leadership. Thus the Scout Master will
not do anything that the boy can do himself, and he will be
continually placing responsibility on the lad. Responsibility is the great maker of men.

Differences, " Scraps " and Misunderstandings.

Fifth, there will be of course noticeable differences among
the boys of the patrol and troop. The most serious differences arise even among men. The boys will " scrap " at
times, and there will sometimes be a tension and rigidity
about their discussions that will approach the breaking point.
Through it all it will be difficult for the Scout Master to keep
himself patiently aloof and allow the thing to work out its
own way. Sometimes an appeal will be made to him to
settle the dispute, and he will be tempted to do so, but often
such action will imperil the object for which he is working.
It is best to allow the boys to discuss, and try out all of their
logic before he begins to make suggestions and, if he can
get the boys to settle the matter themselves, it is to his interest to do so. If a deadlock threatens to exist, then by
wise counsel and judicious suggestions he may be able to
lead the boys out of a quandary in such a way that it will
look as if the boys had gotten out of the difficulty themselves. This will certainly add strength to their organization and they will settle their own quarrels with peace and
dignity. Sometimes the break between the boys will be
so bitter as to cause the formation of intensely hostile fac-
tions, and then the best thing the Scout Master can do is
not to try any new patching or drawing together of the op-
posing forces. There is no use trying to make boys who are
bitterly antagonistic, agreeable to each other. Let them
make new alignments if necessary and in combinations of
their own choosing, even if the result should be the formation of new patrols.

Rules and Infringements of Rules.

Sixth, the boys should make their own rules and provide for the infringement of minor rules, insofar as such action will not be a harm or a hindrance. Boy punishments meted out by boys to boys sounds well enough in theory but does not prove efficient in practice, and should by all means be discouraged or forbidden. The danger of an excessive tendency toward unreasonable action or decisions by the boys is too great. But wherever possible the boys should have a hand in the making of the laws which govern them. Responsibility should be the key-note; and the awakening of such a feeling in the boys should be the goal.

Grouping Standards.

The Scout Master will find it greatly to his advantage to group his boys according to some standard. Unfortunately all standards, so far, are more or less artificial, but approximate success may be secured by using the experience of boy workers in various parts of the country. The standard which is most generally used is that of age. It is also the most unsatisfactory. Boys mature physically rather than chronologically. This makes the age standard a poor guess, because a boy may be physically fourteen when he is chronologically eleven, and vice versa. If the age standard be used, it would be preferable to group all the boys of twelve years together, then the thirteen-year old boys in another group, and the same with the fourteen, the fifteen, the sixteen, and the seventeen-year old boys. This would be rather hard to do in small places, although perfectly feasible in a larger town or city. Because of its impossibility as far as the rural districts are concerned, it might be well to divide the years from twelve to eighteen into three standards,— twelve to fourteen, fourteen to sixteen, and sixteen to eighteen. The age grouping, however, will never be reliable in achieving results.

The height and weight standard is more scientifically correct than the age standard, although it has not been tested out enough to warrant any authoritative declaration in its favor. If this method is used for grouping, the standards for athletic competition among the boys might be used, that is, all the boys of ninety pounds and under might be put together, the same being true for those under one hundred and ten, one hundred and twenty-five, and one hundred and forty pounds. If height is used, boys of fifty-six and a half inches in height and classifying under ninety pounds in weight, might be grouped together. Also boys of sixty-three inches in height and coming within the one hundred and ten pound weight. This standard will doubtless become the real basis of all groupings in the future, but as yet it needs more demonstration in order that the various classifications may be made accurately.

A simple and rather satisfactory way of grouping is by the school boy or wage-earning boy standard. If the boy happens to be in the grammar school, he may be grouped with boys of his own educational advancement; so with the boys who are in the secondary or high schools, and the same may be said of working boys who are forced to earn their own livelihood.

Possibly the best and most satisfactory way of grouping boys is by their interest. Some boys will be mutually interested in collecting stamps, riding a bicycle, forming a mounted patrol, working with wireless, in music and orchestra work, etc., and boys grouped according to such kindred interests as they manifest has proven most satisfactory in general boys' work.

Problems of Boy-Handling Simplified by Natural Standard Grouping.

Grouping the boys according to natural standards makes the problem of handling them much simpler. Boys between twelve and fourteen are in the age of authority, and the word of the Scout Master will settle most difficulties that arise. Boys between fourteen and sixteen are in the age of experience and an opportunity must be given the boys to check up what they are told by what they are experiencing. Between twelve and fourteen, authority may be rigid. Between fourteen and sixteen, it must be giving way to reason. Authority will still continue to settle the boys' disputes but it will be the authority that gives reasons for its action. Boys between the ages of sixteen and eighteen years can only be handled on the basis of coöperation. They have passed from the stage of blindly following what they are told. They have experience enough to know that they are able to do things themselves, and they have discovered enough things to give them a basis of doing things on their own account. The way to handle boys rightly in this group will be by tactful suggestion and coöperation on the part of a Scout Master.

Scouting is More a System of Action Than of Words.

Scouting is not just a lot of lectures or talks to a group of boys; the boy does not want to have Scouting talked into him,— he wants to scout. In early adolescence the boy is all movement and it is a punishment for him to sit very long to hear any kind of talk. The blood is being pumped at a much faster rate through his veins in early adolescence than at any other time, and this increased vitality demands increased movement in exercise. Not only should a boy not be compelled to sit very long at this period, but his activities should be changed every few minutes. A wise Scout Master never keeps his boys at any activity more than fifteen minutes at a time unless they are especially wrapped up in the idea. The boy wants to scout and the proper way to give instructions to boys about Scouting is by the story or yarn method, which has already been spoken of in this chapter.

Neither is Scouting a history of Indian tribes or of any other interesting thing in the community. These may be supplemental and of great value to the Scout, but Scouting first, last and all the time is the development of self-resourcefulness by contact with life and the community through outdoor activities and the daily routine.

The Small Boy Versus the Older Boy in Progressive Results.

A great many Scout Masters have made the serious mistake of starting with smaller boys. Several organizations, splendidly adapted for the development of adolescent boys, have been ruined and discontinued by this very thing. It is easy to get a group of small boys to take up any activity but the fellows whom this movement is going to benefit most are the boys who are somewhat skeptical and have to be shown just what the Scout Master is driving at. A frank, fair statement of the aim and method will meet with generous support from ninety-nine out of every hundred boys. The movement, however, must start with the older boys, and not with the younger.

The Patrol Leader and the Scout Master.

Care should be taken by the Scout Master that the patrol leaders do not have too great authority in the supervision of their patrols. The success of the troop affairs and supervision of patrol progress is, in the last analysis the responsibility of the Scout Master and not that of the patrol leader. There is also a danger, in magnifying the patrol leader in this way, of inordinately swelling the ordinary boy's head. The activities of the patrol should not be left to the judgment of any patrol leader, and if the Scout Master wants to delegate the work of the patrol and troop, the whole group should reach a decision in regard to the plan. Every patrol leader that a Scout Master has increases his responsibility all the more, and the addition of a patrol to his troop, with its corresponding new patrol leader, means just a little more supervisory work for him.

Team-Work.

The question has been asked, " what shall we do with the boy who does not enjoy team work? " If there should be such a boy in the patrol, of scouting age,— twelve years, and over,— you may rely upon it that the boy is really preadolescent, or has been brought up under such conditions as to stultify the natural order of the adolescent boy's life. Either the boy must be given time to reach adolescence or the Scout Master must give him extra attention by developing in him the spirit of service,— the doing of tasks without assistance.

The Spirit of Money-Making.

Although thriftiness and saving is one of the Scout virtues the commercial spirit should be guarded against, because when uncontrolled it has a detrimental effect upon the boys. Boys should not be encouraged to get up plays, entertainments, cut grass, sell articles, or do any one of the thousand things boys can do to earn money for a patrol, when the patrol does not need the money. America is passing through a money-getting age and it is commonly agreed that many of the money-magnates of the United States have caused much of the corrupt government which is existent in so many communities. To promote higher standards the Scout Master must turn the boy's attention from the accumulation of funds to the activities of Scouting.

Advancement through the Scout Degrees.

Now and then a complaint arises because the boys do not qualify quickly enough for the various degrees of Scouting. It seems that the Tenderfoot once having been admitted to the patrol and having become a Tenderfoot is in no hurry to become a Second Class Scout, and a Second Class Scout has no desire apparently to make good as a First Class Scout. This should be the abnormal case and the Scout Master in charge of the troop wherever this occurs should bend every energy towards getting the boys to complete the requirements as laid down in the official manual. Otherwise the boys will be merely Scouts in name, and not in reality.

Lack of Interest in Patrol or Troop Meetings.

Inability to sustain interest in the patrol meetings is given by some Scout Masters for failure to get boys to become enthusiastic in Scouting. The trouble here seems to depend largely on the part of the Scout Master and no doubt, arises from the fact that the Scout Master makes no program for a patrol or troop meeting. The situation will probably change materially just as quickly as the Scout Master knows what he is going to do when he meets his boys.

Parental Objection and Religious Interference.

Parental objection and religious interference may sometimes effect the advancement of the boys, of the Tenderfoot stage. The Scout Master will have to be very careful what he does when it comes to a matter of parental objection. The Scout Master must in no way interfere with the home, but the difficulty would seem to offer an opportunity for a candid talk with the father and mother of the boy showing them just what the idea will accomplish for their son. If the parents still object after this has been done then it is the wisest thing on the part of the Scout Master to drop the boy from the troop.

The Scout Master's Duty, the Sunday School and the Church.

What has been said of the home may be said also of the religious influences of the community. We can not conceive of a church, Sunday School or religious society which can seriously object to the idea of Scouting, if a clear idea is presented of what Scouting gives to the boy. The Scout Master should stand up firmly against making Scouting a mere bait for the boy's attendance at either church or Sunday School. But it should always be the duty of the Scout Master to coöperate willingly and work hand in hand with the boys' religious institutions.

Failure to Keep Engagements.

Failure to keep scheduled engagements is given as another reason for failure. This can only be due to lack of interest on the part of the boys. It may be added that a Scout Master having made an engagement with his boys has no right to break that engagement for another, unless it is of the most serious nature. The boy has a right to expect just as courteous and serious treatment on the part of the Scout Master as the Scout Master has on the part of the boy. Engagements should not be made lightly, and emphasis should be laid not only upon the keeping of the engagement, but its prompt keeping on the part of both the Scout Master and the boy.

The Working-Boy and His Chance for Scouting.

Sometimes the Scouts who are enrolled in the troop or patrols are working boys and have really little time to give to the pleasure and activities of Scouting. The working-boy question is a little difficult in its solution, but there are very few boys who work more than ten hours a day, and a couple of hours' Scouting in the evening, if given in the form of games and recreation, will not only help the boy as a Scout, but will send him back re-created for his work next day.

Need of Strong and Efficient Organizations.

A serious mistake of a good many Scout Masters seems to be the looseness of organization in their patrols and troops. The Scout Master does not insist on the boy's addressing him or the patrol leader in the proper fashion. Anything goes if the boys are pleased, and they are having a good time. No Scout Master will get very far with his boys with such procedure and the insistence on his part of having the boys address him as " Sir " will help him greatly to establish a right kind of spirit in his troop.

Neither should the Scout Master after a Scout meeting

of ten or fifteen minutes turn the boys loose to their own devices. The boys will easily keep themselves busy and fill out the time of meeting but this is not the idea of the meeting. The Scout Master has too big a job on his hands and the problem of making manhood and citizenship is too serious a proposition to be given so little thought and planning. A plan for each meeting and an aim for each plan should be the Scout Master's slogan.

There are some things in connection with Scout work that should be most vigorously guarded against. The Scout Master should by all means guard against athletic leagues of baseball, football, track, basket-ball, etc., within the Scout organization, for nothing will more weaken your development and cause more dissension than an athletic league. Scouting is self-sufficient in itself, and if athletics are substituted for the regular Scout activities in order to keep up a seeming lack of interest in Scouting, something is materially wrong with your leadership or with the temperament of your boys. Athletic games are admirable in theory and usually in practice, and lend a means of excellent development for boys. But competitive athletics have no place in Scout work, and should be assiduously frowned down upon and discouraged. At Silver Bay during the summer of 1910 one hundred and twenty-five boys were present in a Scout camp. They were only one hundred feet from the beach of Lake George, and about one hundred yards from one of the finest amateur athletic fields in the country. In the fifteen days that the boys were in camp, not a single game of baseball was played and but once was there a water meet of any kind. The boys were so busy finding out the things of the woods and were so occupied with the activities as set forth in the official manual that they had no time for the usual play of boy life.

Neither should a Scout Master waste his time and energy on indoor scout meets and demonstrations. A scout meet and demonstration is a good thing once or twice a year but the real opportunity and need of Scouting is the close association of a Scout Master and his boys. The time wasted in scout demonstrations and meets could be more profitably employed by the Scouts learning the things about them and making good in the higher degrees. Linked to baseball, basketball and athletic demonstrations is the idea of a gymnasium. The gymnasium is merely the result of a lack of opportunity to do Scouting. Seventy-five to one hundred years ago when the boys were raised on farms and were in continual touch with everything that tended to build up life, gymnasiums were not heard of. With the development of industrial conditions and the necessity of men, women and children living in towns, the gymnasium came into existence as a preserver of health. The Scout Movement is a step towards the old outdoor life that industrial development paralyzed, and a Scout Master is doing very little for a group of boys by providing them with either gymnasium or gymnasium apparatus.

The Real Solution of Scout Problems.

A Scout Master in speaking of his Scout work and troop management says: "I try to keep myself in the background, as much as possible. I have insisted on the boys who join my troop knowing what the purposes and objective of Scouting really is. I have made them enroll properly and I am making them do the work of the patrol and troop in their own way." This Scout Master's advice is the solution for every problem that can come up in Scouting. A Scout Master who is an adviser and the real leader through suggestions, develops the ideal conditions to be realized in real practice of Scouting. Questions of discipline, questions of interest, questions of uniforms and all the business problems that come up to such a Scout Master and his boys will then be greatly simplified or easily solved.

The Importance of the Daily Good Turn.

It should be remembered by the Scout Master that the daily good turn is the heart and center of all of the Scout Activities. It is the idea to get the boy to look away from himself, and to give some thought and attention to others. The Scout should be urged to do his good turn and once in a while the Scout should tell the Scout Master the things that he has been doing. The boy however, should be discouraged from voluntarily telling about his good deeds as a regular thing. He should be taught to let his right hand do things without his left hand knowing anything about them. Do not compel the Scout to tell you the good turns he has done if he does not wish to do so voluntarily; do not ask him to state the things which he has actually accomplished. However, be continually urging him to do his duty with regard to his daily good turn.

The Importance of Religion.

It is maintained by the Boy Scouts of America that no boy can grow into the best kind of a man without recognizing his obligation to God; it is also maintained that no Scout Master can be the best leader of boys unless his personal life conforms to the requirements of the faith which he holds. His example should be a constant inspiration to the boys of his troop, causing them, no matter of how many different faiths, to be diligent in their adherence to the teachings of the particular religious institution with which they are individually connected. He should see to it that no boy's religion is ever ridiculed by another, and that every boy is encouraged to live his life according to the ideals of his faith.

The Boy is the Main Issue.

The idea that must continually be kept in mind is the boy's good and the boy, rather than Scouting. Half of our teachers in the public schools are trying to teach the subject-matter of the book when they ought to be teaching the boy, they employ static methods. You can get up a goal for attainment and the boy will reach the goal. Generally, however, he will go no higher than you point. Your teaching should be dynamic rather than static.

Aim to secure balanced, symmetrical activities for your patrols. Remember your Scout is four sided, that he is physical, mental, social and religious in his nature. Do not neglect any one side of him, but get the proper agencies to coöperate with you for these ends. *Let the boys do whatever they can. Merely insist on adequate adult supervision.* Above all be patient, practical and business like and remember that old heads never grow on young shoulders. *The Scout Master should take his place in the community by the side of the teacher of secular and religious instruction. He is an educator and is dealing with the most plastic and most valuable asset in the community — boyhood.* Let him take his task seriously, look upon his privilege with a desire to accomplish great things, and always remember that the good of the boys is his ultimate aim.

Chapter IV

THE ADOLESCENT BOY

Need of Reading and Study in Understanding Boys.

The leader of boys to really understand the boy must know something of child life and boy ideals and principles. The making of the boy and his individual characteristics begins early in life, and is attended by two great shaping elements, race heredity and local environment. To understand the application of these principles and their effect upon boy-life it will be necessary further for the Scout Master to know something of the great movements of history through which man has passed and something as well of the problems of the present in the environmental influences affecting boys.

The leader should also be able to recognize the profound mental and psychic changes that accompany the physical development of the boy, as these furnish the best possible clews to the complex adolescent character. Few boys are easy to understand or to handle properly; and the secret of the difficulties often experienced by parents and teachers is that they fail to attach sufficient importance to the physiology of the sexual change as affecting the mental and moral traits.

Physical Changes at Puberty.

From the thirteenth to the sixteenth year, but most commonly in temperate climates from the fourteenth to the fifteenth, begins the change through which the boy is transformed into the man. Though more gradual and less definite in physiological manifestation than in the girl of similar age, this change is far more complete and significant in its effects on the life and character of the boy.

One of the first indications of puberty is the enlargement of the vocal chords, often causing a peculiar breaking of the voice, which is ordinarily deepened about an octave in pitch. This is accompanied by the development of the

" Adam's apple." The heart and other organs enlarge, and the growth of the bones, particularly those of the limbs and extremities, is often so rapid that the muscles are unduly stretched and the boy suffers from what are known as " growing pains." The sexual organs become functional, and the beard finally begins to make its appearance.

Mental Characteristics of the Adolescent Period.

With these bodily changes is associated a remarkable mental development which is apt to cause a shifting of ideals and a readjustment of the boy's ethical and moral viewpoint. Until the beginning of the adolescent change the boy is distinctly individualistic and selfish. Then his whole nature begins to change with the change in his bodily functions, and may occur anywhere between the twelfth and the sixteenth year. It is really determined by his physical development rather than his chronological age.

He begins to see and understand that he is a part of the community in which he is living and begins to understand that the community life is made possible by a disposition on the part of his neighbors to help each other. He also begins to understand the institutional life about him and the family and sex tie on which it is based. He sees also the need of the school, the church and other public institutions. He also begins to appreciate the wider range of things. Nature has greater appeal to him now than ever. The woods and streams and outdoor life get a new significance, and the question of livelihood whether rural and agricultural, or in the line of the various industries, takes a firm hold upon his imagination, and gives him a life compelling purpose. He begins to feel the mating call and at its first impression is attracted to the other sex, with the result that by and by he also becomes a husband and father and a full-fledged citizen among his fellows. Up to the age of adolescence however, none of these emotions stir the boy and since the aim of scouting is manhood and citizenship, the scouting activities ought not to be given to boys who have not reached adolescence or the beginning of the change into manhood.

Characteristics of the Early Adolescent Age.

The early adolescent age from twelve to fifteen years is characterized by a rapid and uneven growth during which vitality and energy alternate with languidness, and the boy is awkward and lazy, with bones greatly outgrowing muscle. The boy also begins to take a new interest in sex and sex relations, his features and voice change, and the inherited tendencies begin to assert themselves. His health is usually at its best, and during his active moments he is boisterous and vigorously energetic. He is selfish but shows signs of altruism; his regard for law increases; the spirit of gang leadership begins to show itself; his longing for friendship is noticeable; his sense of secretiveness is apparent; and his self-assertiveness first begins to be manifested. He is creative in imagination, shows marvelous powers of inference, becomes strongly intellectual, begins to manifest analytic reasoning, imitates the ideal, is uncertain in making decisions, is influenced by suggestions, and possesses generally a strong but not a logical memory. He develops natural religious notions, has strong impulses to do big things, has definite convictions as to his belief in God and Heaven and the understanding of traditional religious terms, shows a noticeable lack of interest in the forms of worship, but a keen appreciation of the spiritual, and is passing through a period when great resolves are most often made.

Characteristics of Later Adolescence.

During the period of later adolescence from fifteen to eighteen years of age, the body nearly attains its maximum growth, the mind begins to show its dominance over the body, and all the bodily impulses grow stronger and more vigorous. Altruism steadily increases; the consciousness of society grows; an appreciation of individual worth and thought develops; the call of sex and the love emotion grows in strength; sentiment is inclined to become strong; boundless enthusiasm manifests itself; and organization and cooperation begin to appeal and be appreciated more and more. There is a growth in logic, a development of skepticism, independent thought, alertness in thinking, and quickness of receptive powers. The boy at this age is in the period of highest resolves and greatest endeavor, is apt to show religious skepticism, and reason often takes the place of his faith.

The Need of Sympathy and Understanding.

While the period of puberty is essentially a time for the exercise of wise and judicious parental influences, the fact that most boys are enrolled as Scouts at about this time makes it vitally important for the ·Scout Master to have a correct understanding and appreciation of the change as it affects the boy's life and ideals. He should be prepared to give counsel as to the care of the body, when necessary, against practices that may be dangerous to health. He should be able to recognize the startling mental changes noticeable in adolescents, and above all he must understand that what may appear to be morbid desires, unworthy thoughts, or ill-judged activities are only outward manifestations of a period of mental storm and stress, and are therefore not necessarily indications of moral deficiency. A boy who in his early years has been friendly and sociable may become shy and reticent, preferring an older companion to the society of other Scouts; and on the other hand, a quiet, well-behaved boy may turn boisterous and unmanageable without apparent cause. There is need for the Scout Master to use the utmost tact, kindness and discretion in handling such cases, for a hard word or penalty unwisely imposed may cause the loss of a really good Scout. It is a time when the qualifications of a leader of boys are put to the severest test, and when his personal relations with his troop must be intimate, wise and wholesome.

Development of the Child and the Boy.

The boy, as a study, is treated by the majority of modern boy-workers, as a product of race development and heredity, recognizing that in his life from its remotest source, the boy relives all the periods of life that stretch into the dim vistas of mammalian and human history. Such a theory of development has been generally accepted by all leaders in the study of race and child psychology. Professor A. F. Chamberlain says: "This view that the individual more or less distinctly repeats at least the chief stages in the development of the race, both mentally and physically, has been accepted as the cardinal doctrine of the newer theories of education which in the form of child study have made their influence felt in America and in the old world."

"Infancy," says Dr. William B. Forbush, "is the rehearsal of prehistoric and feral ages, and the years of early childhood are the reproductions of protracted and relatively stationary periods of barbarian days. It is because these ages were so long and so deep; because man has been a savage so much longer than he has been a Christian, that his subconscious heritage needs to be recognized and the work of habit making, which is the analogue of the past, must during childhood be made the central endeavor of all nurture."

Early Laws of Childhood — A New Era.

Formerly the laws of childhood were framed by antiquarians who had long forgotten boyhood life and who attempted to make the healthy active boys into men even long before the adolescent period. This is what the average, well-meaning father and mother used to try to do with their boys, before the day of open minded child study brought about a new understanding of the boy needs and a new era of development.

Child Resemblance to Savage Civilization.

Child study has brought to notice that the child bears a close resemblance to the savage in his ideas and development. " In many senses it is true," says Professor Geo. W. Fiske, " that the savage is a child and the child a savage. They both live near to nature — give them half a chance — and they know little of the conventions of society. Both live self-centered egotistic lives and are little influenced by public opinion. They live simpler lives, more natural lives than we are apt to live, using simple utensils, and tools; both live in the crude age of culture and intelligence. Both are apt to shun labor, responsibility and care; having little foresight, worrying little and laughing much." Stanley Hall says of the boy: " In his instincts, amusements and associations, his adjustment to " the life of a savage environment is quite stable. " In many ways he resembles the savage and each furnishes the key for understanding both the good and bad points in the other's character."

The Recapitulation Theory.

Based on this close resemblance of child life to the savage life, and because of other likenesses which the child bears at younger periods of its life-stages to earlier ancestral or animal-like forms, biologists and psychologists have deduced the "recapitulation" or "culture epochs" theory. At the very beginning of the human individual life the resemblance is purely biological and physical; but during the growth of the child from two or three years old babyhood into the adult stage, with the consequent mental and moral development, through a series of successive changes in growth, there is a psychological resemblance to the successive social and cultural periods of man-history. Professor Baldwin says, "The individual embryo passes through stages which represent morphologically to a degree the stages actually found in the ancestral animal series." "That is," as Prof. Fiske writes, "the human embryo in the uterus, from the time the ovum is fertilized until birth, passes through various stages of development wherein for a larger or shorter period, it resembles some one of its primitive animal ancestors, or more properly their embryo. Although the early periods are recapitulated very rapidly, and the parallelism is doubtless irregular in different embryos, vestiges of these former epochs of development are plainly seen. Shortly before birth the human embryo greatly resembles the embryo of the larger ape (chimpanzee, orang-outang, etc.), though each speedily grows unlike the other. From this point it is easy to trace backward the progress of development by which life has ascended."

But for the purpose of boy-study, the theory of recapitulation should not be confined to the physical fact alone, but also as well to the psychic and social. According to such viewpoint, what Mosso said in regard to instinct is interesting; "What we call *instinct* is the voice of past generations reverberating like a distant echo in the cells of the nervous system. We feel the breath, the advice, the experience of all men, from those who lived on acorns and struggled with wild beasts, dying naked in the forests, down to the virtue and toil of our father, the fear and love of our mother." Prof. Geo. A. Coe says further, "As the human body before birth passes through a series of forms that correspond in the main to ascending embryonic forms of animal life in general, so after birth, the mind progresses toward maturity through stages which correspond roughly to the stages of human history in the large. In a certain modified sense, the child is first a savage, then a barbarian, then a civilized being."

When this view of boy-life is presented to the student the mind of the boy becomes like an open book. What was once such an enigma to our fathers is now most easily understood, and the work with boys has therefore been placed on a firm foundation of character-understanding and type-knowledge. " Adolescence begins " says Dr. Winfield S. Hall, " in boys about the age of fifteen in the average case, although sometimes the beginnings are distinct in the twelfth or thirteenth year, and again are sometimes not evident until the seventeenth year. As the boy emerges from childhood into youth he passes through a pre-adolescent period that represents the emergence of the race from savagery and fetichism into orderly, tribal organizations, and the beginnings of crude industries and early steps of recognition of the rights of others. It was a stormy period of human history. Petty tribal wars decimated the race. When boys are fully launched in their adolescent period, say from the ages of fifteen to eighteen, they represent the next stage of human development. In that stage government is more or less highly organized. Yet it was a time of monarchial rather than democratic government, though the monarchs were frequently elected." Finally with maturity from eighteen to twenty-four or five, there develops in historical organization, a greater and yet greater spirit of democracy, and general coöperation.

In boy life the first period or early adolescence is the stress period. The boy seeks and worships the physical force, and combines in cliques or gangs under leaders who hold their positions not by intellect but by sheer physical force and cunning. The boy at this period possesses a high sense of honor, though it is sometimes difficult for older people to understand his view-point. He is amenable to suggestion, and it is possible for a tactful leader, step by step, to develop his code of honor and more surely lead him toward a best development of his personality and resources. This is the goal of the Scout Master in his work with his Scouts. Later adolescence is characterized by growth of individual prowess, increased physical and mental activity, and a development first, of self-assertiveness and then of coöperation. The whole period of the adolescent boy-life is one of immense change.

Physical and Intellectual Restlessness.

Physical restlessness is often associated with growing intellectual restlessness and curiosity. "It is a time," says Dr. Forbush, "of stubborn doubts, painful and dangerous, but signs of mental and moral health. This widening of interests, emotional and intellectual, is accompanied by a gradual social broadening. While in the early part of this period egoistic emotions are apt to be disagreeably expressed, vented, sometimes in bullying and again, in an opposite way, by extreme self-consciousness and bashfulness, this sooner or later develops into a clearer recognition of one's self and a finer recognition of others. Adolescence has been termed an unselfing. There is a yearning to be with and for one's kind. This is seen in the growing teamwork spirit in games, and in the various clubs which now spring up almost spontaneously, in the slowly increasing interest in social gatherings, and in the other sex."

Periods of Human History.

The life of man has long been studied in anthropology by dividing his history into several periods of development leading toward civilization. Perhaps the scheme formulated by Morgan is best known. He divided man's history into two great divisions, Savagery and Barbarism,— each composed of three successive periods. Savagery was represented by the three periods, early, middle and later; and Barbarism correspondingly by the three like periods; of early, middle and later. Early Savagery began with natural subsistence on fruit, nuts and roots and ended with the use of a fish diet and the discovery of fire. Middle Savagery, succeeding, ended with the invention of bow and arrow. Later Savagery developed in the mythological period and culminated in the invention of the art of pottery. Early Barbarism developed village life, and many crude household arts and ended with the cultivation of plants and domestication of animals. Middle Barbarism succeeded, developed agriculture and pastoral arts, and introduced the

Editorial Note.— For exceptional help and information in regard to boy-life and boy-characteristics during the adolescent age, Scout Masters should read Chapters I and II of "The Boy Problem," by Dr. William B. Forbush; Chapters IV, V, VI, and VII, of "Boy Life and Self-Government," by Prof. George W. Fiske; "Boy Training," by Mr. John L. Alexander; and "The Boy and His Gang," by Mr. R. A. Puffer.

beginning of a national life. Later Barbarism begins with the use of iron tools and invention of the process of smelting, and developed the art of writing which began literature and led directly to civilization. Dr. Woods Hutchinson has formulated a scheme based on the method of food getting, and showing reference to child development: —

Race History and Boy Life.

	Stage.	Duration.	Culmination.	Characteristics.	Favorite Plays and Games.
1.	Root and Grub	1st to 5th year	3rd year	Mouth as Criterion of everything	Biting and Tasting plays
2.	Hunting and Capture	4th to 12th year	7th year	Fear of strangers; stalking methods; indifference to pain; hero-worship; cruelty	Bo-peep (stealth, stalking, approach, ambush, surprise); Hide and Seek; Black Man; Prisoner's Base — (pursuit, attack; mimic sieges, wars, assaults; gangs)
3.	Pastoral	9th to 14th year	10th year	Fondness for pets; desire to have something "for his own"	Keeping and feeding pets; building huts; digging caves, etc.
4.	Agricultural	12th to 16th year	12th year	Development of fore-sight; passion for Gardening	Watching weather signs; gardening, digging up seeds "to see if they're growing"
5.	Shop and Commercial	14th to 40th year	18th to 20th year	Demanding pay for services; recognition of value and sense of arithmetic	Swapping, selling, trading, exchanging, bargaining

Stages of Evolution of Government and Industry.

Prof. Geo. W. Fiske, in order more closely to compare the boy life to the race-life has formulated a divisional history scheme of comparison, and considers man's history from two view-points,— the evolution of government and the evolution of industry. According to this outline of racial progress the stages of evolution of government are:

1. The Primitive Democracy of the savage kinship Clan Patriarchal.
2. The Limited Democracy of the Barbarian Tribe: becoming monarchial when the single tribes ruled by the "council of braves" come together as allied

tribes, under the increasing authority of a " Chieftain by Prowess."

3. The Tyrannical period of Feudalism; serfdom, despotism.

4. The Revolutionary period which developed the Constitutional Monarchy.

5. The Republican period: — Social Democracy in a self-governing State.

The Stages of Industrial Evolution are: —

1. Industry developed by the Acquisitive and Collectional instincts.

2. Industry developed by the Productive and Destructive instincts.

3. Industry developed by the Constructive and Transformative instincts.

4. Industry developed by the Commercial and Coöperative instincts.

Comparison of Boy-Life and Race-Life.— Fiske.

To compare the boy-life and boy-development according to the theory of recapitulation of the periods of racial progress, the diagram is given on the following page.

Understanding of Parallelism of Boy-Life and Race-Life Makes the Scout Master's Work Easier.

An understanding of the principles which underlie this diagram, as the same are applied in boy work, will go far towards giving to the worker with boys and the Scout Master a deeper insight into true boy-character and a better working knowledge of his personal needs and characteristics. The reasons why boys are so changeable, so restless, and so given to temperamental acts that are so often enigmatical to the adult mind, can be answered by reference to this outline of parallel likenesses between boy life and ancestral race-life. What the boys do is then seen to be natural and most to be expected, and the Scout Master can better foster the greater development of character by building on these race-like desires and appeals, and directing the acquisition of right principles through contact with racial impulses and actions.

In the period of Childhood, corresponding to the Patriarchal or Communal period, the child yields unquestioned obedience to his parents. He forms only narrow attach-

Comparison of Boy Life with Race Life.

			BOY EPOCHS			RACE EPOCHS
No.	Stage of Boy Life.	Age Limits.	Characteristics.	Will-Progress.	Allegiance.	Racial Prototype.
0.	Infancy	Years 0–3	(Before Self-consciousness)	(Self-Discovery)	(Blind)	Pre-Historic Period
1.	Early Childhood / Later	3–6 / 7–11	The Self Period / The Clique Period	Self-Control	Father / Chum	Patriarchal Period / Savage Kinship Clan
2.	Boyhood	10–14	The Gang Period	Comradeship	The Gang	The Tribal Period Limited Democracy to Monarchy 1 — Council of braves 2 — Federated Tribes with Chieftain by Prowess
3.	Early Adolescence	13–15 Grammar School Age	The Chivalry Period	Personal Loyalty (Obedience)	The Hero	The Feudal Period of the Absolute Monarchy
4.	Middle Adolescence	14–18 High School Age	The Self-Assertive Period	Self-Reliance (through struggle)	The Ego	The Revolutionary Period of the Constitutional Monarchy
5.	Late Adolescence	17–24 College Age	The Coöperative Period	Leadership (Resourcefulness)	The State	The Republic. Social-Democracy in a Self-Governing State

ments with other playmates, which will later develop into gang organization. The period of Boyhood or the Gang period corresponds racially to the Tribal period, and is characterized by the development and dominance of gang influence over the boys' whole allegiance. The early Adolescent or Chivalry Period is racially parallel to the Feudal or Absolute Monarchial period with its chivalric virtues, vices and actions. At this time the boys' allegiance passes from the gang to the hero or chosen leader; this is the time when the boy will try most to be like his father or any one of his men friends whom he looks up to and loves. The period of Middle Adolescence or the self-assertive period corresponds historically to the Revolutionary period and Constitutional Monarchy, and is characterized by his struggle for self-reliance and individual achievement. Late Adolescence, or the Coöperative period is parallel racially to the development of Democracy, and is characterized by growing Social adjustment and coöperation in the boy with his fellows and his environment.

Classes of Boy Types.

With these general principles in mind, it becomes easier to recognize and to make a study of the various types of boy with which the Scout Master comes in contact. In the first place there are the psychological types,— the choleric, the sanguine, the phlegmatic, and the hybrid. There are also the types of real life with which we are most familiar,— the masterful, the weak, the mischievous, the backward, the shy, the bully, the joker, the " smartie," the echo or shadow, the quiet or reticent, the girl struck, the self-conscious, the unconscious, and the forgetful. Lastly, we should also consider the different types of the unfortunate boys, including the deficient, the delinquent, the criminal, the dependent, the neglected, the foreign born, the wage-earner, the poverty-stricken, boys of very wealthy parents, over-ambitious boys who have over-ambitious parents, and street boys, who are either loafers or engaged in street trades, or are compelled to use the street as a playground.

The Choleric Boy.

The choleric fellow who is always off at "halfcock," running his head into danger whenever he can, and who is extremely hectic in his make up, is always a problem. He needs a strong hand. Sometimes, he will need even physical repression, but he always demands great care and patience. The Scout Master should deal with each class of boys largely by suggestion, but in the case of the choleric fellow he will often need to use orders and demonstrate that he himself is in the saddle.

The Sanguine Boy.

The sanguine fellow is the normal boy who, having a good digestion, a good home and no cause for worry, sees things as they are and is apt to take them as they come. He will be the easiest kind of a boy to get along with, and the only thing that the Scout Master will have to do may be to provide for stimulation of his interest and ambition.

The Phlegmatic Type.

The phlegmatic chap requires patience more than anything else; generally slow of body he is usually slow of speech and thought. If the Scout Master is not careful he will be apt to call him " dense," and speak to him sharply and at times rather crossly. He cannot do this if he expects to win the fellow. Temperamentally, nature has made him what he is and the Scout Master will have to work harder, make things more concrete that he wants to teach, and hold his impatience in check. Phlegmatic though he is, he will prove solid in everything he does, and he will be either a rock of strength or of weakness to the Scout Master. If he likes the Scout Master nothing will shake his love, but if he has a dislike for him, then the Scout Master is at the end of his endeavor as far as he is concerned.

The Hybrid Boy is a Problem.

The hybrid boy always furnishes a guessing contest,—impulsive to-day, he has to be repressed; phlegmatic to-morrow, he has to be stimulated; and he may be sanguine the next day. There never was a pleasanter boy to work with, but like the chameleon you are never sure of his color.

Just because he is so changeable the Scout Master should show him his best thought and work. It is just such fellows who are inclined to be shiftless and who are generally crowded out in the fight for life. Somewhere in the boy's nature, if the Scout Master is patient, he will find the rock bottom upon which to build manhood and citizenship.

Such achievement, however, comes only by great patience and hard work.

The Masterful Boy and the Weak Boy.

The masterful and weak boys represent the antipodes of boyhood. The masterful boy will see things quickly, will be the leader of his gang, will dominate his patrol, and will run the troop unless the Scout Master is on his job. The weak boy will follow anywhere, be the cause good or bad, and become either a devil or a saint. The masterful boy may be handled by appealing to his sense of leadership. Responsibility should be placed upon him. The Scout Master should make him feel that he is leaning heavily on him. The weak boy on the other hand should be tied up to some steady phlegmatic fellow, the phlegmatic fellow being given the vision of how he can be an older brother to the boy not as strong as himself. The result will be that the weak boy will catch some of the spirit of the phlegmatic chap, and gradually get some depth for himself.

The Mischievous Boy.

Of all the boy types, the mischievous boy furnishes the real pleasure for the worker with boys. The fellow whose eyes can twinkle and who will play a practical trick on the friend he most respects, is always a delight. It is he that keeps the crowd in good humor, who is generally deepest and most abiding in his affection, and who at the drop of the hat would fight to the last ditch for his friend. To handle him rightly does not require a six foot rod, or a half inch rule. But the Scout Master must keep him so busy doing the things that he likes that he will have no dull moments in which to vent his inborn sense of humor.

The Backward Boy.

The backward boy will need to be led out of himself. Give him things to do which will make him forget himself and by careful utilization of his time, gradually he will develop into a normal boy. He is likely to be shy and lacking in self-confidence, so that definite responsibility and normal treatment will bring him to himself.

The Shy Boy.

The shy boy has merely become shy because of lack of association. Usually he has been brought up with his mother and sisters and merely lacks the touch of a man and a man's viewpoint. After he comes in contact with other boys, this will wear away. The problem of the Scout Master is to get the other boys in his troop to pilot the boy into the deeper waters.

" Smartie " and Joker Types.

The " smartie " and the joker types are thorns in the flesh. Just as thorns when pressed in too deeply require a surgical operation to remove them, so it may be necessary for the Scout Master to " sit on " both the " smartie " and the joker. If the other boys of the troop make up their minds to unite in the task, both the " smartie " and joker will become normal boys in less than one season's activities, and the Scout Master will show his generalship to be of the real sort by enlisting the other boys to do the job.

The Echo or Shadow Type.

The echo or shadow type is a serious problem. He it is who generally hinders the good things in life and helps the bad. He can swear by the ward boss in party politics, or he can prove himself an obstacle in the way of civic and national righteousness. The Scout Master's task in his case is to somehow or other strike the chord of independence, teach him to do things by himself, think for himself and stand on his own feet. Along the coasts of the North Sea, they teach boys to swim by throwing them out beyond their depth. It may be necessary to awaken manhood and independence in the echo by swamping him when he is alone.

The Bully.

The bully will be the worst type for the Scout Master until the right boy comes along; there is no use in the Scout Master worrying himself until he does, because of the bully's bluster and bluff. Usually the normal boy will accept him at his face value, and it is only when a lad with self-assertion comes along that the sparks will fly. Then the bully will have to back down or take his medicine. A fight between boys is usually not a good thing, but when it comes to putting the bully in his place it is one of the greatest institutions that the savage man has invented. Once a bully has lost his place, he may bluster, but his bluff is over.

The Quiet or Reticent Boy.

. The quiet and reticent fellow is like the mighty sweeping river. He has depths which have been unsounded, and his life has promise of great possibilities. Just the opposite of the bully, he never blusters but thinks out everything as it comes to him. Every impression is stored away and out of the countless impressions which are made upon him, there emerges a man of real and wide interests. The task of the Scout Master in his case will be to discover his interests and help him to discover himself.

The Self-Conscious and the Unconscious Boy.

The self-conscious and the unconscious boys are merely victims of their surroundings. The self-conscious fellow has no confidence in himself. He is continuously measuring himself by others and is possibly the victim of parental teaching. The constant injunction to act like " Little Willie " next door may have gotten on the boy's nerves and if the lad has a chance without undue embarrassment he will soon reach the normal stage, and be always a little more courteous and respectful and thoughtful than the fellow without this experience. The unconscious fellow on the other hand will plug along doing all sorts of absurd things, because of his lack of knowledge of the fitness of things. He is generally the boy who grows up without any sense of consistency and who has had very much his own way of doing things. He will need to be helped to adjust himself to his environment and to the way that other fellows live. He also will develop as a good man if the Scout Master is a good worker.

The Forgetful Boy.

The same may be said about the forgetful boy and in fact about all boys. The forgetful boy has merely not been interested enough to give his attention to the things that the Scout Master wants him to do. Once a boy has his interest aroused, the Scout Master will have no need of complaint of forgetfulness or of any lack of interest in the boy.

The Unfortunate Boys.

The types which have been discussed will generally work out all right and find their places in the various social strata in the community in which they live. The unfortunate boys, however, are handicapped tremendously by their environment and surroundings, and it will often become a part of the Scout Master's work to help secure a change in these environments. Boys of very wealthy parents and boys from homes of poverty are usually sinned against by their parents. The parents of both are either so busy making money and spending it in the social whirl, or so pushed by the pangs of hunger and the fight for life, that the children who are brought into the world are left either very much to themselves or to underlings who have very little interest in the boy's welfare. It is these neglected boys that oftenest produce our great criminals. Every boy of this type somehow or other is tied together. The neglected boy generally becomes the delinquent and the delinquent boy the criminal, so that what might be said about one, might be also said about all. This class constitutes our national deficit when we come to consider our assets in manhood and the Boy Scout Movement, and the Scout Masters can do a tremendous thing here by helping to form the undeveloped wills of these unfortunate fellows.

The Deficient and the Dependent.

The deficient boy and the dependent are really out of the scope of the Scout Master. The dependent class will have to be taken care of by the charitable institutions of the State, and the deficient boy because of his lack of mental development will always be a ward of the community.

The Wage-Earner and the Over-Ambitious Boys.

The wage-earning boys and the boys of over-ambitious parents or those who are over-ambitious themselves need all the help and sympathy that they can get from a Scout Master. The father who is pushing his boy because of his own ambition will very often need to be talked to by the Scout Master or his friends, and given an understanding of the crime he is committing against his own child. The over-ambitious fellow who is pushing everything aside for a definite thing in life, will often have to be talked to in the plainest language by the Scout Master to get him to see his other responsibilities and duties in life. The wage-earning boy who works from early in the morning until late at night to keep bread in his mouth and breath in his body, will compel the Scout Master, if he is really thoughtful, to give up some of the things which he has already held dearest and possibly lead his wage-earning boy into Scouting activities, even on the half holidays which he would naturally spend in the circle of his own family.

Need of Reading and Study.

An understanding then of boys, such as the leader or Scout Master should have, makes necessary the need of the knowledge of psychic changes and their causes. Work with boys planned in accordance with the principles of the recapitulation theory definitely places it on a solid footing, and makes the handling of the boy groups so much the easier. Scouting concerns itself with boy-life from the pre-adolescent period of boyhood through the changes of adolescence to young manhood, and the Scout Master should therefore familiarize himself with the origin, development, cause, and treatment of the desires and needs and characteristics that form the boy's life during this period of his life. To do this he should seek to augment his knowledge by all such reading as can be obtained on the subject. This foregoing brief outline of boy development should serve only as aid in pointing out the way for a more thorough study of the subject, just as the whole "Scout Masters' Manual" serves as a source of suggestions in the greater field-work.

In the general bibliography the titles listed under the subject of "Boy Work" are merely suggestive, but they include the best of the modern books on this subject.

CHAPTER V

TROOP AND PATROL MANAGEMENT

The Troop Age.

The Boy Scouts of America plan to get hold of every American boy, to improve his general interest in life through Scouting, to weld manly principles into his character, and to make him, through personal and advisory development, fully competent, efficient and coöperative. Scouting is a movement designed to help the boy during the adolescent period of life, so because the greater majority of boys pass through the functional manhood changes between twelve and eighteen years, such limiting ages were adopted in Scouting, and the entering age limit of twelve years most carefully enforced.

The Older Boy.

A Scout over eighteen may continue his Scouting whenever he chooses, and many do continue as Assistant Scout Masters when they have had previous requisite training. But it is not the intention of the Movement to interest and enroll lads over eighteen. Their wants and interests are usually adequately provided for by the numerous adult organizations, clubs and societies.

The Younger Boy.

Some boys develop earlier than others so that physical equals may range in years from 12 to 14, but the greater mass of boys begin to pass through the adolescent period between 12 and 13 years of age. To insure stability, and guard against the evils of admitting the boy who is too young, the Boy Scouts of America have adopted the age of 12 years as the lowest age of Scout admissions and make of it a rigidly enforced rule of admission.

The Problem of Grouping Boys.

In the formation and management of the troop care should be taken that it should be composed of boys of mixed ages. A majority of little fellows will often drive out the older boy, so that the problem of grouping becomes very important in troop management. There is as little toleration for the younger boy on the part of the older fellow as there is for the boy of eighteen or nineteen by grown men.

But in providing for a troop of all ages in Scouting, the age grouping should receive recognition in the formation of patrols. In this case variety of ages is detrimental. For instance the boy of twelve should not be in the same group with the seventeen-year-old boy. In almost everything the interests of the younger boy have no attraction for the older fellow. For this reason it is best to group the boys of similar ages in patrols.

The Problem of Grading by Age.

During the adolescent changes, however, the chonological and physiological ages seldom definitely agree. Often the youngster who is chronologically fourteen may be physiologically ten or sixteen or else ranging somewhere between. For this reason it is absolutely impossible to scientifically grade the Tenderfoot and other degrees of Scouting by age. Some boys mature much more rapidly than others, and because of this a boy should not be held back in the securing of his degree. To hold any boy back by any artificial limits when he possesses the ability to meet the requirements, is a crime against the boy. He should be encouraged to pass the requirements as quickly as possible, and thoroughness should be insisted upon by the Scout Master and the Court of Honor. There are incentives among the scout activities, in the winning of merit badges, carrying on community Scouting, and in leadership development, to hold the interest of the boy after he has become a First Class Scout; and as the Movement grows older, more interest-holding specialties will undoubtedly be developed. No boy will be attracted by any grade or degree, if it fails to arouse his interest. There is a great need of graded work; but this should be provided for by the orderly progressive plan which the Scout Master himself works out as he studies the need of each individual boy.

Starting — The Wrong and the Right Way.

The wrong way to start a patrol or troop of Scouts is to make an announcement in some newspaper or from the platform of some church or institution that the Boy Scouts will be organized on a certain evening, and that every boy in town is invited to be present. This is a very common mistake, and usually results in a large percentage of the boys who join under such conditions, dropping out later on. The right way to start Scouting is to select seven or eight of the leading boys of the community, preferably between the ages of fifteen and seventeen, and beginning with this small group as a patrol, gradually to increase the

MIDWINTER ACTIVITIES — FIRE MAKING ON THE SNOW

size of the troop as the success of the movement in the locality and among the boys seems to warrant. The most successful troop is the one which achieves success with a small nucleus first, and develops in size and progress of Scouting as success continues. At the beginning it is best to present to the boys a full explanation of the scope and purpose of Scouting and its meaning, a personal survey of the Handbook activities, a careful reading of the Scout Oath and Scout Law, a clear idea of the "Daily Good Turn," and possibly a consideration of suggested by-laws and an initiation form, which, if used, should be simple and impressive. How much of parliamentary practices to use will depend largely on the choice of the Scout Master.

Application Forms.

In addition to these first steps, as well as in the case of all other troops, a uniform enrollment blank should be used. This blank should be signed by the parent or guardian of the boy, and should be made a matter of record. The following form has been accepted by National Headquarters as a standard, and is recommended for your use:

Boy Scouts of America

.... Council, City .., State ...

President ....

Scout Executive ....

Application Blank.

No. ......

I hereby apply for membership in the Boy Scouts of America and promise to do my best to keep the Scout Oath and Scout Laws at all times.

Date ....

Name ....

Address ....

Age............Occupation or School.............

(Applicant must not fill out below this line.)

Patrol ....   Troop ....

Scout Master ....

....

I hereby certify that the above applicant has qualified as a
Tenderfoot
Second Class Scout
First Class

...................,
Scout Master.

The above appears in blank on the face of a single sheet, which bears at the head the emblem of the Boy Scouts of America, the names of the local executive council and its officers, and the address of the local headquarters. On the back of the blank is a statement as to what the Boy Scouts of America are, and this is followed by a reprint of the Scout Law, and the Scout Oath, and after that the following:

" I have read the above and approve of the plan and purpose of the organization. This application is made with my knowledge and consent.

Date ....   Signed ....
Parent or guardian.

The Patrol Organization.

Having properly instructed the members of the new troop the next step is to perfect the patrol organization. The necessary thing in the formation of the patrol is the appointment or election of a patrol leader and an assistant patrol leader. In some cases the Scout Master will find it necessary, in order to maintain his authority among the troop members, to dictate the election of or to personally appoint the patrol and assistant patrol leaders; but the best way, perhaps, is to let the boys appoint or elect their own leaders. The patrol formation is directly based upon the gang idea, and is in reality an organized gang under boy leadership and adult supervision, instead of an unorganized gang under boy leadership and no other direction. In the unorganized gang there is always a natural leader in command, and this boy will assert his ability and power for leadership in whatever group of boys he may be. For this reason it is better for the boys to elect their own leaders as this natural leader-type is most likely to be selected by them. Otherwise, if another sort of boy is appointed or selected as leader, the chances are that the natural leader of the group will either oust the other fellow or break up the patrol. The problem of the selection of patrol leaders, whether by official or dictatorial appointment, by proficiency in Scouting, by Scout rank, or by the self-government election of the group, must necessarily be left to the consideration of the individual Scout Master and the needs of the occasion.

Patrol Meetings.

The patrol leader usually presides at all patrol meetings and the assistant patrol leader acts as secretary. The different duties of the patrol officers should be prescribed in the troop constitution and by-laws, which should be adopted by each troop to provide for all group needs. The patrol should meet in business session at regularly prearranged intervals to conduct its own affairs, as differentiated from troop affairs, or, if, as at first, forming the nucleus of the future troop. All rules and regulations for the governing of patrols should be formulated by the patrol members, and the punishments for infringements should also be meted out by them (subject to the Scout Master's supervision). The patrol meeting should be orderly and conducted by parliamentary rules, and a record of everything should be kept. Later when the troop has been formed, or where the troop is already existent, there should be a regular troop constitution and by-laws which should cover and outline patrol activities, meetings, and special deliberations, etc.

Troop Meetings.

At a troop meeting the senior patrol leader usually presides unless otherwise provided for by the constitution and by-laws which the troop members should adopt. The patrol leader ranking second in order of seniority usually acts as secretary, and the third patrol leader in point of service as treasurer. The troop should make his own rules, and as in the case of patrol meetings the members should be orderly in their meeting and governed by parliamentary rulings. In the troop meeting unless otherwise provided for the patrols sit separately; the senior patrol on the right, the second on the left, and so on, with the youngest or last formed in the center. The Scout Master and the Assistant Scout Master sit beside the presiding patrol leader. While in the field, or on the march, the senior patrol usually leads with the others following in order of the length of their service.

Troop Constitution and By-Laws.

The members of each troop should make their own constitution and by-laws. Its chief value is that it is made by them, reflects their standards, ideals and objectives. It is worth more boyishly crude than mannishly perfect. Such a document has authority in proportion as it reflects the actual influence and judgment of the troop members. They will respect it more and enforce it better if they make it themselves. The Scoutmaster's influence in shaping it should be through indirect suggestion rather than dictation. He should furnish the skeleton and let the Scouts do the rest.

Model Constitutional Form for Boy Scouts of America.

CONSTITUTION.

ARTICLE I.— NAME.

The name of our organization should be known as Troop No.— (*III*), (*Seattle*)—, of the Boy Scouts of America.

ARTICLE II.— COLOR.

The colors of our organization shall be (*red and yellow*).

ARTICLE III.— MOTTO.

The motto of our organization shall be (*Our purpose in training is to become prepared and efficient*).

ARTICLE IV.—PURPOSE.

We are joined hand and heart to achieve true manhood. What harms the body, defiles the tongue, or does ill to the mind shall not enter our Council. We will do our best to keep away from the temptations that are ungentlemanly, and will strive ever to attain the efficiency in all things that marks the Prepared Scout. We will be kind to dumb animals. We will try our best to do promptly and cheerfully whatever we are asked to do by our Troop officers. We will always seek to help another in trouble and to do daily some good turn to someone. We will endeavor to promote, maintain, and carry out the principles of the Boy Scouts of America in (*Seattle, Washington*), and to work for the best interests of its members in conjunction with the National and Local Councils. We vow allegiance to our Country and our Flag, and pledge our hands, our hearts and our manly honor to our organization.

ARTICLE V.— SUPREME LAW.

The Supreme Law of our troop organization is the official regulations of the Boy Scouts of America as given in the "Handbook for Boys," and the Constitution and By-Laws of the Local Council of our district. Anything in this constitution in conflict with them is null and void. The entire management of our troop is in the hands of our Local Council, who shall appoint our Scout Master and confirm or reject all appointments made by him. All the actions and duties of our organization will be governed by the rules and body of regulations contained in our constitution, with the amendments added thereto from time to time.

ARTICLE VI.— MEMBERSHIP.

Section 1. Any boy who has attained the age of 12 years, and who lives in our district may become one of our comrades, if chosen by the troop for membership, upon proper application.

Section 2. We shall be grouped by patrols of eight boys each.

Section 3. We are divided into the three ranks of Tenderfoot, Second Class Scout, and First Class Scout.

Section 4. Boys of Scout age wishing to join our troop will make proper application. If the Patrol officers report favorably in behalf of the applicant, the troop shall give its votes concerning him. If he is chosen as a comrade he may appear at our Headquarters in .... weeks.

Section 5. It requires .... black balls on one ballot to reject an applicant from membership.

Section 6. A boy, after passing the proper test, takes the obligation of the Scout Oath. On the payment of his annual Scout membership fee he is then made a Tenderfoot.

Section 7. Comrades from other troops may be admitted on recommendation of their Scout Master and our Scout Master, by vote, without further ordeal, on the payment of the membership fee.

Section 8. Parents, older brothers, and friends interested in our progress and the welfare of our troop may be admitted to our troop as honorary members, with the payment of the annual membership fee.

Section 9. We have four classes of regular members: — members in good standing, delinquent members, suspended members, and honorary members.

Section 10. Members with nothing against them are in good standing.

Section 11. Members with dues unpaid are delinquent.

Section 12. Members both absent and delinquent are self-suspended until dues are paid.

ARTICLE VII.— EXECUTIVE DEPARTMENT.

Section 1. The officers of our troop shall consist of a Scout Master, the members of the local Troop Committee, as provided for by the Boy Scout regulations, one or more Assistant Scout Masters, if properly appointed, a Patrol

Leader and an Assistant Patrol Leader for each patrol, a Scout Scribe or Secretary of the Troop, and any other officer provided for in our constitution or by amendment.

Section 2. The duties of our Scout Master shall be as provided for by the Boy Scout regulations. He serves us and gives us counsel perpetually. He shall be present at all councils. All granting of degrees and transaction of business shall be in his presence. He may reduce inefficient officers. He may suspend or discharge unworthy Scouts, and withdraw their badges from them. He may promote deserving Scouts. He may veto any legislation of the troop. He shall exercise discipline. He shall act as the adviser of the officer in charge of the troop meeting at all business sessions, and shall act with such officer in appointing all standing and special committees.

Section 3. The members of the local Troop Committee may be present at all council meetings of the troop or patrols, and shall act as honorary members of all standing or special committees. They shall assist the Scout Master in carrying out the policies of the troop organization and aid with their advice and help all phases of the troop work. In the event of the resignation of our Scout Master, the members of our Troop Committee will take charge of all troop property and direct the work of the troop until such time as we may be able to secure a permanent Scout Master for our troop.

Section 4. The Assistant Scout Masters shall be over eighteen years of age, and may perform all duties of the Scout Master under the latter's direction. They shall take the place of the Scout Master and assume his duties when that officer is not present.

Section 5. The Patrol Leaders and Assistant Patrol Leaders shall rank in order of seniority of service, and the principal officers of the troop in business session shall be elected from the members of highest rank, consisting of the Patrol Leaders, Assistant Patrol Leaders, Past Patrol Leaders, and all First Class Scouts.

Section 6. The Senior Patrol Leader (*or Senior Past Patrol Leader*) shall be known as the Troop Leader or Troop President. He shall preside at all of our troop meetings with the assistance of the Scout Master. He may call special meetings. He shall countersign all orders for troop money paid out. He has general supervision over the troop and all subordinate officers. He shall appoint, with the advice of the Scout Master, all standing and special committees, when the appointment of the same is not otherwise provided for by special resolution.

Section 7. The Scout Scribe or Secretary will keep a record of all transactions of the troop meetings and of attendance. He will call the roll. He will make out and sign all orders on the Troop Treasurer for money paid out by the vote of the troop. He shall conduct all the correspondence of the troop, and be the official representative of the troop in its relations with other troops. He shall keep a record of all members expelled, suspended, delinquent, or fined, giving the name, age, rank, residence address, and length of service as a Scout. He shall keep a correct mailing list of all the troop members and all the troop officers. He shall notify all applicants elected to troop membership of such fact, and when to appear for initiation, etc. He shall notify all members of their appointment to serve on committees, together with the subject given into their charge. He shall send his name and address to National Headquarters, and keep the National office informed of the progress and special demonstrations and undertakings of the troop. All of his records shall be set down in books of record, suitable for such purpose, and provided for by the troop moneys.

Section 8. The Troop Leader shall appoint, in conjunction with the Scout Master and the Assistant Troop Leader, all committees necessary to carry on the troop business. These committees may be: —

Finance Committee.
Committee on Athletics and Sports.
Entertainment Committee.
Honor Committee.
Yell Committee.
Missioner's Committee.
Library Committee.
Flag Committee.
Drill Committee.
Efficiency Committee.

ARTICLE VIII.— LEGISLATION.

Section 1. The troop may legislate and transact any business necessary for its welfare.

Section 2. All of our members, including the Scout Master and Assistant Scout Masters, shall have equal votes on all questions or measures submitted to the consideration of the troop, and it shall be considered that a majority of all the members present at a Troop Meeting shall be sufficient to enact new measures.

Section 3. Nine members of the troop, of whom at least two shall be elective officers, and either the Scout Master or Assistant Scout Master, shall constitute a quorum.

Section 4. The power of taxing shall be ours.

Section 5. No money shall be expended without our consent.

Section 6. All our transactions shall be parliamentary, and " Robert's Rules of Order " shall be our parliamentary guide.

ARTICLE ·IX.— JUDICIAL DEPARTMENT.

Section 1. The judicial authority shall belong to the whole troop.

Section 2. To expedite matters it shall refer all matters of discipline to a Judicial Committee consisting of the Scout Master, Assistant Scout Masters, Patrol Leaders, Assistant Patrol Leaders, Troop Leaders, and one Member at Large selected by the Scout Master and Troop Leader from each patrol.

Section 3. The Judicial Committee shall hold meetings in special sessions whenever enough business shall warrant.

Section 4. The Scout Master and the majority of the members of the committee shall constitute a quorum for the consideration of business.

Section 5. A majority vote may render a decision.

Section 6. Charges and complaints against a Scout shall be referred to the Judicial Committee.

Section 7. The troop by a majority vote may pardon offenders.

Section 8. A Scout in good standing who considers himself unjustly treated by another Scout or officer may bring the matter before his Patrol Leader whose decision he shall cheerfully and promptly abide by. Then, if he is not satisfied with the decision, he may appeal to the Judicial Committee, whose decision he should cheerfully and promptly obey. The appeal, however, can be carried in like manner to the decision of the Scout Master, and lastly to the Troop

Committee, whose decision shall be final. Failing to obey any decision promptly and cheerfully he forfeits all right to further appeal.

Section 9. A Scout dropped, suspended, or deserting from the troop or his Patrol is not entitled to wear the uniform or badges of the Boy Scouts of America. As the emblems of the Boy Scouts of America are covered by letters patent from the United States, by a recent decision of the Supreme Court of the United States, anyone wearing them without permission from the proper authorities lays himself liable to prosecution and penalty.

Section 10. All badges are the property of the troop and are simply loaned to the Scouts to wear while in good standing. When a Scout ceases to remain in good standing he shall return his badge to the Assistant Troop Leader.

Section 11. A Scout suspended may be reinstated by the vote of the troop.

ARTICLE X.—PATROL MEETINGS.

Section 1. In matters not provided for in the Constitution for Troop Meetings each Patrol shall conduct its own affairs.

Section 2. The officers of the Patrol in business session shall consist of the Scout Master and Assistant Scout Masters who shall act as advisory officers, the Patrol Leader who shall preside, and the Assistant Patrol Leader who shall serve as Secretary. Other officers shall be chosen as needed.

Section 3. Four members and the Scout Master, or the Assistant Scout Master, shall constitute a quorum.

Section 4. A Patrol Meeting shall be called by the Patrol Leader at the request of the Scout Master.

ARTICLE XI.— DELINQUENCY.

A Scout with dues unpaid is delinquent.

ARTICLE XII.— SUSPENSION.

A member both absent and delinquent is self-suspended until his dues are paid.

ARTICLE XIII.— WITHDRAWAL.

A Scout forsaking the fellowship of our troop shall honorably give written notice to the troop, and not be delinquent at the time.

ARTICLE XIV.— DUES.

Section 1. Each Scout shall pay .... cents per week dues.

Section 2. Any Scout failing to respond with his · assignment shall be counted as absent and subject to fine.

Section 3. When a Scout is absent from the meeting without reasonable excuse he shall pay .... cents into the troop treasury.

Section 4. Any Scout failing to try to do what he is asked to do shall be counted as absent, and shall be subject to fine.

Section 5. Fines shall be limited in amount, and never amount to more than .... cents.

Section 6. Each Scout shall pay 25 cents per year as dues for the support of the Local and National Councils.

ARTICLE XV.— MEETINGS.

Section 1. Our Troop shall meet every ...... weeks to practice general Scouting; and every ...... weeks for a business session.

Section 2. There shall be both troop and patrol practices of general Scouting, to be held at times as designated by our Scout Master.

ARTICLE XVI.—RELIGION.

The Scout Master should coöperate with the boy's pastor, parents and church in the religious instruction of the Scouts of his troop.

ARTICLE XVII.— GENERAL PROVISIONS.

Section 1. Our meetings shall at all times be open to our friends, and our parents, pastors, teachers, and members of the Local Council shall at all times be welcome to sit with us at our councils.

Section 2. Nothing unbecoming shall be done in any initiatory or other ceremony, and we will seek to avoid anything in our meetings which may be objectionable to our parents.

Section 3. A Scout always rises in giving his part on the program.

Section 4. A Scout always salutes his Patrol Leader, Scout Master, Assistant Scout Master, Scout Commissioner, and every old soldier. He stands with head uncovered and salutes at the hoisting of our national flag, the playing or singing of our national anthem, and at every funeral.

Section 5. The enrollment and advancement of the Scouts of our troop from one rank to another and the qualification for merit badges and for all other badges shall be strictly in accordance with the requirements of the official manual.

Section 6. The Scout Oath and Scout Law as given in the official " Handbook for Boys," published by the National Council of the Boy Scouts of America, shall be strictly adhered to.

Section 7. Our activities shall be those laid down by the National Council of the Boy Scouts of America in their official manual.

Section 8. Our activities shall be Peace-Scouting in character.

- Section 9. Our troop shall have its flag and special insignia, including Troop Flag and Patrol Flags, displayed in a prominent place in our headquarters. Our American Flag shall always occupy the position of honor.

Section 10. The following books shall be kept in the care and custody of our Scout Scribe or Secretary, who shall be responsible therefor : —

(1) A record of the minutes or proceedings of the troop business meetings.

(2) A book of Constitution and By-Laws, with the signatures of our members.

(3) A visitor's register.

(4) A register containing the name of each member, his birthplace, residence, the date of his initiation as a Tenderfoot, the date of his initiation to the different Scout ranks, and also the date of the termination, suspension of his membership or his delinquency, as the same may occur.

(5) An alphabetical list of expulsions, suspensions, and rejections.

(6) Such books as may be necessary to present clearly the receipts and accounts of the troop.

ARTICLE XVIII.— AMENDMENTS.

Our Constitution may be altered by the troop at any regular Troop Meeting, after the alterations proposed have been read at two regular meetings.

By-Laws.

ARTICLE I.— MEETINGS.

Section 1. Our regular Troop Meeting for general Scouting practice is held on ...... at .... P. M.

Section 2. Our troop business sessions are held on ...... evening every ...... weeks, at .... P. M.

ARTICLE II.— ORDER OF BUSINESS.

Section 1. Our order of business shall be as follows: —

1. Roll-call — Collection of dues.
2. Records of preceding meeting.
3. Reports of Committees (by seniority).
4. Report of members absent at the last meeting.
5. Report of sickness or distress of Troop members.
6. Financial Report.
7. Secretary's Report on awards of degrees, applications to the Court of Honor, Initiations, and Investitures.
8. Report of Committee on Honors.
9. Initiation.
10. Hearing or Presentation of Complaints.
11. New Applications.
12. Balloting.
13. Unfinished Business.
14. New Business.
15. Social Entertainment.
16. Closing Exercises.
17. Patrol Calls.
18. Adjournment.

Section 2. Every meeting shall have proper opening and closing exercises.

ARTICLE III.— AMENDMENTS.

These By-Laws may be changed by a majority vote at any regular meeting.

Troop Politeness and Courtesy.

Chivalry should have its inception in the patrol and troop. The Scouts should under no circumstances call their Scout Master or the Assistant Scout Master by their first names; they should be addressed as Mr. Scout Master and Mr. Assistant Scout Master. The Patrol Leader and his assistant should be addressed as Patrol Leader (*Morris*), and Assistant Patrol Leader (*Hewitt*). In receiving an order from a Scout Master or Assistant Scout Master, the Scout, should answer, "Yes, sir," or "No, sir," as the case demands, and the ordinary rules of courtesy should be observed at all times. In addressing the chair or an officer a Scout should always salute before doing so. Every troop should possess a United States Flag, and each Scout should come to the salute as he passes the national colors, and observe all other respects due to the flag.

Troop Finances.

The matter of finances is one that must always be carefully considered. Sometimes the boys will voluntarily vote

AT THE TRAINING CAMP FOR SCOUT MASTERS AT SILVER BAY, NEW YORK, DURING THE SUMMER OF 1912

a sum of five cents a week per member for the expenses of the patrol. In such case the Scout Master should use a great deal of judgment in the matter and should prevent the boys from such a thing, if there is a single boy in the patrol upon whom the weekly tax would work a hardship. None of the money put into the patrol treasury should be used for the purchase of individual equipment for the boys. One of the cardinal principles of the movement is that each boy shall earn his own uniform and equipment. Patrol funds therefore should be used for patrol expenses. In a few places of the country there are troops or patrols which have set a pace by instituting a treasury into which the boys are permitted to pay small amounts of money which is to be paid out for charitable purposes only.

Troop moneys should be used in the same way as patrol funds — for general troop equipment. The matter of dues is always important and should always receive due consideration so as not to entail any hardship upon any boy. Usually both the troop and the patrol will elect its own treasury officer who will have care of the common funds. However any temptation for such a boy to go astray should not be permitted by the Scout Master, and while trust should be given to the boy, there should be a general rule providing that all moneys of the troop or patrol should be carefully deposited in a local bank, and the account opened in the patrol's or troop's name. Where this is not possible the Scout Master should be the bank receiving the funds, giving the boy treasurer receipts for all funds so deposited with him.

Troop Equipment.

There will always be a problem for the Scout Master to consider in the matter of Scout equipment and uniforms. The ordinary patrol and troop will be composed of the boys of all classes, and how to regulate the uniform and equipment under such conditions will always have to be settled by local needs and circumstances. It should be clearly understood, however, that while a uniform and equipment is a great help to patrol and troop activity it is not entirely essential to the success and progress.

No matter whether the boy is poor or well-to-do he should earn his own uniform and equipment by doing work at a reasonable wage, and it should be impressed upon him that he must work fairly and honestly — that he should not do some very small thing and receive a high rate of pay from parent or guardian,— but that his wage should be the reasonable wage. In this way the boy will obtain an idea of the working value of money. If each boy pays for his uniform and individual equipment, the problem will be largely solved whether the boys are rich or poor.

Patrol Property.

It is best to allow the patrol to have some property in common. Besides affording a lesson in coöperation, it furnishes a tie which will bind the members of the patrol together. Such equipment may consist of the patrol flag, tent, combination cooking outfit, first aid kit, and road maps, etc. Local needs will add many other articles to this list.

Troop Property.

In addition to the patrol equipment, as a means of tying the various patrols more closely together, it will probably be best to have some property owned by the entire troop. There may be a headquarters, a mess tent for field-work, and furniture and paraphernalia for the troop club room are naturally suggested as things for troop ownership. And of course there is also the troop flag. Where troops have their own or permanent headquarters, the Scout Master should encourage the different troop members to make their own stools, boxes, and other handy articles used at head-quarters or in scouting. The property which will be accumulated by the troop will vary in quantity and kind as the life of the troop extends itself, and such features as a library, a natural history museum, a reading room, etc., might be added.

Where the boys show ability or liking for certain trades or mechanical work the Scout Master should seek to tie them up to some expert or tradesman who will be willing to aid the boys in their desire for technical knowledge and experience, each in the work of his choice or adaptability.

Scout Examinations.

Appointed dates should be set for examinations for the different Scout ranks and for merit badges. Such a course should prove more acceptable to the Scout Master and to Scout conditions, than to allow the boy to take his examinations at any time he wishes.

All examinations wherever there is a local council should be conducted by the Court of Honor and not by the Scout Master in charge of the troop. Where there is no Court of Honor, it is best to obtain the aid of another Scout Master or some other known man of the community to serve as such a court. Where the local Scout Master gives examinations to his own Scouts there will always be charges of favoritism, and a general feeling of discontent will be engendered before very long under such conditions.

It should also be the general rule that the Scout should make formal application for an examination. This besides impressing the Scout that the examination is a matter of consequence, will furnish a valuable record of the work accomplished by the various Scouts. The following blank is a suggestion for such an application form: —

.... Council,   **State** ....

Boy Scouts of America

Application for Examination for .... (or
Merit Badge of ....)

Date ....

I, ... age .... Class of
Scout .... Patrol .... Troop
.... Patrol Leader .... Scout
Master .... do hereby make application to
the Court of Honor for a test in the requirements necessary
to qualify for the ....rank or badge.

(Signed) .... Scout
Approved...............Parent or Guardian.
Approved .... Scout Master.

Received and filed .... Date ....
Sec. of Council.

....

The above test was given to Scout .... on
.... and passed to the satisfaction of the
(Date)
Court of Honor.

(Signed) ....
Clerk of Court.

Badge (or rank) awarded ....

(Date)

....
Secretary of Council.

Record System Suggestions.

If possible individual record systems should be kept
showing the progress of each Scout, as well as records showing progress of patrols and troops. In some cities where
point systems have been established detailed records are
kept showing standing of each Scout, each patrol, and each
troop in the individual inter-patrol and inter-troop contests.
As suggestions for similar systems, models of Scout records,
and in order to standardize as far as possible the different
ideas originated, the following records and point systems
have been compiled and are recommended to all the Scout
Masters.

Individual Records.

Scout, ... Patrol, ... Troop No. ...
City, ... State, ...

Boy Scouts of America.

Full Name .... Address, ...
Name of Father, ... Occupation of Father,
.... Business Address, ...
Place of Birth, ...
Date of Birth, ...
Height, ... Weight, ...
School, ... Grade, ... Standing, ...
Church, ... Sunday School, ...
Member of other organization, ...
Qualified for Tenderfoot, ..., 19..... Mark, ...
Qualified for Second Class Scout, ..., 19..... Mark,
....
Qualified for First class Scout, ..., 19..... Mark,
....
Qualified for ...... Merit Badge, ..., 19.....
Mark, ...
Qualified for ...... Merit Badge, ..., 19.....
Mark, ...

....

The following point and honor system for individual
Scouts, patrols and troops, has also been accepted as a
standard and is herewith recommended: —

General Points.

1.	Attendance of meeting	1
2.	Wearing uniform at meeting	1
3.	Non-use of tobacco each week (word of honor of Scout to be taken)	2
4.	Dues and all indebtedness paid up, per month..	1
5.	Passing each test for Second Class Scout.....	2
6.	Passing each test for First Class or Distinguished Scout	3
7.	Passing each test for Honor Scout	4
8.	Each Second-Class Scout in Troop	5
9.	Each First-Class Scout in Troop	10
10.	Each examination passed for Merit Badge	10
11.	Each Proficient Scout	15
12.	Each Distinguished Scout	20
13.	Each Honor Scout	25

14. Each Star Scout 50
15. Scout hikes, per mile .... ½

Proficient Scout.

Each Scout is given a credit of 125 points and must maintain a credit of at least 25 points until the first meeting in ......, 19..... Any Scout may earn 10 points by having a perfect record for one month.

Points are marked off for the following: Points.

1. Non-attendance (without good excuse).. 10
2. Lateness (without good excuse) 5
3. Failure to wear uniform at meeting 5
4. Delinquent dues, or other unpaid indebtedness, per month 5
6. Smoking, swearing or disobedience to officers .... 5 to 25
7. Disorder, failure to properly salute on entering or leaving meeting, or in addressing the chair, or other misconduct at meetings 1
8. Breach of Scout laws, fines to be imposed by committee.

Distinguished Scout.

1. Home: A Scout must submit a certificate from his parent or guardian each month that he has been generally helpful at home for the month past. Scouts must have four certificates by ...... (3 points for each certificate).

2. Work: (1) He must have a general average of 75 at school for at least five months, or submit a certificate of competency from employers for five months. (2) He must read two books recommended by the Scout Master (3 points for each certificate). Books recommended, one on some Scouting or relative subject, and one on a moral subject.

3. Religion: (Optional but counts for points.) He must certify each month to the attendance of church or Sunday School once a week, unless excused by parent for good reason. Must have five certificates by ...... (3 points for each certificate).

4. Scouting: (1) Own new Scout manual and have read it through. (2) Signaling: send a message 25 letters a minute and receive 20 letters a minute. (3) Tie eight

of the knots on pages 50, 51 and 52 of the "Handbook for Boys." (4) Cook a meal for yourself and at least one other Scout over a campfire. (5) Give the names of 10 best trees for wood to use for a cooking fire and 5 kinds that won't burn to use for hangers and log grate. (6) Name 10 wild plants which can be used for food and how prepared for use. (7) Name and identify six poisonous or injurious plants. (8) The four poisonous snakes. (9) The ten most injurious insects and five most beneficial to mankind and explain how useful or injurious. Draw seven out of the nine.

5. Athletics: Qualify in over half of the athletic requirements as set forth in the "Handbook for Boys," or play on a regular school or Y. M. C. A., or other club or athletic team.

6. Handicraft: Must make some article for Scout room or home. (Two Scouts can make something together.) (Points to be awarded, 3 to 10.)

7. First Aid: (1) Demonstrate the rescue of a drowning person from the water by the proper grip. (2) Show how to break any hold a drowning person can get. (3) Resuscitate a person from drowning by the Shaffer method. (4) Pass examination in private health, as required for merit badge. (See "Handbook for Boys.")

8. Social: Propose and teach the troop how to play a Scout game.

9. Special honors: Must earn one Merit Badge in addition to Personal Health.

The awarding of Distinguished Scout must be at the recommendation of the Scout Master.

Three points for each sub-division, except where otherwise designated, are counted under "General Points."

Honor Scout.

(This is meant to be difficult, but not impossible of performance for any Scout.)

1. Scouting: Must be a Second-Class Scout. (1) Have attended one Scout camp for at least one week and contributed to its success, or have slept out of doors thirty nights or taken Scout hikes amounting to a total of fifty miles. (2) Made a grass mattress or camp bed out of willow twigs, and a bow and arrow to shoot 75 yards. (3) Press and mount on paper 30 specimens of leaves of native trees, identify the family and species of each. (4)

Know by sight and song 10 birds. (5) Know by sight, cry and tracks, 10 native animals. (6) Point out and name five constellations and four stars.

2. Camping: Pass an examination on camping, locating a camp, pitching tent and making ditches and latrine and other sanitary arrangements. (See Gibson on "Camping for Boys." Eight Points.)

3. Health: (1) Must pledge yourself not to touch tobacco or liquor so long as you remain a Scout. (2) Must be able to lead the setting-up exercises specified in the "Handbook for Boys." (3) Take these exercises or some other regular exercises approved by Scout Master at least 5 days a week, four monthly certificates required, or (4) take a cold bath at least five times each week each month. Five certificates of either or both (3) and (4) required. (Four points for each certificate.)

4. Chivalry: (1) Must have read two stories of the Knights of King Arthur. (2) Have been recommended by a fellow-Scout as doing a helpful courtesy to a lady or old person or two good turns.

5. Education: (1) Must read a book about one of the American pioneer scouts and repeat it at meeting. (2) Read two other books recommended by Scout Master.

6. Civic: (1) Must have elementary knowledge of the local governments. (2) State. (3) National. Pass examination. (4) Also principal charitable institutions in the community. (5) Must draw a map of locality where you live, showing all the offices of doctors, drug stores, the nearest fire plug to your home, offices of the local officers, police headquarters and firehouses. (6) Know names of your local policeman and officers and members of the fire department, board of health and school directors and their chief duties.

7. First Aid: (1) Must pass elementary national First Aid to the injured examination, and (2) Merit Badge in First Aid; or pass (3) Public Health; and (4) Firemanship honors. See ("Handbook for Boys.")

8. Special honors: Must win three merit badges, besides those already mentioned: Archery, astronomy, athletics, business, camping, civics, conservation, cooking, craftsmanship, bugling, electricity, forestry, handicraft, interpreter, life-saving, music, pathfinding, pioneering, scholarship, signaling, stalking and swimming.

9.   Social: Must get up or give a social stunt at a meeting.

10.   Must have written statement from his mother and his teacher or employer of his helpfulness and that in their opinion he has been sincerely trying to keep his Scout pledge; and must have the approval of his patrol and presiding Scout Master to the awarding of the degree.

11.   Must be proficient or distinguished Scout.

Four points for each sub-division except where otherwise designated, counted under general points.

Patrol Records.

Patrol Number....... Name....... Colors.......

Patrol Leader ....

Assistant Patrol Leader ....

Secretary ....

Treasurer ....

To serve from .... to ....

Patrol meets on .... night.   Time ....

Patrol meets at ....

Have had Lectures conducted as follows: —

.... by ....

.... by ....

.... by ....

.... by ....

Equipment: —

    Uniforms..... Staves..... Patrol Whistles.....

    Signal Flags .... What Kind ....

    Patrol Flags .... National Flags ....

    Bugles or Horns .... Tents .... Drums ....

Members.   Names.   Addresses.

1. ....

2. ....

3. ....

4. ....

5. ....

6. ....

7. ....

8. ....

Honorary Members.

....

Troop Records.

(1)   Scout Master .... Certificate No.........
        Residence, ...:.
        Business Address, ...
        Troop No. ..... Name, ... Colors,
        ....
        Patrol Name, ... Patrol Color, ...
        "   "   ....   "   "   ....
        "   "   ....   "   "   ....
        Meeting Place, ... Day, ...
        Time, ..., Patrol Membership.

1. ....   4. ....
2. ....   5. ....
3. ....   6. ....
        Patrol Leader, ...
        Asst. Patrol Leader, ...

(2)   Wall Record for Troop.

No. Name	Scout Law, etc.	Flag	Knots	Passed	Months' Service	First Aid	Signaling
(Fox) Patrol				1912		Band.	Signal
1. (Smith) P. L.	/	/	/	Oct. 1	/	Bandage	Morse
2. (Cox) A. D. L.	/	/	/	July 20	/	Exam. Bandage	
3. (Williams)	/	/	/	Oct. 15	/		Morse
4. (Johnson)							
5. (Brown)							
6. (Myers)							
7. (O'Brien)							
8. (Griffin)							
(Eagle) Patrol							
1. (White) P. L.							
2. (Adams) A. P. L.							
3. (McRae)							
4. (Edwards)							

Scout Masters' Reports

Monthly Report of Scout Master .... Troop No. ....
of the Boy Scouts of America.

Headquarters at ...... For the month of ......19...

This report will be made up promptly at the end of each month,
and forwarded to the Scout Commissioner of the District.

ENROLLMENT	No. PATROLS	No. SCOUTS	No. ADULTS (over 18)	TOTAL

SCOUT MEETINGS:

1

(DATE)	(NO. PRESENT)

CHARACTER OF MEETING

2

(DATE)	(NO. PRESENT)

CHARACTER OF MEETING

3

(DATE)	(NO. PRESENT)

CHARACTER OF MEETING

4

(DATE)	(NO. PRESENT)

CHARACTER OF MEETING

5

(DATE)	(NO. PRESENT)

CHARACTER OF MEETING

GAINS OR LOSSES:

NAME	AGE Last Birthday	ADDRESS	JOINED	RESIGNED

........................*Scout Master.*

Equipment:
{
Uniforms ....Staves ....Bugle ....
Drums ......Signal Flag ......1st Aid ......
Keys ....Wireless ....Flags ....
Colors ....Tents ....
}

Have conducted......Scouting Trips......Total attendance.

Received at Commissioner's office...... RESPECTFULLY SUBMITTED

................Secretary.

Advisory Committee or Council met......

Competitive Contests.

One of the greatest incentives to Scouting in a troop or under a Local Council will be the independent troop or patrol competition which can be started and continued through definite periods of time. Scoring in these competitions should be on an individual basis, each Scout getting full credit for his accomplishments, each score being put to his credit, if in an inter-Scout contest in the patrol, or for the patrol or troop, if in case of an inter-patrol or inter-troop contest. Interest in the troop competition may be intensified by the Local Council or Scout Master putting up a trophy shield or cup, the trophy to be held by the winner until the close of the next competition. In this way the contest can be continued for three, six or twelve months.

Such contests between patrols in the same troop and also between all the different troops in the district has been very successfully carried out on the point-system basis as suggested by the contest outlined on pp. 269-274. Every Scout Commissioner and Scout Master will see the value in this suggestion, and will perhaps be able to add further to the point-system in order to make and create new stunts, new interest, and a renewal of good results.

CHAPTER VI

TRAINING OF PATROL LEADERS

The Problem of Securing Good Patrol Leaders.

The problem of securing and developing competent patrol leaders is the most difficult, yet the most vital one to which a Scout Master can direct his attention. Furthermore it is peculiarly his problem,— his, because he must discover for himself the controlling motives that actuate his boys, especially the leaders; his, because he of all others must correct damaging influences, divert misapplied energy and develop leadership; his, because the community, expecting much, though helping little, looks to him as the intimate adviser, sponsor and guide. The popular reception accorded the entire Movement shows the strength of the public belief that by means of it, boys' interests are wholesomely directed into channels of true leadership,— such leadership as can be relied upon for honest, unselfish service.

The Scout Master, however, is left to find in the program of the Scout Movement, his opportunity for supplying through play what the boys and the public will generally most value as a means of developing this quality. By the effect of his work just here, the Scout Master's rating is settled. Just here, the permanency of his influence is determined. Success in meeting this problem requires, besides capacity and genuineness in his own make-up, a clear understanding of his task and the ability to deal with it. That his chief aim is to develop character and personality, everyone knows. To further this purpose, he must foster resourcefulness, unselfishness, initiative, acceptance of responsibility and the like. But practically, how is this to be done? What are to be the steps of procedure? Unfortunately no prescribed methods are to be had; for no set rules can be found to apply to any one individual boy or any number of boys of his group. To discover a means all his own is the Scout Master's peculiar and engaging undertaking.

The Approach to the Problem.

As offering a possible, general starting-point, the instructions given in the Organization Bulletin are useful. There one is told to select six boys (from a group of twenty-four that have been brought together at the first meeting) as leaders and assistants, and with them form a special Patrol. " Begin at once to train these boys in the Tenderfoot requirements; when they have passed the examinations call your first regular meeting for organization. Your twenty-four boys may be formed into three patrols of eight boys each, with a trained Patrol Leader and an Assistant Patrol Leader in charge of each. The fact that these leaders have a knowledge of Scouting and have passed the Tenderfoot requirements will give them prestige among the other boys. Give your leaders real responsibility. Let them feel that their special task is to teach, influence and lead the boys of their Patrol and that unless they do it no one else will."

" In grouping boys in patrols it is advisable to form patrols of boys as near the same age as possible, taking into consideration the natural instincts of the boys and their desire for association with one another. This is often a more important factor than age."

" While the patrol leaders are preparing the boys in their patrols for the Tenderfoot degree, continue your instructions of the Leaders and Assistants in the Second Class requirements, so that they will be able as Second Class Scouts to instruct the boys in their patrols. In like manner have them qualify as First Class Scouts."

Selection of a Patrol Leader.

Assuming that a patrol consisting of eight prospective Scouts has been brought together and the preliminary steps of organization taken, that is, that they have been instructed in the activities and duties incumbent upon Scouts and grouped according to their ages, instincts, interests, etc., we find the Scout Master confronted with one of the most important and telling phases of Scout work,— the selection and development of his several leaders.

Whether or not the Scout Master shall appoint a Patrol Leader, or have the members of the patrol select him, or let the entire troop participate in the election, is for him to decide. For obvious reasons different methods should be followed under different conditions. A Scout Master who has no previous experience, either with boys or with the Scout program, might follow one course, while a Scout Master who has had several years' experience with boys, who is, himself, a natural Scout, or who is working with a group that has been previously organized, for some other purpose and because of his experience or view-point might follow a different course. As this is written for those seeking help, it is not out of the way to assume that they have had no large experience with a group of boys and are only slightly familiar with Scout work. A man finding himself in this class should first of all make it his duty to become thoroughly acquainted, individually and collectively, with all prospective Scouts, and spend much time in seeking to learn and understand their peculiar temperaments and interests. All of such time thus studiously spent will in its results become of extreme value to the Scout Master in his later relations with the boys, with their development individually, and with the progress of the troop.

For several meetings, let the members of the patrol or troop work together without installing a Patrol Leader. During this period of, perhaps, three or four weeks, the Scout Master should follow a general program with which he is familiar and which he knows to be useful. At the end of this time, let him adopt one of the two following methods of obtaining a Patrol Leader: —

(1) Appoint a Scout who appears to be the natural and most promising leader, as a temporary Patrol Leader, permitting him to take charge of a patrol (letting it be understood, of course, that he is only on trial).

(2) Have an election in which every member of the patrol participates.

Where Scouts have had an opportunity to work for higher Scout ranking and those who have done the best are likely to be chosen leaders, this latter method is preferable. If a Scout Master follows the first course, he should allow the temporary leader to serve only for a short time, giving others of the patrol opportunities to qualify under the same conditions until such time as an election can profitably be held or until the Scout Master has satisfied himself that a leader can be appointed for a definite term. As a further development of the second method, it has been found practicable to use a competitive examination on all the Scout work covered up to the time of the election. In the final reckoning, this examination would count for two-thirds. The other third would be counted on the boy's popularity, determined by the votes of the other boys.

The per cent of popularity would be credited to each boy on the ratio of the votes he receives to the total number of votes cast. For instance, suppose twenty votes are cast, altogether. If a boy received two of these twenty votes, he would be credited with two twentieths of thirty-three and a third per cent, or three and one-third per cent; and a boy who received thirteen votes would be credited with thirteen twentieths of thirty-three and a third per cent, or twenty-one and two-thirds per cent.

Term of Office.

The term of office for a Patrol Leader should be one year, at the end of which time, he may be reëlected or dismissed as the patrol or Scout Master see fit. In most instances, however, it is better to have him continue in office. In deciding this point, though, a Scout Master, who from his vantage ground can best consider the interests of all the group, should have much influence.

If conditions arise which necessitate a change in Patrol Leaders before the end of the year, such as would occur in the case of resignation, transfer or dishonorable removal, the office should be filled at once, either by the appointment or election of a substitute, or by the advancement of the Assistant Patrol Leader. The term of office of the substitute should expire at the time previously set for the former incumbent.

Development of Patrol Leaders.

The Patrol Leader should be expected to furnish the raw material for his own development. He need not be the best boy of the group, considered purely from moral standards, since it is a Scout Master's duty to develop the best side of every boy's nature; but he must be energetic, alert, and responsible. It may happen that the boy chosen as Leader has the worst reputation of any in the bunch. That in itself is not alarming, for the boy who by others is rated as bad may be of better calibre than one who is popularly recommended as a good boy. He may be more reliable, better principled in essentials, more observant, more agreeable and willing, more unaffected, and on the whole a better fellow among the others of the group than the boy with a less spotted reputation.

Occasionally boys will be found who take upon themselves the role of leader without being so respected by their companions. Such cases are frequently the result of selfishness or an exaggerated sense of individual importance. They are, however, none the less worthy of consideration, and Scout Masters should be careful not to neglect or misuse boys in whom evidence of these faults appear. Such tendencies as theirs are immensely human and can be trained to valuable account. A wise curbing here and there to rightly shape the general course is the Scout Master's function. He will obtain his best results by giving encouragement and making an appeal to the boy's better self.

As soon as a Leader has been selected he should be recognized as special agent of instruction under the Scout Master, helping to teach to the other patrol members what the Scout Master desires to impart. Responsibility, which often makes good material out of what has hitherto been unpromising, is laid upon him now. If the position is new to the boy, and his duties unfamiliar, responsibility should be given lightly and with much sympathetic help at first. As time goes on, he ought to become the Scout Master's right-hand man in relation to his own patrol, helping the Scout Master to provide suitable tasks and to stimulate a desire for progress to the highest Scout ranks. Throughout, the Patrol Leader should be the actual leader of the patrol.

Age and Duties of the Patrol Leader.

For a patrol the members of which average between the ages of thirteen and fifteen, the leader need not be the oldest. He should be elected purely on his merits. When there is a great difference between the ages of the oldest and youngest members,— a condition to be avoided,— one of the older boys should be the Patrol Leader, but not necessarily the eldest. Ability rather than age is the basis upon which ultimate decision should rest. Frequently the two go together.

The Patrol Leader should be given full charge of developing and carrying out the activities assigned to the Scouts under him. It is his duty to arouse the spirit of unity and strength without which the patrol life is impossible. To this end the Scout Master must help the Leader by encouraging the use of patrol competitions and a system of merits by which the advancement of the individual is put to the credit of the patrol rather than to the purely individual account, although individual competitions within the patrol and troop will also help to stimulate interest. (See the Record System Suggestions for Troops and Patrols as outlined in Chapter V; this record or merit system should be used consistently.)

It subsequently becomes the duty of the Patrol Leader to prod the lazy and indifferent and encourage the thrifty and ambitious of his group. If the members of a patrol wish to specialize in any one subject, say First Aid, they should be allowed to do so provided, of course, such extra work is not done to the detriment of their general progress. When the patrol specializes, the Patrol Leader should interest himself especially in the subject chosen, and see to it that the instruction necessary for each member is available. The Patrol Leader should make it his duty to get an expert to instruct the Scouts in the special subject, rather than depend upon the Scout Master; in the case of First Aid the average Scout Master would very likely know less concerning the subject than the average physician, so that instruction from the physician would be very helpful and undoubtedly more thorough and complete. This does not mean that the Patrol Leader is not to coöperate with the Scout Master in getting the physician, but rather that the necessary work of interesting and securing a physician friend for this purpose should devolve upon him as the Patrol Leader.

Patrol Leaders should regularly be given full charge of meetings of the patrols. When the troop is called together the advanced or senior Patrol Leader, or more correctly, the Leader of the patrol doing the best work, should occasionally be in full charge. This honor may occasionally be given other Patrol Leaders, but should not be given in successive rotation. When the Patrol Leader occupies this latter position he is usually designated as Troop Leader.

Duties of Patrol Leaders on Hikes.

When on hikes, the case is somewhat different. Then Patrol Leaders should seldom be given complete charge.

The hike should not be undertaken until an Assistant Scout Master, at least, can be present. Great care should be taken on all such occasions to see that all property regulations, fire-laws, etc., are strictly complied with. For this reason alone, a competent adult person must accompany the patrol. In camp or at any destination, the leaders should be given much the same duties they would have at the regular indoor meetings. Greater discretion, however, in assigning tasks, is to be exercised; yet full and prompt compliance should be insisted upon.

Conference and Councils for Development.

As a means of properly developing Patrol Leaders let the Scout Master have frequently special meetings for Patrol Leaders alone. At such times he should be freely confidential and painstaking in his outlining of problems peculiar to their patrols as well as the problems of general concern to their troop. In all matters pertaining to the welfare of the Troop Scout Masters should be guided to a very large extent by the combined opinions of the Patrol Leaders.

Conferences and councils need not be frequent but should be real. A Scout Master will find his energies better utilized if he can encourage Patrol Leaders to arrange these conferences rather than arrange them himself. The initiative of a Scout Master, if a positive factor at all, will stimulate that of the Patrol Leader. The stimulus should come in other ways, however, than through the direct suggestion of matters of business that are to be advanced for mutual consideration. Many topics presented for discussion at Patrol Leaders' conferences will naturally be reported at later meetings of the patrol and of the troop. In such cases it will generally be desirable to have the Patrol Leaders present the matter rather than to allow them to depend upon the Scout Master. The Scout Master will find it greatly to his advantage to share every problem of troop progress and activity with his Patrol Leaders. At all Scout gatherings the Patrol Leaders should not only be held responsible in carrying out the Scout Master's orders, but should be given a liberal range of authority in originating plans and giving orders of their own.

Use of Patrol Leaders in Teaching Requirements.

Instructions in the simple requirements or in all the regular subjects in which the Patrol Leader is thoroughly proficient should be left to his charge. It should be made his duty to see that all candidates for examination belonging to his patrol are fully equipped to pass the requirements on which they will be examined before they present themselves to the Troop Committee or the Local Court of Honor. The Patrol Leader may call upon his assistants or on any other of his Scouts for help, and, in fact, he should be encouraged to do so in all situations that make it practicable.

Disciplining of Patrol Leaders.

When Patrol Leaders are wisely chosen they seldom require severe disciplining. Nevertheless, whenever it is needed it is highly important that it be administered no less rigorously than the disciplining of ordinary Scouts. It must, of course, be distinctly different and the method of application as peculiar as is the nature of his office. For cases of mild insubordination, which may be frequent with the new Patrol Leader in whom consciousness of his official importance is undeveloped, the punishment should come in the form of kindly, but none the less positive advice. He should be made to realize at the outset that as Patrol Leader he must be a model for other members of his patrol. Failure to live up to the Scout principles must be treated with severity as being a serious offense. Scout Masters should, however, take unto themselves no small share of the punishment for this because it is in the Patrol Leader doubtless due to the same cause that induces it in any Scout, namely, the lack of having these principles made sufficiently plain and attractive. When all Scouts are made to understand that they can retain their Scout name with its attendant positions only so long as they respect and obey the Scout Law and Scout Oath, the Scout Master will have little necessity of subjecting them to any sort of humiliation, because of failure to live as true Scouts.

Decisions on courses of punishment for wanton disrespect and insubordination on the part of the Patrol Leaders must never be placed in the hands of officers ranking below Patrol Leaders. The matter must be adjusted by the Scout Master and his immediate assistants or with the aid or advice of the Local Troop Committee. However, it is very much better to settle such a misunderstanding, if possible, between just the Scout Master, himself, and the offender.

Occasionally a Patrol Leader becomes indifferent to the progress of his patrol; sometimes he, himself, fails to advance to higher Scout ranking as rapidly as he should. Such a Patrol Leader should be treated in one of the following three ways:— (1) his ambition should be aroused by stimulating inter-patrol non-athletic competitions; (2) by depriving him and his patrol of the most attractive Scout work; (3) or (this should be the last resort) by removing him from his office and reducing him to the rank of ordinary Scout. If the plan of using patrol competition is adopted, this competition should be used for instruction rather than for selfish display,— the various features of it being so arranged that his weakness as well as the weakness of his patrol is successfully demonstrated. If the second course is followed,— that of temporary ostracism,— it would be most effective to keep the patrol from participating in any event which they were eager to enjoy. Discretion must constantly be exercised so that the Patrol Leader will have no opportunity to feel that he is being unfairly discriminated against and that no animosity exists.

Self-Government.

A wise leader, recognizing the inherent desire of all boys for fair play and for taking a part in their particular Scout work, will encourage self-government, making it in so far as practical an actual and usable part of their association. Self-government is always good where it is not abused, but valuable only as an object tending toward leadership. So much latitude must be allowed in this for local conditions and previous experiences, both of the Scout Master and his boys, that it is difficult to give definite and clear instructions which can be generally followed. However, one point must be kept always in mind, and that is that *the Scout Master must always be the guiding factor.* When he ceases to become so, he loses his position of leadership. If his influence is felt rather than dominantly asserted, it is far more valuable. Several means might be suggested of letting the members of his patrol know his attitude on subjects. For example, to use two widely different situations,— before the election of patrol officers or before the meeting at which they are to define their attitude toward the question of smoking, the Scout Master should meet the members of his patrol individually and give them a clear, intelligent conception of the importance of their decision, letting them realize how their action can shape the decision of other patrol members, and how it will affect their conduct in the future. The Scout Master can thus enable those who have had no experience in considering such matters to follow the course which would be mutually profitable and satisfactory. Ordinarily it would be unfair for the Scout Master to dictate what the decision should be or baldly emphasize his views, but his outlining and explaining of issues should be so clear that an intelligent solution or conclusion is easily made possible for the boys.

Where it is not feasible to consider such matters with individuals of the patrol the same general course should be followed before the group. Self-government means exactly what the term implies but, contrary to custom, as much emphasis should be placed on the word *government* as on the word *self*. Best leadership is that which governs indirectly or by suggestion so that the boys believe there has been a real self-governing decision. Members of the patrol in every instance must be made intelligently familiar with the subject under discussion and should be encouraged to discuss it to their mutual content. If the Scout Master's patience is taxed and he is subjected to the necessity of hearing what he may consider threadbare subjects discussed to unwarranted lengths, he should take it as an opportunity for studying boyish minds, and only end the discussion when it degenerates into childish quibbling. When groups of boys are brought to the point where they are able to express their own opinions and weigh the opinions of others, then self-government will be made not only possible but distinctly useful. The Scout Master who has brought to his service this valuable asset can also be sure that he is on the right road to the accomplishment of an end which is of large importance in Scouting,— that of handing over to the boy the knowledge he has gained through his longer experience.

Growth of Patrol Leaders.

The metal and the abilities of the Patrol Leader should constantly be tested. No more effective and valuable means of doing this can be found than the unselfish and definite provision of actual responsibility. A Patrol Leader should grow. Constant exercise and work, mental and physical, and giving the needed experience and training, is necessary. By intelligent guidance a Scout Master can turn the energies of his Patrol Leaders to immensely valuable account. Therefore every effort should be made by the Scout Master to give to his Patrol Leaders as much opportunity for individual responsibility and initiative as possible. Toward this end each Patrol Leader should be made to understand that he is responsible for the creation of a Scout spirit among the members of his patrol; that the degree of success each one gains in mastering the Scout requirements depends in a large measure upon him; and that he must constantly maintain both the dignity and enthusiasm which become a leader. If this point of view is well taken the Scout Master may be assured that the qualities he seeks for his Scouts' dependableness, efficiency, and strength of personality are being well fostered and developed.

Selection of Assistant Patrol Leaders.

Assistant Patrol Leaders may be selected by the Patrol Leader, by the Scout Master, or by the members of the whole patrol. In most cases it is preferable to let the Patrol Leader select his assistants himself. The term of office should be for the same period of time as that of the Patrol Leader. This matter is usually regulated by the adoption of a Troop Constitution and By-Laws.

Development of Assistant Patrol Leaders.

. Assistant Patrol Leaders must be developed in much the same way as Patrol Leaders. As assistants they must work under the direction of their leader and coöperate with him in developing and maintaining a high standard of excellence in all branches of Scout activity. If the more menial or servile tasks fall to his lot, as they often will, he should see that they are completed with all the thoroughness and dignity becoming a Patrol Leader.

His duties should be as specific and binding as are those of his superiors. Wherever it is possible for the Patrol Leader to delegate tasks to his assistants he should be expected and encouraged to do so. The Assistant may rightly be considered the go-between for ordinary Scouts and the

Scout officers; as such he should see that the point of view of each group is shared by the other; that criticisms of conditions are either definitely rejected or as definitely sustained; and that rules and courses of action are clearly understood and intelligently accepted before, or at all events, as soon as, they are promulgated. He must represent both Scouts and Scout officers, seeing that the obligations of each are appreciated and accepted.

Cultivating Leadership.

Leadership is contagious. If the Scout Master is a real leader the Patrol Leader will follow the good example, and leadership and growth, being in order and expected, will inevitably result. This is the law of development and the fundamental law of education. It, therefore, devolves upon a Scout Master to employ, quicken, and tax the interests and talents of his boys.

Some Scout Masters fail in this greatest essential because they cannot or do not grasp the understanding of leadership, its relationships or its personal responsibilities. The ability they have to make or mar, to achieve results by real leadership or fail because of the lack of understanding either self or boys and their relationships one to the other, is often very simple of action or occasion, but may be very final in its results. Sometimes the results are what they are because of a well mapped out and studied plan of action, either wisely or wrongly chosen; sometimes they are what they are because of the totally unconscious or intuitive action on the part of the Scout Master.

For example, consider a condition with which many are already familiar. One man can take a group of boys hiking and return with the group feeling they have honored him by taking part in "his hike," while another man can assemble the same group for a similar hike and bring them home feeling they have been greatly favored. The first man undoubtedly meant well and was as interested in the welfare of the group as the second, but he failed to respect certain essential principles of leadership. It is highly probable that when the first man set out he had no definite aim or end in view; the activities they followed were unconsciously made to seem mechanical or perfunctory; his relationship toward them were too familiar and undignified; he lacked that supreme good humor which gave their program a captivating life and zest; and he failed to call out the real abilities of any of them. The necessary elements of leadership in him were sadly wanting. The second man, appreciating the necessity of an attractive purpose, saw that it was provided and that the hikers themselves felt the burden of responsibility in carrying it out. Furthermore, without being austere or supercilious, but by maintaining a natural dignity which invited deference and a certain restrained respect, he called forth an expression of their best natures and made them feel they were really worth while to themselves and others. The one lacked imagination and perception; the second was an educator and a source of inspiration.

To carry out Scout work a man must possess infinite patience, a controlling sense of optimism and a sufficient mastery of every situation. He must be both firm and lenient, secure in purpose, and at the same time resourceful, ingenious, and blessed with a good supply of common sense.

It is the possession of such qualities as these that helps a man discern and develop latent leadership.

CHAPTER VII

SUGGESTIVE PROGRAMS FOR SCOUT MASTERS

Introduction to Programs.

The following programs have been prepared to meet the general and imperative demand by Scoutmasters for suggestions that will help them in planning for their Scout meetings. Scoutmasters should bear in mind that these programs are merely suggestive. In no case is it thought possible to carry out any one of these programs in the course of an evening. Our aim has been to suggest so much more than would be necessary during the meeting period that the Scoutmaster will have ample leeway to choose a suggestion here and there that will fit in with his type of meeting.

These programs have been planned to provide instruction and progressive advancement in Scout work for a troop of twenty-four boys, or three patrols; and present accurate and detailed material arranged in a progressive manner corresponding to the gradual awakening and manifested ability of boy-life.

PROGRAM I

First Meeting

A Pioneer Story — Personal Experiences — Purpose of Scouting — The Scout Oath and Scout Rank — Definite Organization — Use of the Handbook — Announcements — Adjournment.

This program presupposes that a meeting of boys has been called. A number of boys should have been previously instructed as to the object and activities of Boy Scouts.

1. Have an *intensely interesting* tale of the life and early settlement of your community narrated by a pioneer or one of his descendants. *Limit this to fifteen minutes, or omit this rather than have a dry, prosaic recital of uninteresting details.*

2. Have certain boys, good talkers, previously prepared to carry on the local interest by stating personal experience in camp and outdoor life.

3. Incorporate the spirit aroused by these stories into your organization by telling vividly the purpose and objects of the Scout Movement.

A SUMMER CAMP OF BOY SCOUTS

4. Explain the importance and significance of the Scout Oath as discussed on page 15 of the Boys' Handbook. Embody what you have just said into a definite form by displaying the various badges of merit and rank, the troop colors and patrol insignia, and the national flag as emblematic of their pledge of loyalty to this oath and their country. Impress the idea of progressive merit as indicated by the various badges of rank.

5. Develop the idea of a definite organization. Do this in such a way as to arouse their approval and show that it is in response to their personal demand and interest. Show that you mean business. Give the boy application blanks. Explain their use and

purpose so that the boy can answer the questions
which may naturally arise or be put to him by his
parents when their signatures are requested.

6. Pass around copies of the Boys' Handbook for inspection and explain its use.

    a.   Refer to the various sections and topics con-
tained therein.

    b.   Let the boys ask questions. Answer them
from the Handbook.

    c.   Ask questions of the boys. Let them an-
swer from the Handbook.

    d.   Point out the accurate practical information
embodied in the different chapters.

    e.   Close with interest in the Handbook at fever
heat.

7. Arrange a definite time and place for the next meeting.

8. Close your meeting with three cheers for the Scout
Movement and any other good yell which may be
improvised for the occasion.

PROGRAM II

The Creation of Enthusiasm — The Appeal to Interest

Applications — The Scout Yell — Temporary Secretary — Tenderfoot Scout Requirements — Scout Oath, Scout Sign and Salute
— Knot-Tying and Lariat — Announcements — Scout Yells.

*This meeting should be creative of much enthusiasm and
contain as many events of appealing interest as possible.*

1. Call the meeting to order and receive the application blanks given out at the first meeting. Be prepared to answer any questions the boys may ask
as to these applications, and encourage them to
ask for such information.

2. Lead the boys in the Scout Yell, and in any other
good yells which you may deem best for the occasion. Discuss the yell and the reason for it.
Point out its application as a pledge reminder of
the Scout Motto and the Scout Oath, and its value
as serving to create loyalty. The use of the yell
has its chief value in bringing the boys together
into a closer social compact; it appeals directly
to the group instincts of the boy and is corrective
of his self-consciousness. A few yells will serve

to create the get-together spirit, and make each boy feel more closely related to the others. Discipline must always be maintained at the meetings, but discipline among your boys means their constant bottling up of some energy that requires an occasional vent or safety valve. The yells supply such a vent, give rise to an increasing interest, and form an attraction to wilder spirits who would never otherwise join a band of quieter boys. *It would be a very good thing to have one of the boys lead the others in a few yells at this meeting. The yells and discussion should not continue longer than fifteen minutes.*

YELLS

a. The Boy Scouts' Rally:
> Leader: Be Prepared!
> Chorus: Zing-a-Zing!
> Boom! Boom!
> Zing! Zing!
> Boom! Boom!

The boys should stamp or bang something at the last Boom! Boom!

b. America Yell: —
> A-M-E-R-I-C-A!
> *Boy* Scouts! Boy *Scouts! U-S-A!*
> *Use forceful voice on italicized letters and words.*

c. Sky-rocket Yell:
> Leader: Sky-rocket!
> Chorus: Sssss-s-s-ssss!
> BOOM! Ah!
> Boy Scouts!

The Leader's command should be sharp and shrill. The chorus follows in a long drawn-out sizzing sound. Boom and Ah should be given with a very loud and forceful voice.

d. Good Turn Yell:
> Hi! Ki! Wah! Hoo!
> Be prepared! Scouts do
> Some good turn every day.
> Hoo! Rah! Ray!

    e. Scout Rank Yell:
> Be prepared, Be prepared,
> Shout it! Shout it! Shout!
> Tenderfoot, second class,
> First class Scout!

3. Proceed in an orderly and correct way to elect a temporary secretary. Explain to the boys how an election of such an officer is regularly accomplished — what his qualifications should be and then let them conduct the election. This secre-

GIVING INSTRUCTION IN KNOT-TYING

tary should serve until the troop organization is completed.

4. Pass around copies of the Handbook once more and call attention to the requirements of the Tenderfoot class (page 29, B. H.). Emphasize the fact that these requirements must be complete before the Scout Oath can be taken. Point out that the twelve points of the Scout Law must be memorized. Also state where the books can be obtained, and for what price.

5. Turn to page 27 of the Handbook and read the Scout Oath aloud, and explain carefully each part of it. Show the method of taking the oath. Call attention to the Scout Sign and Scout Salute. (See also section on the Scout Oath and Scout Law in the Handbook.)

6. Turn to page 72 of the Handbook and point out the methods of knot-tying and the different knots represented. Explain briefly why the knowledge of knots is important, and the practical uses for the different knots. Have materials ready so that each boy may practice whipping the rope ends and the tying of several knots under your guidance. Go carefully through the preliminary steps and make sure that each lad understands them. Ask questions as to the three qualities of a good knot, and let the boys answer from the Handbook. Also have an upright in the hall, or something similar, and plenty of rope so that the boys can practice lassoing; show them the correct method of preparing the loop, and of holding and throwing the rope. Encourage them to learn as many of the knots as possible and to practice with the lasso at home, so that at the next indoor meeting, contests can be held to see who has become most proficient with the lasso and as knot-tyer.

7. Set a definite time for your next meeting.

8. Close the meeting with three cheers for the Boy Scouts and the Scout Yells.

PROGRAM III

Practical Scouting — First Principles

Opening — New Applicants — National Flag — Drill Practice — History and Composition of the Flag — Tenderfoot Examinations — Games — Daily Good Turn — Need to be Physically Prepared — Hike Arrangements — Yell Practice.

This program presupposes that nearly all of your boys have obtained copies of the " Handbook for Boys," or have been encouraged to do so as soon as possible. By this time those who have books are beginning to use them intelligently, and all want to take up some sort of actual scout practice as soon as possible. So this meeting should be replete with interesting events, and the boys should be told

*that the next meeting will be outdoors in the country or
woods for the practice of actual scouting.*

1. Open your meeting with a few yells.
2. Receive new applications for membership, and welcome such applicants.
3. Display the National Flag and Scout emblems, and ask the boys to explain the Scout's pledge to the Flag. Also explain the drill formation, and have a practice of the drill and Scout Salute to the officer (Scout Master) and the Flag.
4. Relate the history of the American Flag, and explain its composition. Ask the boys what other national flags they have ever seen, and what the colors and emblems represented, etc. Refer them to the first few pages of any Unabridged Dictionary for picture-plates of different national flags, or, if such a book is handy, let each boy have a look at the pictures. If the boys know the tune of the " Star-Spangled Banner " it might be well to sing one or two verses of that song. (For song see page 358 of Boys' Handbook.)
5. Again call attention to the requirements for Tenderfoot, and set the 5th meeting as the definite time for the Tenderfoot examinations. Have each boy repeat as many points of the Scout Law as he has yet memorized, and emphasize the need to *" Be Prepared."*
6. Give the boys something to do in the way of exercise, such as Hand Wrestling (page 303, B. H.), Shop Window Indoors (page 309, B. H), Scouts' Nose Indoors (page 310, B. H.), or any other applicable game or exercise.
7. Speak of the " Daily Good Turn," and emphasize the need of it. Arrange with the boys to be able to give a report of the good turns that they have accomplished during the ensuing days at the next meeting. Impress the value of service.
8. Call attention to Chapter 7 of the Boys' Handbook and the proper carriage each Scout should seek to maintain. Speak of the benefit of bathing and proper eating and the right amount of sleep, and the need for being physically *" prepared."* Demonstrate and practice for a period of ten or

twelve minutes a series of the first four or five setting-up exercises. Encourage the boys to continue the same at a definite time every morning or night.

9. Arrange definitely for the next meeting, which should come on a Saturday or a half-holiday and be held in the country or woods. Outline the program for this first hike, arrange for the proper materials needed en route, and for lunch, and advise the boys as to what sort of clothes and shoes they should wear. Also have it understood that there is to be a preliminary test for Tenderfoot requirements at the noon rest, and that they should "Be Prepared" in all ways. Be sure to set a definite time and place for the start.

10. Close your meeting with a yell practice. Explain the common flag language by demonstration with a flag upside down, at half mast, at full mast, etc., giving their respective meanings. Emphasize the love for the flag, and urge the Scouts to always reverence and protect their national colors. Also refer to the pledge to the flag and explain its significance.

PROGRAM IV
First Principles of Field Scouting

Prompt Start — Scout's Pace — Follow the Trail — Camp Arrangements — Story-Telling — Test — Turn — Nature-Study Observation — Clean Camp — Scout Game — Drill Practice — Announcements — Homeward Walk — Observation Lists.

This meeting should be on a Saturday or half-holiday, and should be definitely arranged for in advance. The boys now expect some actual practice in real Scouting, so get them at it as soon as possible. For this first meeting the hike should be taken into the woods if possible and should not cover a great distance.

1. The appointed time has arrived for the start; get out into the country or woods as soon as possible.

2. You have reached the open land or woods; pick out landmarks in the distance. Advance upon them at Scout's Pace (see page 17). If in the woods make use of Indian signs and blazes (see page 209). Blazes are usually objectionable except in deep woods. Blazing trees injures their

growth. Marking with white chalk or tacking paper to the tree may be substituted for blazing and does not hurt the tree.

3. Select a suitable landmark some distance ahead as a likely place for a day camp, and play " Follow the Trail " to that point.

4. Arrange the camping place for best comfort, and prepare the lunch.

    a. The materials should be brought with you. *See suggested menu and list of utensils on page 152, B. H. for day tramps or hikes.*

    b. If materials are handy, also build a small camp-fire. *Call attention to Forest Fire Warning (page 159, B. H.).*

    c. Give each boy some definite thing to do in preparation of lunch or building of fire, and keep him busy for a while.

5. After the lunch has been eaten, tell a good story or read a couple of chapters from some good book of adventure. Encourage the boys to finish the story and have a report on it at a later time.

6. Have the Preliminary Tenderfoot Test.

7. Receive reports from each boy of his " Daily Good Turn."

7. Ask each boy what he saw or noticed particularly on his walk from his home to the appointed meeting-place. Ask what animals or birds or insects were noticed during the walk into the country. Ask the boys about the different kinds of trees passed en route. *Have someone accompany you into the woods at this meeting who will volunteer to give the boys the correct information concerning the outdoor life. There is someone in nearly every town who would be glad to do this, and who is an authority on animal and plant life in the locality.*

8. Clean up camp and be careful to extinguish the fires.

9. Play the game of Scout Hunting for a little while. (See page 308, B. H.)

10. Practice the Drill, the Scout Sign and the Scout Salute. Practice the Scout Yells.

11. Set the time and place for the next meeting. Remind them that at this meeting the Tenderfoot Examinations are to be held.

12. Set out on the homeward walk, and encourage the
boys to observe the outdoor life about them and to
ask for information of the person who is with
you; he will be glad to give a series of short nature
talks en route. Ask the boys to make out a list of
the new things they have learned about plant and
animal life, when they have arrived home.

PROGRAM V

Tenderfoot Scout Examinations

Opening Talk — Observation Lists — Drill Formation — Tenderfoot Examination — National Flag — Scout Oath — Oral Test — Knot-Tying — Address — Good Turn Reports — Lassoing and Knot-Tying Contest — Knot-Tying — Lassoing — Decision of Judges — Announcements — Adjournment.

*This is an important meeting and should be well prepared.
All arrangements should be completed, and all needed materials should be collected and put in their proper places.
By previous announcement at earlier meetings you have informed the boys that the Tenderfoot examination will be
held at this time. You have also arranged at a previous indoor meeting that this will be the date for the lasso and the
knot-tying contest. You have instructed the boys to prepare for their " Daily Good Turn" reports. And you have
requested them to turn in written lists of their outdoor observations of animal and plant life. Have all these events
as planned.*

*This examination is to be conducted by an Examination
Board known as the Court of Honor. The men who
compose this Board are members of the Local Council, and
are appointed as members of the Court of Honor by the
Local Council. It will therefore be your duty to personally
see that these men are present and that they are instructed as to the amount of work thus far accomplished,
the extent of the examination, what sort of questions to
ask, etc. In communities where the Local Council has not
yet been formed, it will be necessary for you to invite two
or three of the representative citizens of your locality or
a visiting Scout Master to serve as an Examination Board
for the occasion; and it will then be necessary for you to
also instruct these gentlemen in the right way. It would
be a good idea to ask one of the members of the Court of
Honor to deliver a brief talk during the course of the even-*

ing; if this is done, see that he has the right sort of information at hand.

1. Open the meeting with a few well-chosen words of commendation in regard to the boys and their desire to become active Scouts, and for the work so far accomplished. But make your introductory talk pointed and brief.

2. Immediately after the talk, collect the observation lists for future use.

3. Call for drill formation, display the National Flag, and have the Troop give the Scout Salute and the Scout Sign. End with one or two good yells. *The concerted action of the drill and the yells will serve in a great measure to dispel the natural shyness occasioned by the presence of the visiting Board, and will, in a way, lessen the tension of the coming test.*

4. Hold the examination for Tenderfoot Scout.

    a. Have a written test on the National Flag. Ask questions that will require definite answers. Have plenty of writing material handy (pencil and paper) and see that table room is supplied or else have writing-boards. The following questions are suggested: — Where was the first flag made? Who made it? Who planned the design? What is the date of the first flag? Why are there thirteen stripes? What did the stars represent? What do the red and white stripes signify? What was the number of stars? Why? What are the customary forms of respect due to the flag? *etc. It would be a good plan to have posted a week beforehand and in a place where all the boys might see it, a complete list of a hundred or more questions that might be asked on the different parts of the Tenderfoot test. This will give the boy some kind of idea what to expect in the examination, and will insure more thorough preparation.*

    b. Have each boy write down the Scout Oath from memory.

    c. Conduct an oral test. Pick out boys at random to give answers to your questions. Following is a list of suggested questions: — How is the Scout Sign made? What does it mean? Why is the Flag saluted? How is the Scout Salute made? When is it used? What do the colors in the Flag signify? Give the abbreviated Scout Law. What does the Scout Badge represent? What does it signify? What part of it is worn by the Tenderfoot Scout? Repeat the Scout Oath from memory. Ask for volunteers, each to give one complete division of the Scout Law.

    d. Have the Court of Honor conduct an oral examination, picking the boys at random. Let this be the real test of the boy's knowledge.

    e. Have each boy tie his required four knots according to the Tenderfoot requirements.

5. Have the brief talk of the member of the Court of Honor at this time, if arranged for previously as suggested.

6. Call for the "Daily Good Turn" Reports. *The boys will probably be timid or nervous in giving their reports; encourage them and aid them wherever such help is needed. Use tact and good judgment and try to avoid embarrassing the boy. If you think some are badly frightened or if the hour is late, suggest that some of the boys write out their reports, or hold them until the next meeting. Such reports should only be encouraged for the first few weeks until the boy gets the idea. After that reports should only be voluntarily given.*

7. With the Court of Honor as judges, begin the lassoing and knot-tying contest. Instruct the judges as to the different events, and as to the different points to be considered in their decision. Give each boy an equal chance to try out, and encourage each to do his best. *Small ribbon favors might be previously provided for and given to the winners of the three first places in each contest — blue for the winners, red for second place, and white for*

third place. *If it is decided to have such favors,
extra ones should be provided in case there should
be ties for the different places.*

    a. In the knot-tying contest, the following
points of judgment are suggested: —
speed, precision, general knowledge of
knots, best time for tying four selected
knots, and best and neatest whipped rope-
end.

    b. In the lassoing contest, the following points
of judgment are suggested: — ease of
handling rope, precision of cast, and the
best three trials out of five.

    c. Have the judges give their decision as to
the winners, and if favors are given, they
should be given out by the judges as the
decisions are announced.

8. Set the time for the next regular indoor meeting, and
also set the date for the next outdoor meeting.
Announce that at the next regular meeting those
who have passed in the examinations will be sworn
in as Tenderfoot Scouts.

9. Adjourn the meeting by singing " America " (page
357, B. H.), and end with the Scout Yells.

[1] *Note.*— Begin preparation for the next indoor meeting early.
Read paragraphs 2 and 3 of the introduction to Program VII

[2] *Note.*— It might be well to suggest to the boys at this time that
each should get his Boy Scout uniform at his earliest convenience.

PROGRAM VI

Nature Observation — Practical Scouting

**Nature Observation — Cloud Study — Games — Drill Practice
— Fire-Fighting — Patrol-Naming Committee — Observation Reports — Scout Yarn — Land-Marks — Game — Compass Instruction — Assignments.**

*This meeting should be one for practical Scouting and
should be held out in the open country or in the woods.
Be prepared with a good Scout Yarn or a first-class book
to read from.   An excellent list of such books is given in
the Boys' Handbook, pages 387–391.   Obtain or prepare a
brief extract of the Game and Trespass Laws of your section of the country, and take it with you for use at the rest-
ing place.*

1. Get into the country or woods as quickly as possible. On this walk call attention to every bird and un-domesticated animal seen en route, and if the name of the bird or animal is unknown make note of it and have certain boys find out by next meeting.

2. If there are clouds in the sky, call attention to them while en route to the woods, tell what kind they are, and give a brief outline of the different kinds of clouds and what they signify.

3. Have the boys play " Follow the Leader " or " Far and Near " (page 315, B. H.) until a suitable spot has been reached which will serve as the camp. If the latter game is played, the following details are suggested as scoring points:

Each bird seen	1 point
Each domestic animal seen	1 point
Each wild animal seen	2 points
Each snail found	2 points
Each animal track	4 points
Each bird track	5 points
Each different kind of tree-leaf	3 points
Each different kind of flower	2 points
Each different kind of moss	3 points
Each small rock of different composition	2 points
Each small article of man's manufacture, such as buttons, matches, etc.	4 points

4. If the nature of the ground will permit, practice drill formation and Scout Salute. Also have a practice of the first seven or eight of the setting-up exercises.

5. Draw lots, if there are not enough hatchets for each boy, and practice building and lighting a fire, using only two matches. Let the boys do it without advice.

6. Appoint three boys to serve on a committee to select two or three suitable names for the patrols, reports to be called for at a later meeting.

7. Report decision of best written observation list as planned in Program IV.

8. Make use of your story or Scout Yarn. Don't make it too long.

9. Show the boys how to make use of landmarks by noting any particular hill, big tree, forest, or permanent landmarks by which location and direction can be determined and remembered.

10. Play the game of " Stalking and Reporting." (Page 307, B. H.).

11. Have with you a small compass. Show the sixteen principal points, and explain briefly the use of the compass in the field. Refer the boys to the diagram on page 52 of the Boys' Handbook for future study and reference. Explain briefly the difference between the true north and the magnetic north.

12. Send the boys home, two or three in a group, each group to start at a different time and by a different route. Have it well understood that each group is to report at the next meeting what they observed and what they did while en route home.

PROGRAM VII

Tenderfoot Scout Investiture

Opening — Drill — Address — Tenderfoot Examination Reports — Reading of Scout Oath — Address — Investiture — Scout Master — Administering the Oath — Investiture — Questions and Answers — Tenderfoot Badges — Drill and Flag Salute — Announcements — Adjournment.

This is another important meeting and should be well prepared for in advance. You announced at the last indoor meeting that at this meeting those who had successfully passed the examinations would be sworn in as Tenderfoot Scouts. This " Swearing in" ceremony should be invested with privacy and as much dignity as the occasion will warrant. The Boy Scouts as an organization is not in any sense a secret order, but the importance of conferring the different Scout ranks upon the boys will loom large in their minds if the knowledge of investiture is not shared with everybody. Moreover, it would appeal to the boy's inherited social tendencies to invest the ceremony with a formal dignity and use some simple form of initiation.

In preparing for this meeting, care should be taken to have all the arrangements carefully completed. The Tenderfoot badges must be ordered in plenty of time, and all materials needed be in readiness for the occasion. In or-

dering the badges the following rules are to be observed:

1. *Badges should not be ordered until after boys have actually complied with the requirements prescribed by the National Council and are entitled to receive them.*

2. *All orders for badges should be sent in by the Scout Master with a certificate from the Local Council that these requirements have been complied with. Blanks for this purpose may be secured on application to the National Headquarters. Where no Local Council has been formed, application for badges should be sent direct to Headquarters, signed by the registered Scout Master of the troop, giving his official number.*

3. *Scout Commissioners', Scout Masters' and Assistant Scout Masters' badges can be issued only to those who are registered as such at National Headquarters.*

The Tenderfoot badges are seven-eighths of an inch wide and are made either for the buttonhole or with a safety-pin clasp; when ordering state which is preferred. As it will be necessary in a very short time to elect the Patrol Leaders, these badges should also be ordered at this time; the price is five cents, the same as for the other Tenderfoot badges. (See page 13, B. H.)

It might be a good thing to invite the parents of the boys to this meeting, and if this is done, seating arrangements must be made for those who care to come. There should also be present the Court of Honor or at least one member of that body to announce the report of the Tenderfoot examinations, and lend importance to the occasion. If it is decided to have the parents present at this meeting, it would be a very good idea to have some man who is well known and looked up to by the boys to make a five-minute talk on the Scout Movement; if this is arranged for, you should see that he is well posted. The Information Bulletin issued by National Headquarters will serve the purpose. Have present some gentleman well known to the community, a lawyer or judge if possible, who will make a five-minute speech on " Law and Its Place and Value in Good Citizenship."

1. Open the meeting with the Scout Yells.
2. Call for drill formation, and salute the Flag, etc.

3. Have the address on the Scout Movement by the invited speaker, if such an event has been arranged for.

4. Have the report of the Tenderfoot examinations made. The speaker should be prepared with a list of the percentages, and should make a suitable comment.

5. You, as Scout Master, should read the Scout Oath and explain briefly what each phrase means. This repeated explanation of the Scout Oath serves two purposes: It instructs the visitors or the parents who are present as to the meaning and value of the Oath, and it is valuable because by its formal presentation at such a time, when the boy is impressed by the dignity of the occasion, the Oath as a whole and its meaning will appeal to him in a stronger light and attain an increased importance and significance.

6. Announce the address on " The Idea of Law and Its Place and Value in Good Citizenship," and introduce the speaker. The speaker should be previously instructed to read the Scout Law, at the end of his speech, and with a brief comment show how it teaches the boy to become a good citizen.

7. The investiture of the Scout to the rank of Tenderfoot should now begin. The regular ceremonial follows:

    a. The Scouts are called to stand at attention, and the Scout Master asks the following:

        (1) " Scouts, you have given careful attention to the reading of the Scout Oath and Scout Law; you have also passed the required tests and have become eligible to the full rank of Tenderfoot Scout. Is there anything about the Oath or Law that you do not understand?"
Scouts, in unison, answer: " No, sir."

        (2) " Is there any reason why you should not take the promise of the Scout Oath?"

The Scouts answer: " There is not, sir."

b.   The Scout Master then continues as follows:
"In the olden days a knight gave help and protection to other men and women whenever he had the opportunity to do so. A solemn promise upon his honor was always exacted before a man could become a knight. You are the knights of these modern times in America. The promise those men made was called an oath. It was not, however, the same kind of an oath that we make in our courts of law. It was a solemn promise that they would always be pure and honorable, loyal and true, and would help all those who needed assistance. This is the meaning of our Scout Oath, and as you are sworn in as Tenderfoot Scouts, you are to keep this in mind."

c.   The Scout Master then proceeds to administer the Scout Oath as follows:

(*Note.*— *The Scout Master should always administer the Oath and conduct the investiture ceremonial in order to strengthen his influence on the boys.*)

(1)   The Scout Master arranges the boys in a large half circle, so that they stand side by side and all face his position, which should be at least seven or eight feet from the boy immediately in front of him.

(2)   He will then say: "Place your heels together and give the Scout Salute." When this is done by the boys, he continues: "The Scout Salute, with the three fingers upright and together, reminds the Scout of the three promises of the Scout Oath. You will now repeat the Oath after me, in this manner. I

(giving full name), promise on my honor that I will do my best," etc. The Scout Master will then give the Scout Oath with sufficient pauses so that the applicants will have no difficulty in repeating the successive phrases after him. At the time of taking the Oath the applicant will stand holding up his right hand, giving the Scout Sign.

(3) When the Scout Oath has been taken, the Scout Master will say: "Scouts, I now give you the grasp of the Tenderfoot and welcome you into our ranks as members of the Boy Scouts of America. May your progress be ever onward and upward." As he says this, the Scout Master passes around to each boy in succession, giving him the handshake.

d. The investiture to Tenderfoot rank now takes place.

The Scout Master will now ask and receive answer to the following questions:

Scout Master —" What Scout rank do you seek?"

Scouts (in unison)—" The rank of Tenderfoot."

Scout Master —" Have you completed your tests before the Court of Honor?"

Scouts —" Yes, sir." When the examination reports are announced earlier in the evening, each successful applicant should be furnished with a certificate of passing. And they finish the answer to the preceding question by adding: " Here is my certificate of passing."

Scout Master receives the certificates and says:

"You have clearly earned your honor, but before granting it I must ask you a few questions."

e. The Scout Master will now ask and receive answer to the following questions from each boy separately in turn:

Scout Master —" Did you fairly win this distinction on your honor?"

Scout —" I did, sir."

Scout Master —" Have you faithfully kept, to the best of your ability, all the obligations of the Scout Oath and of the Scout Law?"

Scout —" I have."

Scout Master —" Have you kept in mind the "Daily Good Turn" and have you regularly done your duty in this respect?"

Scout —" Yes, sir."

Scout Master —" Of what does the tying of knots remind you?"

Scout —" To do a good turn to someone daily."

Scout Master —" Of what does the Scout Sign remind you?"

Scout —" Of the three promises of the Scout Oath."

Scout Master —" How can you honor your country?"

Scout —" By preparing myself to become a good citizen."

Scout Master —" What is the Scout Motto?"

Scout —" Be Prepared."

f. The Scout Master will now decorate the Scout with the Tenderfoot badge, saying: " Scout (giving name, as John L. Wilson), I take pleasure in decorating you with this badge of the Tenderfoot Scout rank and hope that it may be the beginning for you of greater honors. Be a good Scout always and never fail to do your duty."

8. After the investiture ceremony is finished, call for drill formation and salute the Flag.

9. Have the boys take their seats, and announce the time and place of the next meeting.

10. Close the meeting with a verse of " The Star-Spangled Banner."   *(Everybody Standing)*

Note.— It would probably be best to previously instruct one or two of the boys in the investiture ceremony so that they can lead the others in the answers. It also might be a good thing to practice over the whole ceremony with them.

PROGRAM VIII

Practical Scouting — Instruction

Drill — Observation Reports — Good Turn Reports — Games — Second Class Scout Requirements — Signaling Instruction — Assignments — Adjournment.

This should be a practical scouting meeting indoors, and should be largely instructive.

1. Open the meeting with drill formation and a flag salute.

2. Receive reports of Scout Observation, as arranged for in Section 10, Program VI. *Have as many of the groups report as possible, but do not spend too much time with it. Twenty minutes at the most should suffice, even if some of the groups are not heard from. These Scout Observation Reports were arranged for at the close of your last outdoor meeting, so previous to this meeting you should try to see as many of the groups as possible and advise them as to their preparation of such reports, etc.*

3. Pick out several boys at random to give a report of their " Daily Good Turn." Comment and encourage them in this suitably but briefly.

4. Now before the more serious instruction of the evening, it would be best to have a game of some kind. Cock Fighting (page 308, B. H.), and Hand Wrestling (page 303, B. H.), or Badger Pulling (page 303, B. H.), are suggested, and two of these

games might well be played at the same time by different boys.

5. Call the boys to order once more, and read over the Second-Class Requirements (page 17, B. H.). Announce the practice of the outdoor meeting, with the date thereof, refer to the 2nd, 3rd and 10th requirements, and point out in the Handbook where they are especially treated. (Respectively: Chapter VII, page 255; Chapter IV, pages 202–208; and Chapter I, page 52.) Also call especial attention and comment briefly upon the 9th requirement, and give arguments in favor thereof.

6. Demonstrate the manner in which communication is carried on in the Semaphore, Morse or Myer Codes by means of the wig-wag or flag. This should be brief and only explanatory of the principles involved. *Ten or twelve minutes should be enough time for this demonstration.*

7. Advise the boys to look over carefully the sections referred to, and especially those requirements to be put into practice at the next outdoor scouting meeting. Request that the boys learn by that time the principal points of the compass.

8. Make announcements for the next meetings, indoors and outdoors, and adjourn with a few Scout Yells.

PROGRAM IX

Practical Scouting Practice of Second-Class Requirements

Observation Contest — Requirement 4 — Trailing Practice — Games — Compass Instruction — Compass Games — Fire-Building — Lunch Preparation — Cleaning Camp — Story-Telling — Signal Practice — Scout Game — Map-Making — Announcements — Adjournment.

This is your outdoor instruction meeting arranged for at the last indoor meeting — a practical Scouting practice of the Second-Class Scout Requirements. Among the things needed to take with you in preparation for this practice are wig-wag flags, pencils and score-cards for games, a knife or hatchet for each Scout, plenty of matches, and a good compass large enough to show and give the lettering of the different points (and, if possible, degree marks as per diagram, page 52, B.H.). Plans should be made for an all-

day hike, and a previously prepared lunch taken with you, as before. The distance traversed for these few hikes should not be farther from town than an easy walk, but the practical Scouting and the noon camp should by all means be among the wilds of natural woodland or public park lands. In these Scouting expeditions always strive to get near to nature.

1.   Make a start at exactly the prearranged time, and as you pass from the city or town into the country try out the second part of Requirement 4. That is the satisfactory description of the contents of one store window out of four observed for one minute each,— strictly as observation test. Before you start with such a trial explain carefully the rules that should be observed, and by use of a pencil and score-card let the observation trials have somewhat the nature of a game. Of course the number of windows can be varied in the tests as to the needs and memory ability, starting with one out of two or three and increasing with experience and practice to one out of six or seven. *This observation and memory work is of extreme value to the boy in creating in him through practice a keenness of perception and a quickened mental activity. So from time to time as opportunity occurs in starting out on or coming in from a hike this exercise should be put into practice. Your good judgment is all that is necessary to determine how much time should be given to these tests; usually the distance from your objective point and the needs of the occasion will help you in your decision.*

2.   When the open country or woodland has been reached, practice the first part of Requirement 4. The ability to trail half a mile in twenty-five minutes should be easily accomplished by any boy not a cripple, as the average rate of walking for a man is fifteen minutes per mile. "Scout's Pace," or Requirement 5, already practiced at a previous meeting, might also be used again at this time for a short distance, so that all of the boys may understand thoroughly what it is and learn to do it properly.

3. If a previous location for the noon camp has already been agreed upon, two boys might be selected to serve as " hares " and sent out ahead with their pockets full of confetti paper or shelled corn, and everybody thus join in a game of " Follow the Trail." (See page 310, B. H.)

4. Arrived at a suitable location for the camp, it would be best to have one or two instructive games before the preparations for lunch. As the consideration of the compass is most important, and as the 10th Requirement makes necessary a knowledge of its sixteen principal points, you should proceed to give a practical field demonstration of its use. The following games are suggested as a help in the instruction, to create interest in the practical use of the compass and to engender in the boy a desire for a more thorough knowledge of determining proper directions.

a. " Boxing the Compass "

Take a suitable point as a center and from it take bearings for the principal sixteen points of the compass about eleven paces each from the center point. Since the radius of your circle will then be thirty-three feet, your points will be approximately about twelve feet apart. Instruct the boys how to take bearings and establish the points. By demonstration establish the main points North and South yourself. Have the boys, by group, locate the other points around the circle according to instruction and advice, and then check up to see that the distances are nearly approximate. Mark each point thus established with a stake or something similar and attach thereto a properly labeled card. *These cards should be prepared in advance — heavily inked letters, readable at some distance, on square pieces of cardboard from five to seven inches on side, and each should by its lettering represent one of the compass points, as N., NNE., NE., ENE., E., etc.*

When the points have all been properly marked, have the boys select four of their number to choose up sides, and when this in turn has been done, each side will in its proper turn start at the North point and " Box the Compass " in the proper way with the use of these sixteen points three successive times around the circle. This is done in the following way:

Suppose one side to be lined up at the North point, then the leader will take his position at this point and call out loudly, North, then the second boy will run on to the next point along the outer border of the circle, and call out in the same way North Northeast, and the next boy will do the same with the next point and call out Northeast. There will be a certain time limit established in getting around the circle — a matter for you to determine each time the game is played, because of the changing conditions. If there should be six boys on each side, each boy would therefore occupy eight points during the three times around, and so should obtain a very good idea of the correct sequence of points. Every mistake made in calling out will count as a forfeit and every minute over the required time will count as three forfeits. When each side has had three trials around the compass with marked points, all the card-markers are taken away except the one at the North point, and each side has three more times around in the same manner as before. That side having the least number of forfeits at the close of the game will be declared winners. The rules to observe follow:

(1) Each side will start at the North point.

(2) The run from point will be on the outer edge of the circle and never across the circle.

(3) Each point shall be called out loudly and distinctiy.

(4) The Scout Master or referee shall stand at the center point, and be

careful to score each slight mistake with full count.

When the boys have become fairly proficient in the knowledge and relative position of these points, the game can be made more complex by the use of all the points of the compass — thirty-two in number. They will then be approximately six feet apart. And the game will, of course, be played in the same manner as in the simpler form.

b. Compass Points

This game should be played only after the boys have become more or less familiar with the relative positions of all of the principal points of the compass.

This game is similar to the other compass game and requires the same general preparation in taking bearings, locating points, and establishing a ground plan of a compass. Suppose the points are all properly located and marked with the prepared cards, the game is then ready to begin. Have two boys choose up sides, and have the group that is to begin the game stand ten or twelve feet away from the North point, and outside the circle with their backs thereto. Assign to each boy in the group some one compass point to locate, when the signal is given. At the given signal the boys make a rush for their respective positions, and all those who do not get to their correct places in a certain limit of time forfeit one point. *Of course, the boys might start from the center point of the circle instead of the North point, and if such is the case, they will stand facing the Scout Master or referee at the center point while the location points are being assigned. Since only one side contests at a time, the other side will help the referee in watching out for mistakes. It will be by far the best to have previously prepared cards representing by lettering each a compass point, and after shuffling at the*

*beginning of the game these cards should be
dealt out and pinned on the boys' coats or
shirts at each new assignment of location
points; the letters, of course, should be large
enough to be readable at some distance.*

The time limit for reaching points should
be determined in each case according to the
conditions and distance, etc. The sides will
alternate in trials with different location points
assigned to each boy each time (cards dealt
out, if cards are used) ; there should be two
trials, each with unmarked points. The side
making the least number of forfeitures during
the set number of trials will be declared winners. This game can also be varied by making use of all thirty-two points of the compass,
when the boys are ready for it. The game
will be played the same in each case. The
rules to observe follow in outline:

(1) During assignments the boys will
     stand with their backs to the
     points; any boy caught looking to
     see where he is to go, before the
     signal is given, will forfeit three
     points.

(2) Each mistake made will count for
     two forfeits.

(3) Each contestant will forfeit one
     point if he does not get to his
     place within the limit time.

(4) Each boy caught directing another
     of his own side to the proper
     position will forfeit three points.

5. Demonstrate the correct use of knife or hatchet, and
    the correct way to build and light a fire, giving
    definite explanations as to the best manner of pre-
    paring material, laying wood in place, holding
    match, etc. *Failure to meet the Second-Class test
    is often due to the fact that not enough wood is
    prepared at the start. Success in the fire-lighting
    contest is often due to proper regard of this im-
    portant point. It will be best to read over the ar-
    ticle on page 158, B. H., on the building of a camp-*

fire, as that article contains several helpful suggestions.

6. Have the boys practice building and lighting a fire, using only two matches. Let the boys do it without advice — singly or in groups of two.

7. Prepare for lunch and camp-fire as in the previous outdoor meeting, and be sure to give each boy some definite thing to do in the preparation.

8. At the end of the lunch, clean up the camp, put out the fires in the proper way, etc. And then, if the boys would like it and the time will warrant, tell or read a good camp story.

9. Divide the boys into groups of four each, send them out at proper distances from one another and from your station at the center, and begin the practice of the practical application of the Morse or some other signal code. Each group station should be within sight of your station, where there will also be located one of the groups, and communications by questions and answers carried on from this central location. Each group should have a copy of the Boys' Handbook and a wig-wag flag, and each boy in each group should alternate in the sending and receiving of messages. *The Morse Code and instruction in its use should previously be looked over and explained before the groups are sent out, but the best method of getting instruction will, of course, be in actual practice. For the Code and instructions, see page 202 and top of page 204, B. H. It might also be well to practice at this time the whistle signs and commands as given on page 208, B. H.*

10. If the boys tire of this practice, and there is still time before leaving for home, a game of " Hat-Ball " would be popular and be appreciated. (See page 303, B. H.)

11. Ask each boy to prepare a plat of his locality, with his home as a center, to be turned in at the next indoor meeting. If in the city, to locate on such plat all fire-alarm boxes, hydrants, fire-stations, police-stations, telegraph offices, etc., with the correct direction from the central point or home to be indicated in each case. If in a town

or village, to locate fire-hydrants, telegraph and telephone offices, town hall, churches, and other places of public importance, in the same way.

12. Announce time and plans for next indoor and outdoor meetings, and set out for home. It might be well to have a game of "Far and Near" or some similar game of observation on the way home. (See page 315, B. H.)

PROGRAM X

Health and Care of the Body

Collection of Maps — Address — First Aid Instruction — First Aid Demonstration — Memory Test — Physical Examination — Adjournment.

You should prepare for this meeting by having present a physician, surgeon, or competent nurse who will consent to deliver a short address on the Care of the Body, and give instruction in Elementary First Aid. Several rolls of bandages, splints, adhesive tapes, court-plaster, arm slings, etc., will likewise be necessary, and should be in readiness. If a physician has consented to be with you on this occasion, he perhaps would also be quite willing to conduct a physical examination of all the boys in the Troop; if he is interested in boys, he might consent to act as the regular examiner for the patrols or Troop. A boy should know the condition of his heart and lungs before entering any athletic contest. If he has any defects in his breathing apparatus — nose, throat, or lungs — these should be attended to or they will seriously interfere with his endurance tests and his entire physical development.

It would be a very good idea to have a physical examination of each Scout as soon after he has become a Tenderfoot Scout as possible, and to conduct a similar examination of the same Scout once every six months thereafter and as long as he remains a Boy Scout.

This meeting might be held on any week night, in order to best conform to the physician's time or convenience, but, if on a night other than Friday or Saturday, care should be taken that the boys do not neglect their preparation for the next day at school. The School Boy Scout should remember the Scout Motto — to "Be Prepared" — and should also remember the first point of the Scout Law —

to be honest and trustworthy. Therefore a real Scout cannot be negligent in the preparation of his school lessons, and should be on his honor in such a case to "Be Prepared."

1. Collect the direction plats which were to be handed in at this meeting. Announce that you will look them over and advise as to corrections at the next meeting.

2. Have the address on " Health and Care of the Body."

3. Have a talk of several minutes' duration on First Aid, and demonstrate by use of bandage, splint, slings, adhesive tape, etc. Call the attention of the scouts to the section in the Boys' Handbook on " First Aid for Injuries," pages 273–279. Have the boys practice the methods of applying aid for breaks or fractures of the leg, thigh, and arm under your surveillance and guidance.

4. Demonstrate the proper methods of carrying the injured, and have the boys practice those methods.

5. Call for volunteers to repeat the Scout Oath, the twelve points of the Scout Law, what the Scout Sign means and how it is made, to give the sixteen principal points of the compass, etc.

6. Conduct the physical examination, if it is possible to have it at this time. *In this examination the physician should test the heart and lung action. He will most likely advise you as how best to get rid of the deficiencies that may come to your notice in this way.*

7. Make announcements of the plans in view for the next two meetings, and adjourn with the Scout Yells.

Note.— One announcement that should be made at this time is that the Scouts should prepare for the nomination and election of their Patrol Leaders at a near date, and should have someone in mind who would make good leaders, by that time. And you should announce, further, that those who will be elected at that time will then be eligible to take the special tests given to Patrol Leaders of Tenderfoot Scout Rank, said tests to be secret, to be taken for the purpose of proving special ability and efficiency as a Tenderfoot Scout, and to be given by the Scout Master. And you should announce that the final organization of the

Troop will be completed at that coming meeting. By this time you, yourself, will have noted who in your Troop are the natural leaders among the boys: these fellows will make the best Patrol Leaders, if they can pass the efficiency tests, and are worthy and can be encouraged to strive toward better standards of excellence. Always let the boys choose their own Patrol Leaders by popular vote, subject only to certain attainments of proficiency as Scouts and to your best judgment; never allow likes or dislikes or favoritism to influence you in the approval of their choice. Have it understood, however, that no Tenderfoot Scout can become a Patrol Leader unless he can attain a grade of 90 per cent. in the Tenderfoot Examination Test, and that no Scout can pass the test with a grade of 85 per cent. If the elected leader is not proficient in the special test, the Assistant Patrol Leader elect will become Patrol Leader in his place if able to pass the test successfully. And, further, that if neither elected leader can pass the requirements, another election must take place for two more Scouts to make a trial, etc. It is the natural leaders that will be the best leaders, and that you will want most, if they can be encouraged to make themselves the most proficient, and become best " prepared." In each group of a dozen or more boys there are always a few who come to the front as leaders, and the others will sooner or later fall into the habit of following the dictates or advice or example of these few. These are the chaps you will need to look out for, because, if they can be influenced and guided by your good advice and personal contact with them to develop their natural ability to lead others along the right lines, you will need to look no farther for Patrol Leaders, for you have in them for such leadership in the making the best material in the country.

PROGRAM XI

A Day in the Field — Practical Scouting

" Scouting "—" Hat-Ball "— Tree-Study Contest — Signaling — Compass Games —" Stalking" and Reporting "— Lunch and Camp-Fire — Fire-Building Contest — Camp Yarn — Map Reports and Assignments — Homeward Bound — Star Study.

This meeting should be on a Saturday or half-holiday, and starting shortly after the noon hour should continue along into the evening and end with the homeward walk. If the trees are in leaf, have each boy take with him on the

hike any sort of a magazine or booklet so that it may be
used for the collection and storing of leaves for your tree-
study contest.   A prepared lunch should be taken along
— such as meat and egg sandwiches, cheese, cookies, etc.,
and each Scout should likewise have with him his staff, a
plate and a cup, matches, a candle, and a knife or hatchet,
and suitable straps to attach the little pack thus collected
to the back; before starting out you should see that the
packs are properly adjusted, and demonstrate the correct
manner of carrying any sort of a pack on the back.   It
would be best for each boy to have a haversack by this time
(see page 363, B. H.), for there will soon be need of one
for the over-night hikes, and it proves very handy as an
easy and adjustable pack.   Another handy thing, of course,
to have along on the hike is the individual mess-kit (see
page 364, B. H.)   For information in regard to the neces-
sary staff, see page 365, B. H.   Several small coffee-pots
should be taken with you, as well as enough ground coffee
or cocoa to supply the Troop (also a can of condensed cream
and a small quantity of sugar in cans).   Among other
things, you should also be supplied with wig-wag flags and
several small compasses, if the latter can be obtained for
the occasion; likewise, you should have previously looked
over and made what corrections you thought best on the
maps or direction-plats which were handed in at the last
meeting, and these should be taken along for discussion dur-
ing the afternoon.   For this afternoon hike some place
should be chosen that is already fairly well known to all
members of the Troop, and before starting out you should
make a rough sketch or map of the chosen locality, showing
directions from known landmarks, trend of streams, roads,
fence-lines, etc.   This little map will prove of great value
for use in scouting games, and serve as an excellent demon-
stration of the working value of such a sketch in practical
scouting.

1. By the aid of your previously prepared map, study
    the locality into which you are going, so that be-
    fore the actual start is made each Scout in the
    Troop will have some knowledge of the lay of the
    land, possible directions to be taken, etc.   When
    this has been done pick out some well-known place
    on the map that will serve as a rendezvous, and
    play the the game of "Scouting" (page 298, B.

H.) by sending the Scouts out in groups of two or three and at different intervals in different directions, each group to arrive at the rendezvous within a certain limit of time, to report all animals or birds noticed on line of route taken, to report fully in the best manner what they saw and did, etc. *You will need to judge in each case, according to existent conditions, the method of point-scoring to be used, for what things to allow points, etc., and it will of course be imperative for you to get to the rendezvous as soon as possible after the groups are all sent out, so it will be best to give roundabout routes to the boys and keep the shortest and most direct route for yourself.*

2. As it will probably take some little time for all of the groups to arrive and report, as soon as two or three groups arrive and finish reporting it will be best to start a game of " Hat-Ball " to keep those occupied who have finished. However, before the boys start playing the game they should be instructed to dispose of their packs and staff, and lay the same aside in a neat and orderly manner. The game should be continued, taking in the later comers as they arrive, until all the groups have reached the rendezvous and properly reported.

3. Propose a tree-study contest and outline its principles and procedure. Such a game or contest ought to prove interesting to the boys and certainly would be highly instructive in observation and nature-study. Announce that the contest will be continued for the next four or five ensuing meetings, and set a definite date at which the results of the contest will be decided. *The suggestions as to plan and principles of the contest follow: Have the boys collect leaves from as many different trees and bushes as they can find. The leaves, while in the field, can be kept between pages of a magazine taken along for that purpose, but are to be posted each on a separate page of a note-book when the Scout again reaches home. Beneath each leaf in your note-book are to be recorded the date of collection, the name of the tree — genus and species — the period of leafing (when leaves*

of that kind of tree first appear and when they disappear) and all other information about the leaf and the tree from which it comes, that the boy can obtain. The best note-book for general use would probably be one about eight inches by twelve; in this the leaf should be laid flat and firmly pasted in about the center of a page. On the opposite page to each leaf should appear its record, all the information in regard to the genus or species that the boy can obtain. The Scout who collects and records the largest number of different kinds of leaves, who gathers the best information for the record, and who makes up the neatest looking book will be declared the winner of the contest. Encourage the boys to come to you between meetings, if they need further information in regard to planning the book and affixing the leaves. In such cases merely paste in one or two leaves and point out the place for the record; let them do the rest, as it is their own work and experience in this that will help them most.

4. Have a practice of the signal code by means of the wig-wag, as suggested in Program IX.

5. Play one of the Compass Games with all thirty-two points of the compass in use. *Let the boys lay out the ground circle and locate the points themselves, with the aid of the small compasses. Do not give them advice unless it is absolutely necessary. In order to ascertain what information the boys have gained as to direction, it would be a good thing to pick several out at random, and placing a small compass in their hands, ask them to explain its use.*

6. If there is still time before dark, it would be excellent scouting practice to have such a game as "Stalking and Reporting." (Page 307, B. H.)

7. As evening shadows begin to fall begin preparation for the lunch and camp-fire. As there will be need of several smaller fires for boiling coffee, as well as the larger camp-fire, there will be plenty to do in looking for wood and preparing it for use. Give each Scout some definite thing to do that will keep him busy. Have a fire-building contest by

groups of three boys each, best fire and speed to be counted. The winning group should be given the privilege of building the larger camp-fire; while the best of the others can be used for boiling the coffee, etc. As there will probably be need of six such small fires for this purpose, it would be best to assign four Scouts each to a fire. Give each group a coffee-pot and the proper amount of coffee, and explain to them how to "make" it; let them do the actual preparation in each case.

8. After the lunch has been eaten, tell one or two good camp stories. Call for volunteers to relate camp experiences or stories. Call for a number of "Daily Good Turn" reports.

9. By the light of the fire, spend a few minutes in a consideration of the direction-maps previously referred to, point out corrections made, and criticise and praise where such criticism or praise is due. Assign different centers in the locality to each Scout, and ask for a similar plat to be drawn and filled in as before.

10. Set out on the homeward walk, and as you go it might be well to relate a scout yarn or have such a game as "Follow the Leader," etc. If the stars are coming out and can be seen, tell the boys about the planets and real stars and their differences, and point out as many constellations as you can find. Briefly outline the Nebular Hypothesis, and see how many of the planets you can locate.

PROGRAM XII
Signal Practice

Signal Practice Stations — Station Duties — Semaphore — Signals — Signal Code Practice — Assembly — Adjournment.

This should be another half-day in the field, if at all possible. If, however, weather conditions will not permit, upper windows of several houses about town will do almost as well, provided the houses are so located that signaling can be easily carried on between them. As this is to be mainly a signal practice, a sufficiency of wig-wag flags and other signal apparatus should be on hand. If the practice is to be in the open, there will be no need of taking lunch or spending more than a couple or three hours in practice.

1. If in the woods, get out into the country as quickly as
    possible, and divide the Troop into several groups
    as on previous signal practice, and station these

SIGNAL CODE PRACTICE

groups some distance apart, so that at the most one
group can be within sight and communication of
only one other group; if in town divide the Troop
into groups of four or five, and station them at

upper windows of houses, previously arranged for, so that communication can easily be carried on between the houses by signaling.

2. Each boy in each group should have some definite thing to do, and should rotate in their duties in a certain fixed and prearranged order. One should handle the wig-wag flags, another should act as the bearer of messages or assignments from group to group, another should serve as the receiver of messages, with Boys' Handbook, note-book and pencil, and another should serve as a reserve, helping to receive messages or to carry out instructions. The Scout Master should have his headquarters at the central station, but should, at least, visit each station in turn, to inspect and to give instructions.

3. If in the open there should be from 30 to 50 minutes given to signal practice of the Semaphore code, with the use of short commands given out by the Scout Master, and sent on from station to station.

4. As many of the signals as can be conveniently used should be put into practice in arranging stations, giving commands, etc., as given on pp. 208–209 under Whistle and Hand signals.

5. The remainder of the time should be taken up with Signal Code practice with the wig-wag flags. To aid in this practice, and to keep each boy busily employed, orders should be turned in at one station by the Scout Master to send a certain message by roundabout route to another station, out of sight of the sending station, and have the messenger of the receiving station bring in the message in written form to the sending station or headquarters. Also certain duties should be assigned as to reporting descriptions of the surroundings of each station, locating by compass the different points of interest with each station as a center, making a rough sketch of immediate surroundings and location of stations, etc. There should be innumerable methods and means of keeping the interest of the boys aroused, by suggestions that are bound to arise, according to the locality, the time, and the place.

6. The boys should all be called together in one place before leaving for home, and instructed as to the plans for the next outdoor and indoor meetings, and for the collection of station sketches, and for the giving out of new assignments, etc.

7. Adjourn the meeting with the Scout Yells. Send the Scouts out two by two, at different intervals, to their homes, each group to report at the next meeting what was noticed en route, all animals, birds, men and women, principal public buildings, and things of especial note.

PROGRAM XIII

Troop and Patrol Organization

Talk on Organization — Organization — Troop and Patrol — Patrol Names and Calls — Appointment of Constitutional Committee — Election of Patrol Leaders and Assistant Patrol Leaders — Address on Efficiency — Tug-of-War Contest — Refreshments — Troop Formation and Salutes — Adjournment.

This is another important meeting and should be well arranged for and carefully planned in advance. The following general suggestions may help out considerably, but you as Scout Master should be on the lookout for something interesting to add to the list of events of the evening, something of appealing interest to the boys, and something that will, of its own nature, lead to a greater efficiency of organization. It is suggested that the evening program be divided into parts, the first part to consist of entertainment and exercises. A speaker should be secured beforehand who will consent to give a short address on "Efficiency in Organization." It will make a very pleasant evening, and be doubly enjoyable to the boys, as an aftermath of the business program, to arrange for the serving of light refreshments during the latter part of the evening.

By this time you will have observed which ones of your boys are the leaders among the others, and are best fitted by ability and efficiency to become Patrol Leaders. You have made previous announcements to the boys to think over the situation and have in mind the best suitable candidate among them on patrol names, and they should be ready to give their final report at this meeting. Where it is thought best to have a constitution and by-laws for the troop organization you, as Scout Master, should be ready with the draft of a suggested simple form. The use of such constitution and by-laws will serve to promote the ideas and duties of citizenship and should prove of valuable service. Arrange for the speaker to come later in the evening, arranging therefor a definite time. And have the business meeting called (at the prearranged time) as early as possible.

Read italicized note of section 7.

1. Call the meeting to order, and in a few brief words state the need for a very definite organization, the election of Patrol Leaders and Assistants, patrol names and calls, constitution and by-laws, a regular order of business, etc.

2. *It is presupposed in this program that there is now the full number of Scouts in your troop, and therefore there will be three patrols, composed of eight Scouts each.* As each patrol in the troop has its own name and call, together with its own officers, you will now call attention to the difference between troop organization and patrol organization, showing how the same rules and regulations that govern the larger body necessarily apply to the different patrols, wherein the duties of the Patrol Leaders coincide and how the strength of the entire troop organization is built up and made compact by the well-organized and efficiently conducted patrols.

3. Call for a report of the Committee on Names, and when this has been given allow five or six minutes for the free discussion of the names by the different patrols, and then call for the adoption of a name for each patrol in order by majority vote.

4. If it is decided to consider the adoption of a constitution and by-laws, let it be understood that such conditions shall apply to the entire troop organization, and that the rules and regulations so adopted shall apply equally to members of both troop and the different patrols. It is suggestively urged that some simple form of constitution be considered, and if this is done, the Scout Master will appoint two or three members of each patrol to confer with him as to the suggested draft

already prepared, and to any new measures that may be considered. Arrange for the report of this meeting at the next indoor meeting, and the adoption of the constitution and by-laws at that time.

5. Conduct the nomination and election of Patrol Leaders and Assistants.

    a. Explain just what is meant by using parliamentary language, and call for nominations. Each patrol to turn in its own nominations.

    b. Give plenty of chance for free discussion. Explain how a Patrol Leader or Assistant must be an example to his own patrol and to the other patrols in the troop as well.

    c. Conduct the election by ballot, with one teller for each patrol. As Scout Master, you will be judge of elections and will instruct the Scouts as to proper method of voting by ballot system. You will also appoint one of the Scouts of the troop as clerk of the elections and instruct him in his duties. *In cases where there is only one patrol, two tellers will still be necessary.*

    d. When the votes have been counted the Scout Master will say: "As Judge of Elections I call upon Scout ——, who is Clerk of Elections, to give the report of the Tellers."

       And the Clerk of Elections replies: "For Patrol Leader of (Buffalo) Patrol the tally stands:

       Scout ————— —————votes
       Scout ————— —————votes

Scout —— is therefore declared by will of the members of ————— Patrol their Patrol Leader.

       For Assistant Patrol Leader of —— Patrol the tally is:

       Scout ————— —————votes
       Scout ————— —————votes

Scout —— is therefore declared by will

of the members of the —— Patrol their Assistant Patrol Leader.

For Patrol Leader of —— Patrol the tally is:

Scout ————————— ————————votes
Scout ——————— ————————votes

Scout —— is therefore duly elected Patrol Leader of —— Patrol." *And the same procedure applies for the other officers of the other patrols.*

e. When the report of the tellers has been completed, the Scout Master will then say: " Scouts of Troop ——, of the —— and —— and —— Patrols, these are your elected leaders, who are now ready to undergo the efficiency tests. If they successfully pass these tests and so show their ability to become leaders of patrols, they will be installed at the next regular indoor meeting, and become your first leaders and representative Scouts. Scouts, as men congratulate their officers upon their election, you now have the opportunity to congratulate the officers of your choice."

6. Recall the meeting to order and proceed with the second part of your program. With a few appropriate remarks introduce the speaker on " Efficiency in Organization."

7. It would be best now to enliven things with some sort of physical exercise such as a Tug-of-War contest. Select two of these recently elected Patrol Leaders to choose sides, and see that the size and strength of the troop are as evenly divided as possible. *There should be a good, strong, heavy rope provided in advance for this contest — preferably a soft cotton rope of some thickness.*

8. If refreshments have been previously prepared, have them served at this time. *Ice cream and cake should be very suitable for this occasion.*

9. Call for Troop Formation, with the newly elected Patrol Leaders in position, and have the Scout and Flag salutes given. Make announcements for the

next indoor and outdoor meetings. State at this time that the next indoor meeting will be very important because of the Patrol Leader Efficiency Tests, the Patrol Leader Installation, and the adoption of the constitution.

10. Adjourn with a practice of the Patrol Calls and the Scout Yells.

PROGRAM XIV

Patrol Scouting

Observation Reports —" Stalking and Reporting "— Fire Building — Compass Games — Scout Games — Scouting — Patrol Practice — Announcements — Adjournment.

This should be another afternoon for practical scouting out in the open country. Inasmuch as the Patrol Formation has been more perfected by the recent election, this will be a good chance for the new officers to become used to their positions and duties. At the last indoor meeting the boys were sent home in groups of two, and were told to report at the next practical Scout meeting: one of each group should now be prepared to give that report. Before starting see that each Scout is properly provided with a knife or hatchet.

1. Get out into the open country as quickly as possible, and as you go receive reports of observation, as assigned at the last outdoor meeting.

2. When a suitable spot has been reached, play some game of practical scouting, such as " Stalking and Reporting." (Page 307, B. H.)

3. Have a fire-building contest. (Page 315, B. H.)

4. Play " Box the Compass " with thirty-two points.

5. Play " Stalking " and " Scout Hunting." (Pages 307 and 308, B. H.)

6. Pick out certain landmarks about a half mile or a mile apart, and send a patrol to each, with instructions to make a sketch of their position and correct directions of all principal objects from their station. *Each patrol should have, of course, one or two small field-compasses to work with.* Having completed their sketches, each patrol is to work toward a certain definite point about equally distant from all. Here you will station yourself, and the patrols will try to reach you unseen. The first

Scout of any patrol with a copy of the sketch of
his assigned position, who reaches a spot within
ten feet of you unseen, will be declared winner of
the stalking contest, and his patrol be declared
the winning patrol.

7. Make announcements for the next indoor meetings.
8. With Patrol Leaders as leaders play " Follow the
Leader " (page 315, B. H.) on the way home.

PROGRAM XV

The Constitutional Convention

**Order of Business — Report of Constitutional Committee —
General Discussion — Adoption of Constitution and By-Laws —
Scout Games — First Aid Instruction — Installation of Patrol
Leaders — Announcements — Adjournment.**

*This meeting has been largely arranged for by the sugges-
tions of previous programs but there are a few things
that will need special attention and preparation before the
meeting. As suggested in Program XIII, you have appointed a Constitutional Committee to prepare a draft of a
constitution and by-laws to be submitted at this meeting;
by this time you will have conferred with and carefully advised the committee at some special meeting with them, and
you will also have ascertained what further business might
be necessary or wanted other than that already suggested
in your own submitted constitutional form. For those to
whom it might be helpful, a model constitutional form for
Boy Scouts is given in Chapter VI.*

*Besides the discussion of the constitutional measures and
their subsequent adoption, there is also to be the installation
ceremonies of those Patrol Leaders and Assistant Patrol
Leaders who have been successful in passing the efficiency
tests. The boys should understand that the positions are
both elective and competitive; this knowledge of the aspirants
for the different offices that there are to be competitive tests
ahead of them will serve to eliminate the fellows who are
natural shirkers, to deter those from seeking or accepting
the positions who are not efficient to serve as Patrol Leaders, and who, having attained their positions by popularity,
might later not live up to the responsibilities of their positions. You should have no trouble of this sort, however,
if your judgment in the picking out of the right boys has
been correct.*

These efficiency tests should be held in secret, with only those present who are actually concerned in the outcome — the six elected leaders (or less) and the Scout Master or Assistant Scout Master. For this purpose a special meeting should be called either at the Scout Headquarters or at your home or office a day or so previous to the night of this general meeting (Program XV). It should be previously understood that the special tests are to consist of a special Tenderfoot Scout Requirement examination together with a general test in the efficiency of the most practiced Second-Class Scout Requirements, to show that the candidate for office is up to date in all his knowledge. Further, that Patrol Leaders must pass the Tenderfoot Scout Requirement test with a grade of 90 per cent. to be eligible for office, and the Assistant Patrol Leaders must have a grade of 85 per cent.; in the general test for Second-Class Scout Requirements the former should pass with a grade of 60 per cent. and the latter with a grade of 50 per cent. If the elected Patrol Leaders fail to pass, the elected Assistant Patrol Leaders, if making the correct grade, will then become the Patrol Leaders. And new elections must be held at a near date to fill all offices not filled by the outcome of the first trial.

1. Call the meeting to order with a few brief remarks as to the order of business, the importance of the adoption of such a constitution, and the methods to be employed in its adoption.

2. Call for the report of the Constitutional Committee, and the reading of the proposed constitution and by-laws.

3. Call for a free discussion of what has been suggested by the committee, urging everyone in the troop to express his views of the measures.

4. Proceed with the adoption of the constitution and by-laws by majority vote. *Be careful in this; and be sure that the will of the majority will not hurt a single Scout, at least in money matters.*

5. Devote fifteen or twenty minutes to playing any game the Scouts may choose, such game to be suitable for indoors, and suggestive of Scout Practice.

6. Explain briefly what is meant by fainting and by shock, and demonstrate the treatment therefor. (See pages 261 and 270, Boys' Handbook.) Ex-

plain what is meant by sunstroke and exhaustion, freezing and frost-bite, poisoning, and fits, and outline general treatment of each. Call attention to the discussion of the same in the Boys' Handbook, pages 271 and 272.

7. Conduct the installation ceremonies of the Patrol Leaders and Assistant Patrol Leaders who have successfully passed the efficiency tests.

The Scout Master will say:

" The Scouts who have been duly elected leaders of their patrols by popular vote, and who have proved their efficiency as Tenderfoot Scouts and their ability to serve as leaders by special test, will please present themselves before me.

" Scouts of Troop (9) of the State of (*Virginia*), you have balloted for and elected these Scouts to be your officers for a period of —— months. You have used the method that men use to elect their officers and are thus in keeping with the laws of your country. They have been duly elected, and have successfully passed the special tests proving their ability and proficiency. Does anyone know any reason why these Scouts should not be acknowledged as your officers?"

If there is any objection, it should be settled rightly and at once.

" Then in accordance with the power the Boy Scouts of America have conferred upon me, I will now proceed to formally present these Scouts with their respective offices.

" Scout Leaders, you have been faithfully elected by your fellows, and qualified by your own efforts and ability — you, Scout (*Brown*), as Patrol Leader of the (*Buffalo*) Patrol; you, Scout (*White*), as Assistant Patrol Leader of the (*Buffalo*) Patrol; you, Scout (*Menser*) as Patrol Leader of the (*Bear*) Patrol; you, Scout (*Lee*) as Assistant Patrol Leader of the (*Bear*) Patrol; you, Scout (*Eubanks*), as Patrol Leader of the (*Owl*) Patrol; and you, Scout (*Wilson*), as Assistant Patrol Leader of the (*Owl*) Patrol. This means that your fellow Scouts give you the responsibility of looking after the interests of your

patrols. As leaders, you will be looked upon as
our representative Scouts, and you must therefore
guard the honor of your patrols with great care.
In the field and on the march, while out scouting,
your business is to see that the members of your
patrol do their duty by the Scout Oath and Scout
Law, by themselves, and by each other. You are
also to be watchful of yourself not to be bullying,
or to think yourself a better Scout because of your
office. You are leaders in order to serve your
patrol and fellow Scouts. Do you understand
these instructions?"

Answer: "We do."

Scout Master: "Do you promise also to keep the
Scout Oath and the Scout Law, which you have
already sworn to, and to do all you can do to up-
hold the principles of the Boy Scout organization
and continue a representative Scout, good and
true?"

Answer: "We do."

Scout Master: "Repeat after me the following, one
at a time: I —— Scout (*Menser*) ———— accept the responsibility ———— that my fellow
Scouts ———— have put upon me ———— and
will to the best ———— of my ability ————
perform the duties ———— of Patrol Leader (or
Assistant Patrol Leader) of the (*Bear*) Patrol."
*The Scout Master will repeat slowly with pauses
at the dashes, and repeats the same ceremony with
each candidate.*

Scout Master: "I, therefore, in acknowledgment of
your promise and election, give you the Scout Grip
and declare you Patrol Leader (or Assistant Patrol Leader) of the (*Bear*) Patrol. I take great
pleasure in decorating you with your badge of
leadership."

*This foregoing ceremony is to be repeated for each
Patrol Leader and Assistant Patrol Leader, making the appropriate changes for each Scout and
Scout-office. The Scout Grip consists of a handshake with the right hand, with the fingers in the
same position as in making the Scout Sign. One
Scout shakes hands with another by a good warm*

*handclasp, with the three middle fingers extended
in a straight line along the other's wrist, and with
the thumb and little finger clasped around the other's fingers.*

*Suitable bars of white braid should have been previ-
ously prepared by the Scout Master, with temporary fastenings. (See pages 44--45. Boys' Handbook.) The Patrol Leader's arm badge consists
of two bars, 1½ inches long and ⅜ of an inch in
width, of white braid worn on the sleeve below the
left shoulder. In addition he may wear an oxidized silver Tenderfoot badge. The Assistant
Patrol Leader wears one bar of white braid in the
same fashion.*

Scout Master: " Scouts of Troop (9), of the
(*Bear*), and (*Buffalo*), and (*Owl*) Patrols, these
are your leaders. You have asked them to be so.
You now have the opportunity of congratulating
them as men do their elected officers."

8. Make announcements for the next indoor and outdoor meetings.

9. Adjourn with the Scout Yells, and a Patrol Call Practice.

PROGRAM XVI

Trailing

**Tracks and Trailing — Special Talk on Tracking — Track Ob-
servation — Special Talk on Colors — Color Test — Scout Games
— Announcements — Adjournment.**

*This should be preferably an indoor evening's instruction
and entertainment. Have present some trapper or naturalist
who will talk to the boys on " Tracking and Trails." Have
present as much material or books on tracks and tracking as
you can secure for the occasion. Be ready to refer to a
number of good authorities on the subject. In connection
with the color test have banners or cards of red, green, and
black on white, the latter arranged in the form of a large
black circle on white background. If possible have present
some good optician who will talk on the eye and the carrying power of various colors.*

1. Refer to Chapter IV of the Boys' Handbook, and ask
the boys to read the information given therein in
regard to tracks and trails. Point out the salient
points in the discussion of the subject by Mr. Er-

nest Thompson Seton in Chapter IV, just referred
to.   Show other books or information on the subject, also pictures of animal and bird trails, besides
those given on pages 198, 200, and 201 of the
Boys' Handbook.   Give a list of books on the
subject, suitable for reading or study, and indicate
where they can be obtained.

2.   Have the talk on "Tracking and Trails," by the trapper or the naturalist, and, providing the boys seem

FIELD STUDY OF TRACKS

interested in the talk, urge the speaker to tell some
tale of the forest or wild-animal life that has to
do with the subject under discussion.   If the
speaker does not object, let the boys ask questions
on the subject.

3.   Assign track-observation work to each boy, said work
to consist of picturing as neatly and as accurately
as possible the tracks of three known animals or
birds; said sketches to be handed in at the next
meeting.

4.   Introduce the speaker who is to give a short talk on

the carrying power of colors, and their effect upon the eye, the physical composition and peculiarities of the eye, etc. Urge the boys to ask questions on the subject, and try to have in the room, either from an optician or a physics laboratory, a good color chart, so that the eyes of each boy can be tested for colors, etc.

5. Place the three colors — red, green, and black on white — certain distances from the boys and have them test the vividness of these colors as they appeal to each boy individually. If possible step out of doors and have these colors carried farther and farther away and see which will longest hold the eye. Then explain why red is used as the danger signal; why green is next in importance in its appeal and why black on white is usually rated third. For a further test secure if possible advertising cards such as are used in street cars. Have a variety representing each color. Study them in their relative appeal. Carry out this study of colors into an imaginary forest or jungle. Have birds and insects named whose plumage or tissues bear one color or another.

6. If there is still time enough left, have a few such games as "Cock-Fighting," "Hand-Wrestling" and "Badger-Pulling" to relieve the tension of the previous hour or so of lecturing. (See B. H., pages 302 and 303.) Or else have some quick action game of Scouts' choice, such as will be applicable for indoors and yet strenuous enough to give the needed exercise, and so lessen the tension of inactivity.

7. Make announcements for the next two meetings and request each to obtain the written consent of his parents or guardian to be allowed to accompany the troop on the overnight hike (see Program XVIII), said written consent to be turned in to the Scout Master at the next regular meeting (see Program XVII).

8. Adjourn the meeting with a yell-practice of the Scout Yells and Patrol Calls.

PROGRAM XVII

Tenting Instruction

Meeting Place — Tent Instruction — Tent-Raising Contest — Tent Cloth Demonstration — Reports — Scout Game — Announcements — Adjournment.

For this meeting obtain the use of some unused yard or lot about town, preferably where there is a tree or two standing in the lot, but even a vacant city lot will serve the purpose fairly well. Also obtain just for this occasion the use of several tents of different kinds; there will probably be several owners of merchandise in your locality who will be glad to loan their property for such a purpose, providing due care of it is taken. If you are not yourself familiar with tent raising get someone who does know about tenting and camp life, who will be willing to give a demonstration on the methods of putting up tents and their practical uses. Read carefully the article in the Boys' Handbook on "Tents," pages 164–173, and study well the diagram on page 169. Obtain three pieces of unbleached cotton cloth, 90 inches wide and 5 yards long (one for the use of each patrol), and see that proper rings are attached for demonstration purposes. Be sure to obtain also a sufficient supply of ropes and pegs, etc. See that the Scouts take with them their knives or hatchets for use in making tent pegs, where needed, etc. Before the day for the meeting it would be best to practice using the tent-cloths as per direction in the article just referred to, so that you may become proficient in the art of setting up the different tent styles, and can give proper demonstrations without any bother or hindrance of inexperience. This meeting will require the greater part of an afternoon.

1. Having all met at a certain place, or at the vacant lot to be used for the meeting, get to work as soon as possible. There is plenty to be done.

2. Give a demonstration of raising and taking down different kinds of tents. Let the boys ask questions. When the boys have watched proceedings a couple of times, set them to work by patrols in setting up and taking down the same tents. Do not give any more advice than is absolutely necessary. If there are three tents (if there is only one patrol, the patrol might be divided into two parts), there might easily be a tent-raising contest for speed and abil-

ity, after the boys have experimented by raising
and taking down the tents a couple of times.

3. Proceed to give a demonstration with the tent-cloths
as per directions in Boys' Handbook, pages 165–
169, explaining the construction and uses for each
tent so made. After each demonstration, especially in the more simple forms, have the patrols
(or half patrols) construct the same sort of tent.
Encourage and direct these attempts and urge the
boys to construct similar figures from paper when
they get home. Ask them to read carefully the
article in question.

4. Have any outstanding reports or assignments handed
in at this time, and make due comment upon them.
Collect all written consents of parents, as requested at last meeting.

5. If there is still time enough left, have some such a
game as " Hat-Ball " for exercise.

6. Make full announcements as to plans for the next
meeting, the first overnight hike. Instruct the
boys in what is expected of them, what to take
with them, etc. Ask them to read carefully Chapter III on Campcraft in the Boys' Handbook, especially pages 145–149. Announce too, at this
time, the date of the Second-Class Scout Examinations (see Program XXII) and admonish the
boys to make themselves as proficient in all the requirements by that time as it is possible to do.

7. Adjourn the meeting with Scout Yells and Patrol Call
practice.

PROGRAM XVIII

First Overnight Hike

Start for Camp — Tent Raising — Bed Preparation — Signal
Practice — Game of " Hat-Ball "— Camp-Duty Assignments —
Supper — Good Turn Report — Scout Games — Camp Duties —
Around the Camp Fire — Lights Out — Morning Assembly —
Breakfast — Cooking Instruction — Camp Duties — Scout Games
— Instructions for the Day — Cleaning Tents — Observation
Hike — Dinner — Cooking Instruction — Rest Period — Clean
Camp — Scout Contests — Afternoon Swim — Scout Games —
Supper — Camp Duties — Around the Camp Fire — Announce-
ments — Home.

*This is one of the most important of meetings, and will de-
mand careful attention as to details and a well-developed*

plan of action. The Scouts should be carefully instructed in what you expect them to know and to do, and the Patrol Leaders should have a perfect knowledge of their powers and duties. You will need to be strict in discipline, and firm in your decisions, but kind and considerate withal. Upon the success of this meeting and its proper management depends in a way your whole future success as a Scout Master and leader of boys. So; therefore, you will have need to " Be Prepared:"

Discipline is especially necessary in camp, for the boys are so much inclined to consider the whole meeting in the nature of a great lark. It will be necessary to largely eradicate this idea, and at all times insist positively on order, but let the boys get as much pleasure in being out in the open as they can, as long as their pursuit of that pleasure does not interfere with the life and discipline of the camp.

Before starting on the " hike " you should have received personal communication by card or by note from the parents of each Scout giving him permission to go, and in case of their refusal you should take means to ascertain the reasons therefor.

Among the things that need definite attention and prearrangement for you should carefully note the following, as in reality a carefully planned and carefully prepared camp is its key to practical success:

(1) Choose a suitable site in advance, and have the camping ground cleaned.

(2) Whatever tents shall be needed should be on the grounds, and also all cooking utensils, and food supplies.

(3) Latrine or toilet facilities should be prepared for.

(4) The material for bedding, stakes for tents, etc., should be gathered and on the ground.

(5) The boys should know the entire program and what is expected of them to the least detail. And the Patrol Leaders and their Assistants should be carefully instructed in their duties and obligations.

(6) All materials needed for practical field scouting should be taken along — staves, knives, hatchets, packs, camping kits, compasses, wig-wag flags, etc.

(7) There should be enough wood on hand, either of dead limbs and trees on the ground, or taken to camp by wagon from another place; wood for cooking and camp-fire purposes is a necessity.

1. Having arranged a definite time for a start — about an hour and a half past noon — get out to the camping grounds as quickly as possible in marching order — practicing Scout's Pace and Requirement 4 for Second-Class Scouts when en route. *Of course such a camp and hike should be arranged for on a holiday if possible so as to give two full days for preparation and experience. But if not on a holiday, the " hike " should start immediately after the close of school on Friday, and end Saturday evening. If such is the case some of the arrangements should be attended to with the*

A TROOP ON AN OVERNIGHT HIKE

help of the Scouts themselves, on Wednesday and Thursday evenings preceding.

2. Group the troop into bunches of four each under leadership of Patrol Leaders and Assistant Patrol Leaders and have the tents pitched in orderly arrangement. You will act as inspector, and pronounce judgment upon the results. *The tents in use should be large enough to accommodate at least four Scouts to the tent. This would arrange matters so that there would be a Patrol Leader or an Assistant with each group. Also erect poles for the American camp flag, and for patrol flags.*

3. Detail each half-patrol with its leader to make their beds of fallen timber, fir boughs (if handy), bush

sprays, grass, leaves, hay or straw. Then have the bedding placed neatly on this superstructure. As inspector and instructor you should insist firmly on thoroughness of work, efficiency and neatness. *If there is room to take single-cot ticks or mattresses to the camp in the supply wagons,* these laid over the boughs and leaves or straw beneath make most excellent beds when the covers are added. Enough covers should be taken along for each Scout to insure warmth if the night in the field should be cold or chilly.

4. If the start is made shortly after noon on a holiday — there will be time enough left after these arrangements have been completed to have a wig-wag practice. In such case, deploy the Scouts in different directions in half-patrols, and proceed with Morse Code or Semaphore signal practice. If, however, the start is made after school on a Friday afternoon, and there should still be some time left over, play a few games like " Hat-Ball " to liven things up a bit, and to more likely secure enough weariness to insure at least some sleep during the night.

5. Divide the troop into four groups or details, and assign them each their separate camp duties. One group shall be under your command or the Assistant Scout Master's for the preparation of supper, the other three each under a Patrol Leader, and one assigned to duty as camp police or dog soldier, one to gather and prepare wood for the cooking-fires and camp-fires and to pack water, and the other squad or group to do duty as camp cleaners.

6. As soon as supper is prepared, all will sit down at some place near the camp-fire to enjoy their meal. During the course of the meal you will give out final tent and bed assignments, and outline camp rules for the night.

7. Have a " Daily Good Turn " report from all the Scouts.

8. Play the night game of " Will-o'-the-Wisp." (Page 317, B. H.)

9. After the game, the camp-fire squad should gather

more wood to be used during the night, and they should be assisted in their work by the camp police squad. In the meantime the other two squads should be busy with their own duties, one in cleaning up the supper remains and cleaning the utensils for to-morrow, and the other in cleaning up all the mess occasioned by the establishment of camp, the disposal of the supper refuse, etc.

10. Then all gather around the camp-fire, where you should outline the program for the morrow, and make a short talk on the "Object and Practical Benefit of the Camp." Then have ready several good camp stories. Encourage the boys to tell any good camp stories, too, that they may know; either that or of tales of adventure. Just before bed-time a prayer is found effective in some camps. Prayers should be encouraged where circumstances are appropriate.

11. Let 9:00 P. M. be the time for bed, and lights out. *The boys should require at least nine hours of sleep, although as a matter of fact in an ordinary camp, unless the boys are tired, the excitement and the strange surroundings will keep them awake for some time into the night. You should insist on a Scout's honor on perfect quiet between lights out, or taps, and rising time, or reveille.*

SATURDAY, OR THE SECOND DAY.

1. Arise at 6:30 A. M., and assemble the troop for setting-up exercises. One of the Patrol Leaders should call the roll.

2. Prepare breakfast at 7:00 A. M. Detail one squad to build cooking-fires, one squad to gather and prepare firewood, one squad to carry water for drinking and cooking and make themselves handy in any way needed. When enough wood has been gathered, and the fires are burning nicely, detail to each fire half-patrols to prepare their own breakfasts. Instruct the groups in the preparation of say, the model breakfast (page 152, Boys' Handbook), substituting cocoa for coffee for those who wish. Such a breakfast should be sufficient. (See Fireplace instructions, page 149, B. H.)

3. 8 A. M. Detail the squads appointed the night be-

fore, for morning work — one to wash dishes and clean up the scraps, one to put out the fires, lay by more wood for the noon hour, and get things ready for the events of the day; one to clean up camp, putting all trash and refuse in the proper place, and one to put all bedding in the sun for airing, and clean up the tents.

4. 8:30 A. M. Have one or two lively morning games such as " Poison," or " Hat-Ball," or " Duck-on-Rock " (pp. 303, 304, B. H.).

5. 9:15 A. M. Call for Troop Formation, and give instructions for the day.

6. 9:20 A. M. Have all bedding neatly rolled, each Scout his own bedding, and deposited in the tents. Order preparation for a " hike."

7. 9:40 A. M. Presuming you are familiar with the country and location of camp in distance-relation to other points, send the patrols off in different directions on four-mile hikes, two miles out to certain points. All should return by noon. These should be observation hikes, and each patrol should take note of all different (known) types of trees and shrubs, all birds, and all animals seen en route. If tracks are found in sandy or muddy places, record of the fact should be made, their location, and probable origin, and, if possible, a diagram of same made on the spot. At the end of the hike, when the patrols have returned, a half-hour should be spent in giving in reports of observation, and for the rough sketching of the route traversed, from notes taken en route.

8. 11:45 A. M. Begin preparation of dinner, a half-patrol at each fire. *You and your assistants will carefully direct the cooking, and specially instruct the boys in the knowledge of Requirement 8 for Second-Class Scouts.*

> (1) *Put a clean, flat stone over the fire, and when hot, lay beefsteak upon it. Turn the steak from time to time. Or hold the steak on pronged stick before the fire until cooked. Bake the potatoes with their skins on with the use of heated stones on the edge of the fire.*

(2) *Clean potatoes, peel, and boil in a tomato can.*

(3) *Scrape and cut up the potatoes, and boil with meat in a tomato can.*

9. Have a half-hour or more of complete rest. *Insist on rest and quiet.*

10. Wash the dinner dishes and cooking utensils, clean up camp, and put out the cooking-fires.

11. 2:30 P. M. Have a series of inter-patrol, inter-squad, and individual contests. *The following are suggested:*

Water Boiling	*Tent Pitching*
Knot Tying	*Signaling*
Lasso Throwing	*First Aid*
Fire Building	*Compass Work*
100-Yard Dash	*Broad Jump*
Relay Race	*220-Yard Dash*

Counts and honors should be kept track of, and some sort of point system established such as 5 for first places, 3 for second, and 1 for third place, the whole added up, the number of points completed for each individual squad and patrol, and winners declared.

12. 4:00 P. M. If weather and facilities will permit, have a half-hour's swim. In such case, the utmost *care should be taken to guard against loss of life. There should be row boats handy, and a life guard of the best swimmers appointed to provide against danger. All should be out and dressing by 5 p. m. For those who cannot swim or who do not care to; games can be started, giving the boys their choice. After the swim all should join in some good, healthful, active game. Where weather and facilities will not permit the swim, have a game of "Man Hunt" or "Deer Hunt." (See pp. 301, and 291, Boys' Handbook) at this time.*

13. Begin preparation of supper at 4:30 P. M., with same arrangements as before. Proceed with the cooking instruction.

14. 5:30 P. M. Break-up of camp. Put the whole troop at work striking tents, rolling canvases, packing goods and tents and bedding in camp wagons, filling in latrine, and collecting rubbish

for camp-fire. Make a thorough clean-up of camp.

15. 6:00 P. M. Gather around the camp-fire for some such program as the following:

COLLECTING AND BURNING CAMP RUBBISH

(1) Reports of contest and special honors.
(2) Opinions of Scouts on camp.
(3) Complaints and suggestions.
(4) Talk by Scout Master (ten minutes or less) on "Scout and Camp Life."
(5) Camp-fire story.

      (6)   Roll Call. Each Scout will respond to his name by giving his patrol call.

      (7)   The Scout Yell.

      (8)   The National Anthem —" America."

16.   7:00 P. M.   Make announcements for future meetings.

17.   7:10 P. M.   Put out the fire with water, and be careful to see that it is all out. Then set out for home. *The start homeward should always be made early enough so that the boys will arrive home by 9:00 P. M.*

PROGRAM XIX

Observation Practice

Talk on Observation — Leaf-Study Contest — First Aid Practice — Observation Games — Facial Differences — Identity — Finger-Prints — Announcements — Adjournment.

From now on, until the Second-Class Scout examinations, as much time as possible should be given to practice with the signal code and first aid to the injured, as these are the most difficult requirements to master. Accordingly practice either in one or the other should be given at every meeting, where possible, up to the time of the actual tests.

For this meeting you should also have in readiness a small metal plate or flat and smooth metal surface, a small quantity of printer's ink, and a small rubber roller with which to spread the ink on the metal surface. A round piece of glass, such as the side of a drinking glass will do as well as the metal plate. If possible too, try to find and glance over some book treating of physiognomy or facial features, usually there will be some such books in every fairly equipped library.

Before the meeting send each Scout word that he will be expected to bring his "leaf-contest" book to the hall with him for purposes of examination.

1.   Open the meeting with a few brief words on the subject of the evening —" Observation," and its practical use and application in every-day life.

2.   Collect the "leaf-contest" note-books, and glance over the contents of each. Comment upon the great diversity of the leaves in shape, color, marking, system of views, etc., and also the marked difference in leaves of the same tree. Drive the

point home that Nature does not duplicate herself in identical looks or marking or shapes not even in the leaves of the trees, that each leaf has its own identity, and by careful observation can be easily told from all other leaves on the same tree or any other tree. *Hold the books over for one meeting for more careful examination into the sort of results that are being obtained in nature study.*

3. Have ready sufficient supplies for a " First Aid " practice. *Let this last some little time so as to give the boy enough actual practice in the requirements as will give him a fair knowledge of the different methods to be used. Have a number of contests between the different Scouts in applying bandages and giving first aid to any one or two of a series of accidents.*

4. Play the observation games such as " Scout's Nose Indoors " and " Kim's Game."

5. Call the attention of the boys to the difference in their identity, how that each one differs from the other in shape of head or nose or skin, in color of eyes and hair, in stature, in manner of speech, etc. Point out the differences in shapes of the head, colors of the eye, colors and texture of hair, shapings of the ear, and show how any Scout can be easily identified from any of the others by an observation of just any one of these physical characteristics. Make out a number of cards on which descriptions are given of certain physical characteristics of the face and head, etc., and distribute these cards without names to certain of the Scouts in order that they may try in a limited time to find the subject of the description among the other Scouts present. If these Scouts fail or any one of them fails, let others have a trial either with the same or new cards. Score points for the Scouts who are successful.

6. Briefly discuss finger-prints, and their use as a means of identification. Have the boys examine the markings of the lines on the finger tips, and point out how different they are in arrangement not only on the same hand, or the same person, but on any number of hands of different persons. Show

method of taking record of finger-prints and the simple materials needed for use. Take an impression of the fingers of each Scout, with his signature, and pass them out to them respectively as mementos of the occasion. *Spread the printer's ink on the metal plate with the rubber roller, press the tips of the fingers with a slight pressure to the metal surface and then to a piece of blank paper. If the glass is used, the rubber roller is used to roll the ink on the glass, then the finger tips are rolled slightly on the glass, and the glass in turn rolled on the paper. A little practice makes the taking of impressions very easy, and either method should give good results. The glass method is the one most in use in the United States Navy. Printer's ink takes the best impressions as the other ink is liable to blur.*

7. Make announcements for the next two meetings.
8. Have a practice of the Patrol Calls, Troop Formation and Drill. Close the meeting with a salute to the flag, and the Scout Yells.

PROGRAM XX
Field Practice — Efficiency

Start — Practice of Requirements 4 and 5 — Requirements 6 and 7 — Compass Games — Signal Code Practice — Scout Game — Adjournment.

As this is to be the last actual practice before the preliminary tests for Second-Class Scout requirements, you should spend at least a whole afternoon in actual scout practice in the field or woods. See that all paraphernalia necessary for the field practice of outdoor requirements is taken with you. Have a suitable spot already selected as a good location for the scout practice, and begin work as soon as possible.

1. Get out into the field and arrive at your selected camp as soon as possible.
2. In getting to your location give orders to the Patrol Leaders to see that each Scout can successfully fulfill Requirement 4, tracking half a mile in twenty-five minutes, and also Requirement 5 — knowledge of the Scout's pace.

3. Immediately upon arriving at your destination organize a contest for practice of the 6th and 7th Requirements. This should be a time limit contest, and account taken of speed and ability.

4. Give orders to one Patrol Leader to have a ground compass laid out, and when that is finished play the Compass Games. See that each Scout knows accurately at least the sixteen principal points of the compass, fulfilling Requirement 10.

5. Divide the troop into its patrols, and the patrols into groups of four each, one under the command of a Patrol Leader, and the other under the Assistant Patrol Leader. Then deploy the groups to suitable distances and have the signal-code practice. Pay principal attention to the Signal Code, and see that each Scout, during the practice, has his equal chance of sending and receiving messages. Have the groups do as much as possible without the book or written copies of the code system. Also a practice of the Semaphore signal code. Also make good use of the occasion for a practice of the Whistle Signs, and Hand and Flag Signals as given on pages 208–209 of the Boys' Handbook.

6. Call Scouts together and have a game of " Hat-Ball," or some similar game before leaving for home.

7. After the game, make announcements for the next two or three meetings, and adjourn.

PROGRAM XXI

Preliminary Tests for Second-Class Scout Requirements

Opening — Roll Call — Oral Quiz — Scout Game — First Aid Practice — Scout Game — Signaling — Announcements — Adjournment.

This should be an indoor evening meeting at the Scout Hall or Headquarters, and as a preliminary test should, in the main, be oral in its nature. Your desire in this case is to ascertain how much of actual knowledge of the different requirements the Scouts really have. This meeting, because of its nature, will probably make the boys restless, so your plans should be laid so as to intersperse a needful game or two at the proper places in order to relieve any tenseness the boys may feel.

You should have examined the corrected "leaf-contest" books with advisory notes and added instructions in the note books of the "leaf-study" contest, and these books should be given back to the boys at this time with the announcement that the contest will end by the date of the next indoor meeting of the troop and that the books shall at that time be handed in for final judgment upon the results. For the results of the contest, the boys should understand that each and all who take part will receive a certain number of honors according to condition and qualities and neatness of his collection and study.

1. Call the meeting to order with Flag Salute in Troop Formation.

2. Have roll call, with each Scout answering to his name with patrol call. After roll call have a few Scout Yells, under leadership of the senior Patrol Leader.

3. Have an oral quiz, asking questions at random, first here, then there, and skipping from one subject to another as follows:

(1) What is the treatment for fainting? Explain.

(2) What is Scout's Pace?

(3) By position of your arms show method of making a, b, g, and 1 by Morse system.

(4) Explain method of building fire, using not more than two matches.

(5) What is meant by boxing the compass?

(6) What is the tourniquet?

(7) With wig-wag flag spell out the words "Be Prepared."

(8) Repeat the twelve points of the Scout Law.

(9) What is a fracture? Bruise? Sprain? Burn? Scald?

(10) Show or explain method of carrying injured.

(11) Give the sixteen principal points of the compass.

(12)   Explain method of cooking meat and po-
       tatoes without ordinary cooking uten-
       sils.

(13)   What is the Semaphore Code?   Illustrate.

(14)   Explain treatment for fracture, for burn,
       for sprain.

(15)   What is the use of observation?

(16)   What is meant by efficiency?

(17)   Explain use of the triangular bandage.
       Demonstrate.

(18)   What is telegraphy? Explain the princi-
       ple in use.

(19)   With wig-wag flag spell your name.

(20)   Demonstrate the use of the roller bandage.

(21)   What is a compound fracture? Explain
       treatment for dislocation.

(22)   Show method of using the Semaphore, by
       spelling your name.

(23)   What is sunstroke and how caused?
       How is nose-bleed treated?   Sunburn?
       Hiccough?

(24)   Repeat the Scout Oath.

(25)   How is it possible to show that you have
       fulfilled Requirement 9?

*Each Scout should have his turn and the other Scouts
should be admonished to listen to questions and answers,
and ascertain if the same have been correctly answered.
This will give them an idea of what to expect at examination time, and how to prepare therefor. Anything that is
not understood should be explained, and each question given
should be fully answered, if not by the Scout questioned,
then by volunteers, and in the last resort by your explanation. If a Scout fails to answer a part or the whole of any
question, he should be given another chance.*

4. Play a game or two to enliven things a bit. Try
    some such game as " Hunt the Coon " (page 301,
    B. H.), or " Spear Fights." (page 302, B. H.).
    Also try exercises such as " Hand-Wrestling,"
    " Badger-Pulling," or " Poison " (page 303, B.
    H.).

5. Have a " First Aid " practice.
    1. Use of bandages and tourniquets.
    2. Methods of treatment for shock or fainting.

3. Methods of treatment for bruises, fractures and sprains.
4. Methods of treatment for burns and scalds.
5. Methods of carrying and taking care of injured.
6. Have another indoor game of Scouts' choice.
7. Have each Scout spell his name in turn with the wig-wag flag — Morse Code.
8. Make announcements for next two meetings, and outline methods of examination.
9. Adjourn with Patrol Call and Scout Yell practice.

PROGRAM XXII

Second-Class Scout Examinations — Outdoors

Start — Requirements 4 and 5 — Requirements 6, 7 and 8 — Requirement 10 — Compass Games — Scout Games — Signal Code Examination — Roll Call — Announcements — Adjournment.

Inasmuch as the principal part of examination tests can best be made outdoors, this will of course be the more important of the two examination meetings. Most of the examination tests can be cleared up at this time so that the bulk of the next indoor meeting can be made useful in other ways with new instruction and entertainment. If it is at all possible for you to do so, you should have with you at this time a visiting Scout Master from an adjoining locality or district, to act as official examiner. If a Scout Master cannot be obtained, try to have present one of the members of the Court of Honor or the Local Council of Boy Scouts, and if this fails you, at least have with you in the field some interested citizen or lodge member who will consent to serve as official examiner.

The location for the outdoor examination should be in the woods or fields only a short distance away from your town or in the vacant lot used in the tent-raising practice, if in the city, and if it is large enough to serve all purposes. Of course in every case the woods or fields would make the best location.

All materials should be in readiness, and enough supplies for use in Requirement 8 should be taken along.

If the examiner is a stranger to the requirements, he should be most carefully instructed in the methods of

*judging results, and in the outline of the afternoon's work.
The examiner and the Scout Masters should keep record
of all grading decisions made, with proper entrant name of
Scout and his contest grades in a small note-book to be used
for the occasion.*

1. Get to camp location as quickly as possible.
2. With examiner acting as time-keeper, take the troop
   by patrols and try out Requirement 4. Then try
   out Requirement 5. *Measure off roughly for
   these trials, making distance cover as circular a
   track as possible.*
3. Detail one patrol to lay out requirements for compass games, one patrol to prepare material to carry
   out Requirement 8, and one patrol to try out in
   Requirements 6 and 7. In latter case each one of
   the eight in the patrol should work alone, and the
   examiner should give his attention to the grading
   of results. As soon as this first patrol have finished in this examination, they should continue
   in trial of Requirement 8, working this time in
   pairs — one preparing the meat and the other the
   potatoes. At the same time the second patrol —
   those detailed for preparing material for Requirement 8 (opening packages, and distributing appor-
   tionate supplies) — should be given their examinations in Requirements 6 and 7, under the same
   rules as the test for the first patrol in these requirements. When the Scouts of the first patrol have
   finished in the trial test of Requirement 8, they
   should be given a chance to play a game of " Hat-
   Ball " or one of their own choice; and second
   patrol, finished with Requirements 6 and 7, should
   then continue with Requirement 8, in the way already outlined, and the third patrol — those detailed to lay out requirements for the compass
   games — should be given their chance with Requirements 6 and 7. As soon as the Scouts of one
   patrol finish with the two tests, they should begin
   with a game, and as each of the other patrols
   finish, they, too, should join in the game.
4. When all the Scouts have been examined in Requirements 6, 7, and 8, and the examiner and Scout
   Masters have made an examination of the cooked

products of Requirement 8 to test the thoroughness in cooking, then "Compass Point" game should be started, with thirty-two points. Every mistake made in calling points should be noted, and applicable grading made therefor. In addition each Scout should be called aside separately, some time during the course of the game, and bidden to repeat the sixteen principal compass points in their due order. This will constitute the trial of Requirement 10.

5. Two patrols will then engage in a game of their own choice, or in the various Scout exercises, according to their own inclinations. In the meantime, the eight members of the other patrol are sent out a definite distance from camp in different directions, each with a wig-wag flag. Then the examining board will send out a message in the Morse Code from camp to each Scout, and receive in turn as correct and appropriate answer as possible. This will constitute the test of Requirement 3. The patrol will be called in by whistle commands as soon as finished, and each of the other patrols sent out in the same way, for their examinations in this requirement.

6. Reassemble the troop, and have the roll call.

7. Make announcements for the next two meetings.

8. Adjourn with the Scout Yells, and depart for home.

PROGRAM XXIII

Second-Class Scout Examinations — Indoors

Opening — Roll Call — Oral Quiz — First Aid Examination — Signal Code Examination — Address — Special Talk — Announcements — Adjournment.

This meeting should be held during the evening of the next day after the outdoor examinations, or at least, if you have used a Saturday afternoon for the last meeting, this meeting should be scheduled for Monday evening or just as soon thereafter as possible. The reason is that the examinations should be over as soon as possible, and if a visiting Scout Master is with you at the first meeting he might also be induced to stay over for the second.

The meeting, as an examination, will be one largely of memory tests, etc., and proof of practical knowledge of

" First Aid." *It would be well to have with you a member
of the Court of Honor or a member of the Local Council
of your district, whether the Scout Master is with you or
not.*

*If the Scout Master is with you, you can probably count
on him for a few words in regard to Scout work, or as a
bearer of a message from another troop — if the Council
member is present, he cannot only act as a judge of the
examinations, but also will probably help out in a few interesting and well-chosen words of good cheer and inspiration.*

*As something special in the line of entertainment for this
meeting, it might be well to have either a telegrapher or
despatcher present, who will tell the boys something about
practical applied electricity as used in telegraphy, and
demonstrate by use of telegraph instruments and storage
batteries, showing the use of the Morse Code in telegraphy.
Or if you cannot obtain such an expert, it would be a good
idea to have the mayor of your town or city or the chief of
the fire department present for a talk on efficiency in their
lines of work.*

*If a despatcher can be present, you should see that the
proper instruments with all needed paraphernalia and supplies are ready at hand and in place for demonstration purposes.*

1. Open meeting with Flag Salute in Troop Formation.
2. Have the acting Secretary call the roll, giving time of
   service as Tenderfoot Scouts and dates of enlist-
   ment. The Scouts will respond to their names
   with the answer —" Present " and give the name
   of their patrol. This will be proof sufficient of
   having fulfilled Requirement 1.
3. Give an oral quiz with questions similar in part to
   those suggested in Program XXI.
4. As an examination in Requirement 2, each Scout
   should give a demonstration in applying triangular
   and roller bandages and tourniquets, and in addition a written examination should be given in
   which each Scout will explain the nature and treatment of fainting, fractures, sprains, burns, scalds,
   etc.
5. Have an oral quiz on the Morse and Semaphore
   Code system. In this case the Scout Master will

make a letter with the wig-wag, and call some Scout at random to give the letter. In same way tests can be made with a number of simple words.

6. Have address as made by the visiting Scout Master, or member of Local Council, or Examiner.

7. Have the address on " Telegraphy," if possible, and the accompanying demonstration. *Or an address by the Mayor, or Fire Chief, can be used here.*

8. Make announcements for the next meetings, and let it be known that at the next indoor meeting following, those who have been successful in the examinations will be " sworn in " as Second-Class Scouts.

9. Adjourn with Patrol Calls and Scout Yells.

PROGRAM XXIV

First Principles of First-Class Scout Requirements — Map and Nature Study

Map Instruction — Roll Call — Lunch Hour — Signal Practice — Nature Study Information.

This meeting should be on a Saturday or holiday, and should be spent in tramping. This should be a nearly continuous hike of five or six miles at the least, and proper precaution should be made for the protection of the feet by wearing proper tramping shoes, and all unnecessary articles should be left behind. Lunch, already prepared, should be taken along with each one of the party, as well as the Scout staff, and knife or hatchet. Read the instructions for hikes as given on pages 145–146 of the Boy's Handbook, and follow the suggestions given therein, as to shoes, kit, extra shirt (if needed), and map study.

If at all possible take along someone on this hike, who knows the woods and the birds and animals, and who can give accurate and definite information concerning the wild things in field and forest. There should be a naturalist or science-teacher or woodsman in every locality who would be glad of taking such a chance to increase the interest of the boys in nature study and nature lore.

One or two wig-wag flags should be taken along by each Patrol for practice use.

1. Call a meeting of the troop for a half-hour's map study before starting on the " hike." Give in-

struction in use and reading of different sorts of maps.

FIELD STUDY OF THE FERNS AND GRASSES

2. Make a start on the "hike" at the appointed time, after calling the roll.

3. At lunch hour, in as favorable location as you can find, make announcements for the next two meetings. State that at the next meeting the Scouts

successful in the examinations will be "sworn in" as Second-Class Scouts. And that at the next meeting following will be a troop business session, and that every Scout should be present.

4. Make use of wig-wag flags for signaling, wherever possible to do so.

5. Encourage the Scouts to ask for information about the wild things — animals and plants.

Note.— Government maps of your locality can be secured by addressing Director U. S. Geological Survey, Washington, D. C. Enclose 10c for each map wanted.

We would recommend that Scout Masters use the conventional signs used in the U. S. Army surveys. These conventional signs can be secured by addressing the Army War College, Washington, D. C. Also see Chapter II.

PROGRAM XXV

Second-Class Scout Investiture

Opening Talk — Roll Call — Address — Announcement of Successful Applicants — Investiture Ceremonial — Announcements — Refreshments — America.

All of the Scouts that have worked persistently since their initiation as Tenderfoot Scouts, especially if these programs have been consistently followed in general detail, will now have easily passed the Second-Class Scout Requirements Tests, and are ready to be vested with the rank of Second-Class Scout. If there are those in the troop who will not put forth any appreciable effort to progress from rank to rank, and seem content to remain as Tenderfoot Scouts, something is wrong either with the management of the organization or with them. All reasonable inducements should be held out to them to work on upward in the ranks, and the training as outlined in these foregoing programs, should prove plentifully sufficient for such purpose. It will be your business to watch out for natural laggers and shirkers, and to so instill the idea of progression in the minds of the majority of your Scouts as to cause a general movement forward through the force of public opinion. And if all else fails to arouse the shirkers to move onward, his case should be turned over to a special committee of inquiry appointed by the Troop Leader, whose duty should be to assist him either to mend his ways or resign from the troop membership. Shirkers of the persistent sort are not wanted, and the sooner the organization is rid of them to make room for " climbers," the better it will be for all concerned. Of course, though, a reasonable time should be given for each Scout to make good, each should have the same approximate time to serve in each rank with more or less the same training — this applying especially to new Scouts, either enrolled late or taking the place' of those Scouts dropped out; moreover a . certain definite date after the first Second-Class Scout examinations, another special examination of the same sort should be given for those who have failed the first time, or for new Scouts. Scouts of any rank should never need more than three trials to make good at any test,— so after the third failure to attain progressive rank, such cases should be looked after with special attention.

This is another important meeting, and should be well prepared for in advance; in general form it resembles the Tenderfoot Scout Investiture of Program VII, and the same general instruction and explanations in use in that program applies here equally as well.

If it is decided to invite the Scouts' parents to this meeting, proper seating arrangements should be made; in this case such duty should be turned over to one of the Patrol Leaders. As another excellent means of entertainment, and something really needed on an occasion such as this, especially if the parents or visitors are to be present, is a public address on some applicable subject by a public man, — a judge, statesman, or well-known attorney. Such a good address would be one on " Good Government." Also you should see that a member of the " Court of Honor " is to be present, who shall make announcements on examination results, and say a few words as to the development and importance of the Boy Scout organization in the locality.

It will also be necessary to attend to the ordering of sufficient Second-Class Scout badges. (See instructions of Program VII.) The Second-Class Scout badges are made of gilt metal, in safety-pin style, and are to be worn upon the sleeve. The price is 10 cents. The Patrol Leader's Second-Class Scout badge is made of oxidized silver, but otherwise resembles the other badges in finish and in price. The badge is a representation of the scroll of the complete Scout badge, upon which is the Boy Scout motto —" Be Prepared."

1. Open the meeting with a few brief remarks as to the plans and purpose of the meeting.

2. Call for Flag Salute in Troop Formation. Then have the roll call, with each Scout giving his Patrol Call in answer to his name.

3. Have the address on " Good Government " as prepared for. *Limit to ten or twelve minutes.*

4. The member of the " Court of Honor " will follow with a few brief remarks on the development of the Boy Scout organization in his locality, and follow that with the public announcements of the names of the successful applicants for Second-Class Scout rank.

5. Proceed with the Investiture ceremony as follows:

    a. The Scouts are called to stand at attention, and all repeat the Scout Oath in unison.

    b. The Scout Master will then say:

        " Scouts, you have repeated the Scout Oath, and I am confident that you do your best in living up to its principles; you have also passed the required tests which enables you to progress one step onward. You are now to become Second-Class Scouts."

    c. The Scouts then salute, and the Scout Master continues:

        " You will now repeat in unison the twelve points of the Scout Law."

    d. The Scouts repeat the points of the Scout Law.

    e. The Scout Master then arranges the boys in a half-circle formation, so that they stand side by side and all face his position which should be at least seven or eight feet from the boy immediately in front of him.

    f. The Investiture to Second-Class Scout rank now takes place. The same ceremonial is used exactly as in Program VII, making proper changes of rank classification, where necessary.

6. Have the boys take their seats, and make announcements for the next two meetings. Announce that the next meeting will be a Troop Business Session.
7. Have refreshments, if they have been arranged for.
8. Adjourn the meeting with a couple of verses of the National Anthem —" America."

PROGRAM XXVI

Troop Business Session

Instructions — Patrol Meetings — Entertainment.

This meeting was announced at last meeting as the regular evening set aside for discussion of troop and patrol business. Having seen that the officers of the meeting are properly instructed in their duties, and having discussed the new business of whatever nature it is intended to bring up for discussion here, it will be best to take a back seat, as it were, for this occasion, giving control of the meeting to the boys, and acting only as mentor or friend or counselor, as prescribed by the Constitution.

1. Open and conduct the meetings as prescribed in your Constitution and By-Laws. (See Article II of By-Laws, as suggested.) *As a first regular business session, it will necessarily be the duty of the Troop Leader or President at this time to appoint all standing and special committees, so arrangements should have been made, consultations held, etc., for this purpose. After the said committees have been appointed and instructed in their duty, they should be encouraged to hand in at this time orally, a temporary report. This will awaken and hold up the interest of all.*
2. *Under the head of new business — a first meeting time should be determined upon and announced for the organization and perfection of Patrol Business Sessions, preferably within the following week.*
3. *The Stunt or Entertainment Committee should have previously arranged some planned-out program of their own, providing for the entertainment of the troop in session. Stunts will be popular.*

PROGRAM XXVII

First Class Scout Requirements

Drill Instruction — First Aid Drill — First Class Requirements — Computing Practice — Nature Hunt — Game — Semaphore or Signal Practice — Setting-Up Instruction — Announcements — Adjournment.

This meeting should be held in the open, preferably in the afternoon, as soon after Investiture and Business Meetings as possible. Proceed this time only as far as it is necessary to find a rather flat open space of some size for drill work,— either in the woods, open fields, or park lands. Any new instruction in Scout Drill should be given at this time. It will also be best to have along a few copies of the Boys' Handbook for use, both in First Aid Drill Work and the reading of the new requirements for higher rank.

Some of the Scouts already know how to swim; the others should be encouraged to learn at the first opportunity, and all told how necessary to preservation swimming really is. In the new drill-work in first aid instruct the boys in artificial respiration and call attention to the explanation on the subject in the Boys' Handbook.

Have materials ready at hand for use in the Semaphore practice.

1. After coming together at the appointed place, proceed immediately to your intended drill ground, and arriving there call for troop formation and proceed with drill exercises. Give any new instruction necessary.

2. Have First-Aid Drill for practice. Call the Scouts' attention to instructions on swimming, and the accidents and treatment thereof. Instruct in the methods of artificial respiration, etc. Explain to the Scouts how necessary to self-preservation it is to know how to swim, and encourage those who have not yet learned to do so whenever the opportunity arises, under a proficient instructor.

3. Read over carefully and explain each of the requirements for the rank of First Class Scout.

4. Try out Requirement 9. With a little ingenuity and thought this exercise can be made highly interesting and instructing. Test the Scouts in the open on distance, size, and height. A handy tape-

line will check results of the Scout estimates and guesses.

5. Send each boy out separately to find some specimen of plant life. The boys have already had several nature talks on trees and wild life. Now give each some one thing to find and bring in as quickly as possible, such as an elm leaf, a bit of oak bark, a hickory leaf, a snake flower, etc. Your knowledge of the local herbage will suggest proper assignments. Request, too, each Scout to bring in a leaf from some other plant than that assigned to him, to name the tree from such leaf, and give a general description thereof, etc.

6. Have Scout-choice of games, and let the play continue as long as possible.

7. By whistle commands or bugle call Scouts to attention and to " come together." Instruct in the use of the Semaphore code. Heretofore attention has been given chiefly to one of the several code systems, but now it is time to continue advancement and learn the other codes also.

8. Have a setting-up drill, and give instructions to those in need of it in the methods and needs of the exercises.

9. Make announcements for the next three meetings. Make sure to announce the date of the next overnight hike.

10. Adjourn with Flag Salute and Scout Yell.

PROGRAM XXVIII

Scout Reporting

Report Assignments — Message Delivery by Code — Information Gathering — Trip Report — Botany Study — Street Mapping — Time Limit Hikes — Good Turn Reports — Nature Study — Announcements and Adjournment.

This meeting can be arranged for handling from indoors, so that using the Headquarters as a central station, rendezvous, or camp, the Scouts can be instructed, given assignments, and sent out from there on their various duties and Scout work. While giving attention to this reporting practice, one patrol or perhaps at least four Scouts should be kept close by at all times, and these to be changed every so often, so that all may have a chance of reporting. It is

*needless to suggest that too long or arduous an assignment
would be unwise at this time. All paraphernalia needed for
the occasion should be at hand.*

1. After having met at Headquarters, and given instruc-
    tions, give out assignments for scout-reporting, to
    each Scout or squads of two as the needs of the
    occasion and duty may suggest. Following is a
    suggestion of some such assignments:— Send one
    Scout with code flags to a certain point 1 with a
    message to deliver to another point 4 in town, and
    to return with message received from point 2.
    Send Scout No. 2 out with similar instructions to
    send message to point 1 and receive message from
    point 3. Scout No. 3 with message for point 2
    and to receive message from point 4. Scout No.
    4 to send message to point 3 and receive message
    from point 1, etc. *Each Scout should be given a
    different message separately and secretly, and the
    points should be far enough away in opposite di-
    rections to preclude any other sort of communica-
    tion than code signaling, and yet in plain reading
    view of each other.*

    Send several Scouts out to collect information re-
    garding movements of people, or any particular
    occurrences in different parts of town.

    Send some with messages to friends, requesting
    answers, and ask for detailed account of trip of
    Scouts to and from, etc.

    Send several Scouts out to collect tree leaves,
    bark, pieces of wood, etc., as in Program
    XXVII, asking for trip reports.

    Send Scouts to map certain street sections or
    squares, showing location of known buildings, and
    give information of movement of people, carriages,
    street-cars, etc., and anything of note in progress
    thereon.

    Send Scouts out with time limits on certain
    hikes about towns, giving instructions to visit and
    note certain activities at certain points, etc.

2. Call for "Daily Good Turn" reports of the yester-
    day and day before.

3. Give Scouts at Headquarters, books with illustra-
    tions showing leaves and appearance of different

local trees and plants, as well as the animals and birds common to that part of the country. Also some book showing animal and bird tracks, etc. Have them make diagrams of the leaves, tracks, etc.

4. When enough time has been given to this sort of practice, call in all Scouts, and make announcements for the next meetings, and adjourn. Give date and information as to next over-night hike. (See Program XXX.)

PROGRAM XXIX
Scoutcraft — Evening Instruction

Roll Call — First Aid Practice — Map Assignments — Address on "Banking"— Scout Games — Requirement Practice — Requirement 5 — First Aid — Announcements — Adjournment.

This meeting is important as the means to bring attention to details of certain First Class Scout requirements, and explanation thereof. Have all materials ready to give instruction and try out methods for First Aid as outlined in Requirement 10. Also have materials handy for practice of Requirement 9. Arrange with a banker or financier to give the boys a short talk on "Banking" and the needs of "Creating a Savings Deposit," etc.

1. Call the meeting to order with Flag Salute and Roll Call.
2. Have First Aid regular practice.
3. Call attention to Requirement 7 and give out assignments to each Scout to make a rough sketch map of a certain locality in town, city or country, naming a different locality or square for each Scout. Announce the need to have this ready by the next regular indoors meeting.
4. Announce by a proper introduction the speaker of the occasion and the importance of his subject as a Scout Requirement. (See No. 2.)
5. Have a few minutes' recess in games of Scouts' choice,— suitable for indoors.
6. Try out Requirement 9, making note by contest-scores the results of each Scout's estimates.
7. Call attention in the Boys' Handbook to the section covering Requirement 5. Read over the informa-

tion and explain, where necessary, and answer all fair questions. Demonstrate treatment where necessary, and have a tryout of the same among the Scouts.

8. Call attention to the importance of the next meeting as an over-night hike, and explain the regulations for camp governments given in that program (XXX). Call attention to the need of perfect order, and obedience of Scout officers and rules to insure the success of the meeting, etc.

9. Adjourn with Troop and Patrol with Scout Yells.

PROGRAM XXX

Overnight Hike

The Start — Pitching the Tents — Preparation of Beds — Flag Poles — Supper — Conduct — Clean Camp — Camp Duties — Scout Games — Around the Camp Fire — Camp Rules — To-morrow's Program — Scout Yarn — Stunts — Songs — Indian Dance — Lights Out —" Taps "— Lowering the Flag — Reveille — Morning Exercise — Flag Salute — Morning Dip — Breakfast — Camp Duties — Morning Game — Drill Practice — Signal Practice — Lunch-Cooking Instruction — Camp Duties — Contests and Games — Swimming — Supper — Camp Duties — To-morrow's Program — Around the Camp Fire — Scout Yarn — " Taps "— Reveille — Nature Study Hike — Dinner — Rest Period — Nature Study and Walk Assignments — Supper — Packing up — Camp Fire Council — Homeward Journey.

In preparation for this program it would be best to read over the preparation instruction of Program XVIII. All arrangements for the camp should receive careful attention, and all details thought out and planned beforehand, previous to the start of the troop to the camping grounds

It is presumed in these overnight hikes that only one or two nights, making up a week end, will be spent in the field, and therefore suggestions are outlined for only such a length of time. Longer periods of camping will be fully treated in the programs for Summer, Winter and Permanent Camps now in preparation. Each short-time camp will necessarily be much the same in general plan and outline of Scout requirement practice, games, etc., and arranged as they are only for temporary use; so that a general outline of each will do as well for any other, the changes being in the details of Scoutcraft practice. But nevertheless, the outline of plans, duties, stunts, and rules should always be carefully prearranged for each such week-end or overnight outing.

In addition to the preparatory suggestions as offered in Program XVIII, the following should also be noted:—

   1. In choosing a location for a camp site, do not place your camp near a marsh, cemetery, swamp, stagnant water, in a punch bowl depression, or in the midst of a dense vegetation. Choose rather an

A SCOUT CAMP IN THE WOODS

   open clearing of unplowed land on natural sloping ground, with a sandy or gravelly top soil.

   2. Careful inquiry should be made as to purity of water supply near your chosen camp-site. Information from people living in the neighborhood is fairly reliable as to presence and location of springs, sources of streams, contaminating influences of lakes, streams, and wells, and the purity of the waters from each of these sources for drinking purposes. Some such investigation should always be made by the Scout Master.

   3. In preparing for latrine or toilet facilities, care should be taken that the toilet be well removed from the rest of the camp, preferably hidden by a screen of trees or bushes, and that it shall not be in the direction from which the prevailing wind comes toward camp. A little carelessness will cause disagreeable as well as dangerous results. It should be an imperative rule that no other place besides the latrine shall be used, and there should be rigid prohibition of the pollution of the ground surface and constant care of the latrine.

4. *All garbage should be kept in a covered can or pail and disposed of before decomposition takes place. Upon the break up of such a short time camp it should be buried in the ground, and covered over with several inches of earth. In longer time camps, the garbage should be so buried every one or two days.*

5. *Cleanliness should be insisted upon. Everybody should be taught the value of good and safe sanitation and encouraged to coöperate to make sanitary rules actionable.*

6. *The camp-site should be chosen, if possible, near a place suitable for swimming, and in such a favored locality, proper arrangements should be provided for the swim or bath. Those who do not know how to swim should be encouraged to learn, but great care should certainly be taken in giving the proper instruction, and precautionary measures should be taken that none of the Scouts should be allowed to go swimming without the presence of the Scout Master or some leader.*

7. *Choose your camping place far enough from the town or city or village to be free from visitors and the temptation " to go to town " on the part of the boys.*

The first part of the chapter on "Campcraft" in the Boys' Handbook by H. W. Gibson is extremely valuable as information for short-term camps, and it would be best to read over the following points:— Introduction; the Scouts; the bed; hot stone wrinkle; camp lamp; building the fire-place; water supply; sanitation; general hints; water hints; weather signs; building a camp fire, etc.

Prepare a definite program of duties and events for so long a time as the camp is planned for, covering the full

*period of time and providing for " something doing " during
each part of the day. The general outline of this plan
should have been reviewed at the previous meeting so that
the boys might know what is to be expected of them, understand the rules and different duties, etc., all beforehand.
The following outline of events is suggested.*

FRIDAY AFTERNOON OR IST DAY.

1. At the appointed time for the start march out to the
   camping grounds in Patrol formation.

2. Arrived at the camp, have the tents pitched by Patrol
   team work in an orderly arrangement. *For these
   short-term camps the kind of tents for use would
   of course differ in different localities and at the
   option of the Scout Master. Ordinarily the lean-
   tos should prove ample, but in all cases provisions
   should be made for protection against rain both
   in selection of the tent and their erection. Tents
   should accommodate at least four Scouts each;
   there should be with each such half patrol, a Patrol
   leader or Assistant Patrol Leader.*

3. When the tents have been pitched satisfactorily, proceed to have the beds prepared. (See suggestion
   3, Program XVIII. And also see the articles on
   bedding in the Boys' Handbook.) Also have poles
   fixed for the raising of the American flag, the Boy
   Scout emblem, and the Patrol insignia.

4. Prepare Supper. *Local geographical conditions will
   suggest or demand a variety of dishes, and the
   sort of menu served at this first supper, of course,
   will depend upon your selection of food stuffs,
   cooking accommodations, etc. There should be
   plenty of milk to drink, and good bread and butter. Cake and sweets or fancy dishes are not
   necessary, and in such a short-term camp, are not
   expected. The bill of fare should be elastic to
   meet local and geographical and weather demands;
   your judgment of such local conditions will be
   all that is necessary for suggestive selections.
   Weather conditions will demand warm food when
   the weather is cold or rainy and cold dishes, as a
   rule, when the days are warm. Also the nature
   of the food will depend upon the location of the*

troop,— *in the Southern States, or in the North, in the East, or in the West, etc. For suggested menus for overnight and week end camps, see the Boys' Handbook.* Take plenty of time for the eating of the meal. Encourage wholesome conversation and natural pleasantry, but discountenance any signs of ungentlemanly conduct or "rough house."

5. After supper, have a clean up of camp, dishwashing, removal of supper remains, etc. Then call the Scouts to "Attention," and give out camp duty assignments. *For such a short-term camp these camp Committees should be chosen to serve permanently during the term length of the camp, and some means of creating a desire or honor to serve on some such Committee should be engendered or developed by the Scout Master. With this purpose in view the following plan has been suggested: Provide four committees for purposes such as Sanitation, Policing, Wood-gathering, and Camp-cleaning. The duties of the Sanitary Committee will consist of looking after the proper disposal of garbage, disinfection, care of latrine, etc.; the Policing Committee will see to proper obedience of camp rules, to getting water for cooking purposes, to picking up and disposing of all papers and trash about camp, the raising and lowering of the flags, etc.; the Camp Cleaners will prepare vegetables for cooking, wash and dry dishes, pot and pans, clean up around the cooking fires, clean the boats, if any are to be used; and the Wood Gatherers will provide wood for the camp-fires, gather fire-wood for cooking, build and light the camp-fire, etc. Have the assembled Scouts elect the four leaders from among the members of the Troop by popular vote. Then have each leader, except the Chief Camp Cleaner, at this same meeting choose four other Scouts to serve with him. And have it understood that Chief Camp Cleaner's committee will consist of the Scouts found guilty of misbehavior, breaking of camp rules, rowdyism, etc.*

You probably have some other method of handling these camp assignments, some regular camp

organization, or other arrangements, which would
prove generally acceptable for such purposes, if
sent to others through the Scout Magazine,—
" Boys' Life."

6. If there is still time, have some good Scout game to
    enliven the boys,— a game of Scout's choice, and
    suitable for the time of the day, etc.

7. Gather the Scouts around the Camp-Fire, after the
    ceremony of building it has been performed, and
    proceed with a camp-fire ceremony.

    1. Outline the camp rules for the night and
        those for the days following.
    2. Outline the program for the morrow, and
        explain any detail asked about.
    3. Tell some good Scout Stories. (See refer-
        ences to Scout Stories in Boys' Handbook,
        and the Scout Master's Manual).
    4. Have volunteers do stunts for amusement.
    5. Have a number of college or old time songs.
    6. Have a competitive Indian dance around the
        camp fire, by group or by Patrol.

8. Let 9:00 P. M. be the time for bed, and lights out.
    Some of the boys probably come from homes
    where they are used to evening prayers. Always
    give them the chance for the evening prayer before
    turning in, and discountenance any interruption
    from other boys not used to this custom. At the
    time for lights out have the troop bugler, if you
    have one, blow " taps." *You should insist on a*
    Scout's honor on perfect quiet between " lights
    out " or " taps " and arising time or " reveille."
    Also before " taps " is sounded have two of the
    Scouts lower the American flag and put it away
    properly.

SATURDAY OR 2ND DAY.

For daily camp programs see suggestions of Program
XVIII, and of Boys' Handbook, page 153. The following
program is also suggested:

1. Arise at 6:30 or 7 A. M. *The boys should previously*
    have been cautioned to remain quiet on their honor,
    if they awaken earlier, and not make any noise until
    regular arising time, or until " reveille " is sounded.
    Consideration should be shown toward those desir-

ing to sleep. When "reveille" is sounded, or some other means is used of announcing arising time, have everybody turn out in pajamas, swimming suits, etc., for a brisk, snappy five-minute setting-up exercise. After the exercise the flag should be raised, and the Scouts should salute the flag. Then where swimming facilities are possible, everybody should take a morning five-

SETTING-UP EXERCISES IN A SCOUT CAMP

minute dip. This should be understood to be a bath plunge and not a swim, and the boys should take soap and towels for a clean scrub and rub down, and a tooth brush for cleansing the teeth. Then the boys should dress hastily and prepare for breakfast. Prepare breakfast as suggested in Point 2, of Program XVIII, selecting some such menu as that proposed in B. H. list; and it may also be well to have a tryout of Requirement 5 (F. C. S.) in the preparation of pancakes or flapjacks, hoecakes, etc.

2. 8 A. M.   Set aside this half hour for Camp Committee duties, making use of all boys not on some regular assignment in sunning the bed-clothes, cleaning up the tents, etc.

3. 8:30 A. M.   Set aside this hour for morning games,— something lively and popular.

4. 9:30 A. M.   If type of field will permit, use this next hour in practice of the troop drill.

5. 10:30 A. M.   Send out patrols into the field in different directions under orders of Patrol Leaders for signal practice of Semaphore, and International Morse Code.   Also for practice of troop secret codes, if any have been developed.

6. 11:45 A. M.   Have the Scouts themselves prepare their own dinner under your direction, or with the aid of the Assistant Scout Masters.   Give instructions in the methods of cooking one or two articles as those given for Requirement 6 (F. C. S.).   Also give instruction in the use of cooking fires, construction of fire places, etc. *For Information see Boys' Handbook.*

7. After the dishes have been cleaned off and washed, new firewood brought in, and any other little duty attended to, have a half-hour of absolute rest, during which it might be advisable to give advanced instruction in First Aid, etc.

8. 1:45 P. M.   Have a number of inter-patrol contests planned for to take up the afternoon hours, such as lassoing, tomahawk throwing, bandaging, fire-lighting, tent raising, signaling, archery, tug-of-war, running, tilting, jumping, First Aid drills, etc.   Or else give such time to some good outdoor games, such as "lion hunting," "hostile spy," "man-hunt," "flag-raiding," "deer hunt," "bear hunt," etc.

9. 4:00 P. M.   If there are swimming facilities near the camp, a half hour should be given at this time to swimming instruction, water games, etc. *In such case, of course extra precautions should be taken to secure the best means of safety to the different Scouts, such as having watchers on the bank or in boats, a life-saving crew organized among the best swimmers, etc.*

10. Begin the preparation of supper at 5:30 or 6 P. M. and proceed with cooking practice and instructions in a similar manner as at noon.

11. After supper and just before the camp committees begin their duties of straightening up camp, remaking beds, etc., outline the morrow's program and explain details, etc.

12. As the camp-fire is being built and started burning outline the plan of Camp-Fire Council or Pow-wow

SCOUTS AT MESS — THIS TABLE WAS MADE ENTIRELY WITHOUT NAILS BY THE SCOUTS IN THIS PATROL

which should be proposed for camp-fire gatherings, and then continue around the fire with the carrying out of such outlined program. The following number of points for such program are suggested :—

1. Opening of Council by an elected Camp-Fire Chief.

2. Roll Call of Scouts responding with Patrol Call.

3. Reports of the day's contests, award of honors, if you have an honor system developed, etc.

4. Reports of Scouts on different subjects, assignments, etc.

5. Opinion of Scouts on camp life, organization and management.

6. Suggestions proposed for new stunts or events.

7. Complaints.

8. New Scouts proposed for membership.

9. Challenges for inter-patrol and inter-scout contests given and accepted.

10. Short talk by the Scout Master or Assistant on some suitable subject.

11. Social doings, stunts, dances, stories, songs, general entertainment, etc.

12. Challenge contests in such games as " spear fight," " cock fighting," " hand-wrestling," " badger pulling," " forfeit," " bunt bear," " tilting," " pole star," " wolf," " scrum," " poison," etc.

13. If there is still time, tell a good Scout story.

14. 9:30 P. M. " Taps," time for lights out, lowering and furling the flag, and turning in.

SUNDAY OR 3RD DAY.

1. Reveille. Continue the morning program as for yesterday as far as suggestion 3. This should include the swim, setting-up exercise, and raising of the flag.

2. Plan for a morning hike through the woods for the study of woodcraft, noting all tracks, birds, animals, and different sorts of trees as seen en route. Also play some adaptable scouting game while on the move.

3. Arrange to get back to camp before noon and prepare lunch or dinner.

4. After dinner is over, have a rest period of at least an hour, in which the Scouts should remain inactive, listening to Scout stories, comments of trip, outlining of plans, etc.

5. Spend the afternoon in nature-study, or signal practice, or walk assignments, or any such exercise or activity which will be conducive for quiet and orderly action. Have it understood that the boys shall return promptly at supper time or 5 o'clock

(or, at swimming time, if there are such facilities, say at 4 P. M.)

6. 5 P. M.   Begin preparation of supper at this earlier hour in order to have plenty of daylight time for breaking-up and cleaning camp.

A KNOT-TYING PRACTICE IN CAMP

7. Assign to all those not employed in regular camp committee work, the duty of striking tents, rolling canvas, packing camp goods and bedding, and collecting all rubbish for the camp-fire. If a large amount of material is on hand, a wagon might be hired to pack things home, and in such case this

part of the plans should be previously arranged for, and the wagon started homeward at this time.

8. When everything is in order about camp, and the latrine has been filled up, and the camp-fire started, gather around the fire for a final Camp Council, following the same general plan as on the night before, although it would be best not to continue later than 7:00 P. M.

9. Carefully put out the camp-fire in obedience to camping rules, and make the start homeward. Start early enough to arrive home by 9:00 P. M.

PROGRAM XXXI

Scoutcraft Practice

Roll Call — Talk — Map Reports — Requirement 12 — Information — Knot-Tying Contest — Lassoing Contest — Tomahawk Trials — First Aid Contest — Signaling Contest — Bandaging Contest — Estimate Contest — Announcements — Star Study — Adjournment.

This should be an evening meeting, and preparation made therefor at Headquarters with all the exercise materials ready for Scout drills in first aid, signal practice, and patrol formation, as well as games. Contests should be given at this meeting to enliven the boys, and quicken the general interest, provision therefor being made partly by announcement at the last meeting. It would also be well to have a list of the indoor contests posted, or given out at the last meeting as suggested, so that the boys could practice up a bit. These contests might be carried on individually, by choosing sides, or by patrols, and records or score-cards of simple material should be provided for the occasion. It would be best too to have this meeting on a night when no clouds are in the sky, and all the stars are out, so that the Scout could study the heavenly constellations as part of the evening exercises. If this is decided on, either you should prepare yourself sufficiently to point out several of the better known constellations, stars of the greater magnitude, planets, " Milky Way," " North Star," etc., or else get someone to be with you for the evening, who does understand a bit about Astronomy, and who might act also as a Contest Judge for the practice trials.

1. Open the meeting with roll call and flag salute, asking each Scout as his name is called to answer by giv-

ing his Patrol Call, and immediately thereafter to salute the flag.

2. Give a short summary of the results of last meeting, observations of same, etc.

3. Gather in the map assignments as given out at the second meeting back. (See Program XXIX.)

4. Ask how many Scouts have begun to carry out the instruction of Requirement 12. Get definite information, and encourage the Scouts who have not given attention to the same, to start as soon as they can.

5. Have the knot-tying contest. *In counting points it is suggested that you count 5 for first place in any one contest, 3 for second place, and 1 for third place.* In this contest such counts are suggested as: — (1) largest number of knots; (2) most skill and ease in tying; (3) fastest time in tying certain knots of choice, or in completing all knots, etc.

6. Have the lassoing contest. Counts: Best three attempts out of five; method of throwing, etc.

7. While these two contests are going on, and especially while awaiting results of the lassoing contest, it would be interesting to have a tomahawk throwing contest. *For this a large upright board target should be provided and caution should be used not to stand too far away at first. If your target is not wide enough to take all the blows, this might prove too destructive for inside practice, but it will always prove an interesting outdoor event.*

8. Call for volunteers to answer queries as to knowledge of First Aid,— Counts: general knowledge; largest number of questions answered, etc. *It would not be wise to have too many, lest the boys grow weary, but certainly since this is so vital a subject and so absolutely necessary in Scoutcraft, that at least as large a number of questions should be asked as will demonstrate the Scouts' general knowledge, and emphasize in their minds the importance of the subject.* The following general questions are suggested:

    1. What is the need of First Aid knowledge?

    2. What is meant by " presence of mind "? How should a Boy Scout use it?

3. How can you put out burning clothing?
4. How can you help in case of an electric shock?
5. What is the best way of stopping a runaway?
6. How would you treat a person for vomiting?
7. What is a fracture? What is the proper treatment for it?
8. What is a bruise? How is it treated?
9. What is a sprain? How is it treated?
10. What is the treatment for dislocation?
11. How is bleeding treated?
12. What do you suggest as the treatment or first aid in case of poisoning?
13. How would you help someone who is burned or scalded?
14. What is fainting? How treated?
15. What is the first aid for sunstroke or exhaustion?
16. What is the method in treating sunburn?
17. How treat for a bite or a sting?
18. What is the treatment for something in the eye?
19. How treat for cramps or stomach-ache?
20. What should you do for earache? Toothache?
21. What is artificial respiration? When should it be used?

9. Have a signaling contest by teamwork. Send and receive a message by semaphore, and then one by the International Morse Code.
10. Have a contest in first-aid and bandaging by teamwork. Count for skill, time, efficiency and aptitude in the best three out of four bandages applied, etc.
11. Have an estimate contest on Requirement 9 for First Class Scouts. Count for two best estimates out of three for distance, size, number, height and weight.
12. Make announcements for the next two meetings, and arrange for an outdoor athletic contest for the next outdoor meeting.
13. Adjourn to a place where the sky can be clearly seen

and the stars show to best advantage, and proceed
with the instruction in elementary astronomy.

14. End meeting with the Scout Yell and Patrol Calls.

PROGRAM XXXII

Scoutcraft Practice — Outdoor Sports

Announcements — Troop Drill — Lassoing Contest — Toma-
hawk Contest — First Aid Contest — Stretcher Drill — Quarter-
Mile Run — Javelin Contest — Rest Period — Fire-Lighting and
Water-Boiling — Dinner — Camp Duties — Fire Making — Tent
Raising — Signaling — Swimming — Archery — Jumping — Yell
Contest — Tug-of-War — Tilting — Indian Dance — Announce-
ments — Adjournment — Assignments.

*The greater part of a Saturday should be given to this
meeting, and you should have given some special attention
towards arrangements and plans therefor. It is suggested
that some few field events be added to the day's program
other than those mentioned and explained in the Boys' Handbook,— events such as short races, spear or javelin throwing, high jump and broad jump, Indian war dances, etc. If
there is any racing of whatever sort planned for, care should
be taken that such Scouts who want to run are in such
healthy condition that a short sprint or other similar exercise will not be harmful. Each Scout should be requested
to bring his own food supply along, and his individual kit for
preparing the same if he has it. In the sport events materials should be arranged for in plenty of time ahead,—
such as wig-wag flags, tent paraphernalia, poles for high
jumping (if planned for), javelins or spears, bows and arrows for archery contest, lassos, etc. The counts should
be the same as arranged for in Program XXXI and the
same general rules and regulations observed. The field
should be in open and rather flat ground, and not too far
away from your Scout Headquarters, so that materials can
easily be taken to and from the field. But it would be best
to select your field as much in the country as possible.*

*It is presumed that by this time all the Scouts enrolled in
your troop have a full outfit of uniform, mess-kits, etc., as
given in the appendix of the Boys' Handbook: (See pages
359–368, inclusive). The Ax (page 360) will do excel-
lently as a tomahawk.*

1. Having arrived on the grounds or field, start the program with an assembly and short talk outlining

the purpose of the day's exercises, the rules and regulations to be followed, and an outline of events in their approximate order.

2. Devote a short time to troop drill and instruction.

3. Start the regular program of sports with a lasso contest. Use a tree stump or post at suitable distance, and also a moving Scout.

4. Then have a tomahawk contest at 20, 40 and 50 foot spaces. Use a tree stump or board target; *never* use a living, growing tree.

5. Have a First Aid contest by team work in resuscitation drill,— for artificial respiration, etc.

6. Have a First Aid contest by team work in a stretcher drill.

7. Next have a quarter-mile run open to all whom it is perfectly safe to let race.

8. Have a javelin or asegai contest. *In making these spears or javelins some harder wood should be used and sharpened to a point on one end so that when thrown it will stick into the ground. These spears should be about eight feet in length, and slender and light, as in the regulation spear in use in college field-sports. They may even be pointed with an iron head to lend weight to the point. Almost any encyclopedia will give a fair description of such a light spear.*

9. Now have a half hour rest. *The boys will need such a rest both because of the previous exercises, and of the other events still to come. But care should be taken in having the rest, that the boys do not catch cold because of cooling off too rapidly or in the wrong place. Care should always be taken to so arrange the events that health and the bodily interests of your Scouts shall always be best secured.*

10. During this rest or immediately thereafter it would be a very good time to have the fire-lighting and waterboiling contest. *Each competitor should gather his own wood (if in a woodless field, such materials should be furnished), light his fire using not more than two matches, carry his water in a can provided by himself, which should contain as nearly a quart as possible.*

11. When the fires are built, dinner should be prepared,

scout style. *Each Scout should provide and prepare his own food; but all the scouts should plan to eat together.*

12. After dinner is finished, orders should be given to "Clean Camp." *Everything should be left as nearly clean as it was found, and in true scout style and safety.*

13. Now have a fire making contest by rubbing sticks together. (*For instructions, see B. H. pages 70–75*).

14. Next have a tent raising contest by team work, providing materials have been arranged for this event.

15. Then have a signaling contest also by team work. Deploy the Scouts advantageously, and have the trials consist of taking and receiving messages from your central station. Test out both code systems so far made use of.

AN ARCHERY ENTHUSIAST

16. If accommodations and weather will permit it would be well to have a swimming contest for those who know how to swim. *Great care however should be taken in case of this event, and every precaution taken against any accident. Do not allow the boys to stay in the water longer than a half-hour.* If the swimming contest is impossible, have in its stead a 100-yard dash, open for all with exceptions as in the quarter-mile race.

17. As a rest after the last event it would be best to have the archery contest. *If the boys have not already been instructed in the use of bows and arrows and the method of making them (see B. H. page 75–81), their use now will be an incentive towards an awakening interest in this fine sport.*

If the boys have no bows and arrows, such materials should be furnished for the occasion and instruction given in their uses.

18. Now have a running broad jump contest, and while this event is going on have also the high jump, if arranged for. For these events the boys should be arranged in two classes according to size, age, and physical development, etc.

19. Now have another half hour's rest, during which a Yell contest by team work could well be planned for,— the yells to consist of troop yells and Patrol calls, etc.

20. Then a Tug-of-war contest by team work would be fine as another event, to keep up the interest and keep the boys busy.

21. Then have a tilting contest. *For this purpose the staves sufficiently padded at one end can be used as tilting poles. Small rings can be drawn on the ground and the contestants standing in these will try to push one another out of the ring boundaries.*

22. Then have a team work Indian dance contest, by patrol or by group. *This is heavy exercise and cannot be kept up very long at a time, but will certainly prove popular and interesting. It will tire the boys out quicker than any one event if followed with the vim and energy that the usual boy gives to this sort of sport.*

23. Make announcements for the next two meetings, and announce also the results of the day's contests.

24. Adjourn at an early hour with a good ripping Scout Yell, and send the boys home in groups, each group to report by a spokesman of their choice what they noticed en route,— such reports to be due at the next meeting.

PROGRAM XXXIV

Troop Business Session

Order of Business — Entertainment — Star Study — Scout Games — Announcements.

You have already had one business session of the troop, and it should now be time for another, lest the boys forget the parliamentary principles through lack of practice, and in

*order to dispose with accumulated troop business affairs.
As long as you are training the Scout in civic duties, and
the knowledge of parliamentary practice, however simple in
form, such meetings should not come too far apart. Give
the boys a chance to learn by actual practice, and, if the full
Constitution is taken as a model as suggested in Program
XV, there will be need of added instruction at each such
parliamentary session. In such case a business session
should be scheduled, as suggested, for every eighth or ninth
meeting.*

1. Open and conduct the meeting according to your Constitution and By-Laws, proceeding regularly with
   your adopted " Order of Business."

   Under the head of Social Entertainment provision
   should be made for a rest by games, volunteer
   stunts, etc., such as the needs of the occasion seem
   to demand.

2. Since this is an evening meeting, if it should be pleasant, and the sky all alight with stars, it would be
   an excellent opportunity to continue with the study
   and instruction in elementary astronomy. If the
   night is disagreeable without, and there is time, the
   meeting should be followed by a few applicable indoor Scout games, as suggested in B. H.

3. Before the final adjournment, the proper announcements should be made outlining the plans or programs for the next two or three meetings, as
   far as formulated.

PROGRAM XXXV

Field Scouting — General Practice

**On the March — Signal Practice — Rest Period — Lunch —
Use of the Ax — Estimate Practice — Nature Study and Woodcraft — Map-Making Assignments — Adjournment.**

*Get as far out into the open as possible, or take a long
hike putting into practice such of the requirements as will
prove adaptable and sufficient for your purposes. If your
choice is the former suggestion, divide the time about
equally into instruction, scouting practice, and games. Requirements 3, 6, 8, 9, 10 (F. C. S.) can be put into practice
in the field, or on the hike as well. In advance of
this meeting the Scouts should be asked to bring along a*

*younger boy or brother for instruction in Scout principles
as outlined by Requirement 12. Have the boys prepare
for the hike by taking along notebook and pencil for practice in stalking as per Requirement 10.*

1. Go into the fields or woods in Patrol Formation, or
   if circumstances permit play some observation
   game en route such as " Far and Near," " Window
   Observation " (a part of Requirement 4 S. C.
   S.), etc. Or send out two Scouts giving them
   secret instructions as to general route taken, rendezvous at a certain distance, etc., and play, en
   route, such games as " Hare and Hound," " Deer
   Hunt," " Indian Trail," " Lion Hunt," " Through
   Mail," etc. (See B. H. on Games.)
2. Having reached a camp or rendezvous, deploy signal squads in different directions for a series of
   messages. If younger boys are along instruct
   them in what is going on, or else have some of the
   Scouts give this instruction, one new boy each to
   an older Scout.
3. Call in all of the Scouts by whistle or bugle signal,
   and have a half hour's rest or more, during which
   time the Scouts can instruct the younger boys in
   the requirements for Tenderfoot rank, or tell
   stories, or do easy stunts, etc. *If arrangements
   are previously made to have something to eat en
   route, this will be the time to prepare and enjoy
   the lunch. Only a light lunch in this case will be
   needed,— things easily carried and easily prepared.
   For suggestions see menu lists in articles on
   " Camping " in B. H.*
4. If facilities are at hand, and circumstances permit,
   also give instruction at this rest period in the proper
   use of the ax in felling and trimming light timber
   as per Requirement 8 (F. C. S.).
5. Also a try-out can be made either at the rest period,
   or partially while on the hike, of Requirement 9
   (F. C. S.) as to size, number, height, distance, etc.
6. While on the hike call attention to all different trees,
   shrubs, bushes, grasses, mosses, lichens, birds, and
   animals, or their tracks, etc. If flowers are in
   bloom have the boys become familiar with the
   flower construction, also with different plant and

wood smells. The boys should also become familiar under your instruction and caution with the poisonous and nettle plants such as poison ivy in the East, the poison oak in the West, " buck brush " where encountered, and with the stinging nettles. Birds should be kept track of when seen, by such notes as suggested in B. H. p. 86, descriptive notes

READING A SIGN OF THE TRAIL — TURN TO THE LEFT

of wild animals and their tracks should be recorded, etc. For excellent outline form for bird-study see the Boy Scout Diary.

7. When the hike is over, ask the boys to make a map of the country covered from their memory, showing route taken, characteristics of country, location of land marks, courses of streams, etc.— such map to be completed and handed in for use at Headquarters, at the earliest opportunity, or next meeting.

8. Make announcements for the next few meetings, and adjourn with the Scout Yells and Patrol Calls.

PROGRAM XXXVI

First Aid Practice — Elementary Astronomy

Opening of Meeting — First Aid Drills — Address — Emergency Instructions — Games and Announcements — Star Study — Instruction — Field-Observation — Adjournment.

This evening's meeting should be given over to First Aid practice during the first part of the evening, if the sky is clear enough to study the stars, but if the sky is overcast with clouds, a few games should be interspersed between part of the First Aid practice, and the latter work receive fairly concentrated attention during the whole evening. In case the stars can be studied, and it is clear enough to pick out the different principal constellations, the boys will need no intervening exercise, but should find plenty in this sky-study to create and hold the interest. A good book for the boys to read, if so interested, and excellent for the use of the Scout Master is " Starland " by Robert S. Ball,— a book of exceptional suggestions and important information set forth in a simple, clearly defined manner,— just the thing in fact, for the boy. For more advanced information for the Scout Master and as an aid in constellation study see J. D. Steele's " Popular Astronomy," especially Part III, and " Astronomy with the Naked Eye" by Garrett P. Serviss. If circumstances permit a study of the stars, one or two telescopes or field-glasses should be borrowed to aid the eye in seeing further and clearer and enlarging the planets; a telescope, though, is not necessary for first study,— only an excellent help. In the larger cities, large tripod telescopes are usually found on street-corners or in park squares, whose owners charge only five or ten cents for a look at the planets and the moon. Tell the boys of this, so that they may take advantage of the opportunity, should their interest be aroused.

In preparation for First Aid practice, all bandages and appliances should be at hand for demonstration instruction and practice in all the different First Aid drills and methods. It might also be a good thing to have a speaker for this meeting, a physician, surgeon, or nurse to talk on some physiological subject, such as " The Bones," " Health," " The Body in Action," " The Nervous System," " Mind and Body," etc. Or it might be a good suggestion, also, to get some authority or student of astronomy to help out in the star-study.

1. Begin the meeting with a few words outlining the program of the evening, or with a short yell practice, or roll call with Patrol call answers, etc.

2. Have a few of the regular First Aid drills by assignment, such as stretcher drill, head bandage, arm bandage with splints, leg with splints, collar bone, resuscitation drill, etc. (Only roller bandages should be used.)

3. If a speaker has been arranged for as suggested, have the talk at this time. *This should be well understood to be brief,— not more than ten minutes' duration,— and right to the point.* After the talk, allow a few extra minutes in which the Scouts may ask questions, if interested.

4. Go over the treatment for accidents and emergencies as outlined in the Boys' Handbook, and explain all hazy points. Have the boys tell by assignment or voluntarily what to do for treatment of the most common emergencies, such as cuts, bruises, sprains, burns, eye troubles, toothaches, poisons, dog bites, snake bites, insect stings, fits, freezing, etc. *Two most complete and excellent small books on First Aid for Scout Masters and Scouts alike, replete with explanations, illustrations, and descriptions are "Emergencies" by Charlotte V. Gulick (Ginn & Co., 1909), and "Emergency Notes" by G. R. Butler, M. D. (Funk & Wagnall Co., 1889). A more complete work on the same subject, though of same size, is "Johnson's First Aid Manual, 4th edition (paper covered, Johnson & Johnson, 1909).*

5. If there is to be no star-study this evening, close the meeting with, or else intersperse before suggestion 4, a few suitable indoor Scout games. End the meeting with announcements and the Scout Yells.

6. If it is clear enough for star study, the announcements should be made for the next meeting, and then all should adjourn to some suitable open place where the astronomy study should begin. If telescopes have been procured, it would be best to have at hand some simple affair to serve as a rest for the glasses so that they may be held as steadily as possible. From charts pick out the positions of as

many of the planets as can be seen, and have all the
boys understand the difference between the planets
and the stars proper. Outline simply the main ideas
of the planetary or Copernican theory of evolution,
and briefly explain shooting stars, meteors, comets,
nebula, etc. Tell about the different moons, the
method of measuring star distances, the coldness
of the earth's moon surface, the reason for eclipses,
and reason for changes of the seasons, etc. Tell
about sun spots, rotation, revolution, "Milky
Way," and constellations; and answer as many of
the interested questions as possible. Pick out the
main constellations of the month. *These can be
learned usually from students of astronomy, are
outlined in the book by Mr. G. P. Serviss.*

7. Adjourn the meeting with the Scout Yells and Patrol
Calls, or with some of the old well-known songs.

PROGRAM XXXVII

Cooking Instruction — Requirement 6

**Cooking-Squads — Cooking-Fires — Requirement 6 — Try-Out
— Scout Games — Precautions — Adjournment.**

*This special meeting has been suggested because of the
real need of cooking practice in the open under careful leadership and instruction. In this case as much time as possible should be given to the proper trials of this requirement,
trying the preparation of every article. This should be out
in the open in the woods or fields, and all materials should
be made ready beforehand, each Scout packing along his
own rations and kit. Such a meeting, needing so much instruction, will probably require both your close attention
and also that of your assistants.*

1. Get out into the open, and divide the troop into
squads of two for the cooking practice.

2. Give instructions in the proper building of a cooking
fire, and a fireplace. Have the boys follow your
instructions, and point out their errors. (*See B.
H., page* 149.)

3. Have a try-out of the proper cooking of different articles given in the requirement,— all the articles, if

there is plenty of time. (*For instructions see B. H., pp.* 149–151.)

4. If there is still time have some one or two good active Scout games of choice.

5. Make the usual announcements, and in this case take the usual precautionary methods against spread of fires, accumulation of trash, etc. Put out the fires carefully, and clean up the refuse and odds and ends.

6. March home in Patrol Formation.

PROGRAM XXXVIII
Scout Reporting
Announcements — Assignments — Games.

This meeting is similar in purpose to those of Programs XXXIII and XXVIII, and therefore the same suggestions will apply as well in this case. A good plan also would be to arrange to visit some museum or zoölogical garden for observation of birds and animals, each Scout to make a brief report of animals and birds observed, personal impressions, etc. Also at this time the Scouts should have their attention called to Requirement 4 (F. C. S.), and urged to fulfill this necessary test as soon as possible.

1. Make announcements for the next two meetings, before giving out assignments for observation reports.

2. Look over the assignment suggestions of Program XXXIII. Or instead of these suggestions have a game such as " Scouting " (p. 298 B. H.), " Flag Raising " (p. 306 B. H.), " Stalking and Reporting " or " Spider and Fly " or " Stalking " (p. 307 B. H.), " Across the Border " or " Surprise " (S. M. M.).

PROGRAM XXXIX
Scout Instruction — Efficiency Percentages
Opening of Meeting — General Instruction — Games — Drills — Estimate Contest — Announcements — Adjournment.

The purpose of this meeting should be general instruction and demonstration in regard to any points not clearly understood in any of the First Class Scout requirements. In order to ascertain from the Scouts themselves just what things to consider, it might be best to ask each Scout to hand in before the meeting a list of the points which are not quite clear to him, so that the needed instruction can be given collectively or individually, or else to have a general question quiz. Some of the First Aid information should be reviewed, and also nature observation of living things and starland, and topography or map making.

A system of efficiency percentages is also a good subject to introduce at this time. It will help out in the final tests, and may prove of great interest to the boys in their desire to become best versed in Scout principles and proficient in Scout activities. Kept individually or by patrol it will also serve as an excellent record system for reference use by Scouts, Scout Masters and other officers, and by parents. Quite a number of Scout Masters already have some sort of honor system or efficiency records, such as this scheme proposes and includes, and the majority are having exceptional success with the idea. Such a record can be kept in a great number of ways, ranging all the way from simple unit marks to such a system as used in baseball records of league standings, batting averages, etc.

Of course too much time should not be taken up with continual attention to the necessary instruction. A good start, fifteen or twenty minutes of concentrated attention with persistent effort, a little play, and a bit more of work with mechanical action or movement, a closing with a feeling of free spirit and fellowship, a creation of enthusiasm, a binding of ties toward one another and to the organization,— that should always be the general plan and the purpose of every meeting with boys. Therefore during the evening, interspersed between parts of the instruction, there should be suitable games and exercises, drills and practices, etc.

1. Open the meeting in some suitable way by roll call in which each Scout will do some stunt at the call of his name, or each shall give his Patrol Call.

2. Proceed with whatever needed instruction is required, in whatever way is deemed best.

3. Have one or two suitable indoor Scout games of choice.

4. Proceed with the evening instruction. Have a few practice drills in First Aid and Signaling.

5. Have a Requirement 9 (F. C. S.) contest.

6. Make announcements of the plans for the next few meetings.
7. Adjourn with Scout's choice of closing exercises — yells, songs, stunts, etc.

PROGRAM XL

Swimming and Athletics

Swimming Instruction — Substitutions — Water Games — The Natatorium — Salt Water Versus Fresh Water — Stroking — Water Emergencies.

There should be at least one meeting before the Final First Class Scout examinations at which swimming instruc-

A SWIMMING RACE — READY

tion should be given. Of course there are some parts of the country where there are no facilities for such sport, either natural or artificial, but the majority of American boys have a chance of learning to swim at some time or another during the year. As a substitute plan for this meeting in place of swimming instruction, the troop might get out into the fields for a signal practice, have an athletic contest under your instruction in proper methods, or a visit might be taken to some interesting place in the city or country.

In case swimming is to be the purpose of this meeting, it would be best to have along several older fellows for the occasion, to give instruction in the proper methods and in water games, and also to provide for plenty of protection against accidents. If the boys care to do so, it would be a good stunt for the whole troop to visit the nearest baths or natatorium for this afternoon swim. The price is very reasonable in most places, safety is provided for, and care is usually taken that the water is of the right temperature for the time of the year.

Quite a number of boys will have opportunity to learn swimming only at salt-water baths or at the ocean beaches. Salt-water swimming is exhilarating and excellent, but because of the difference in the floating qualities of the waters, boys are better able to cope with every sort of water accident, if they have first learned to swim in fresh water.

As much instruction should be given at this meeting as possible. Probably the majority of the boys who can already swim only know one or two strokes at the most, while for safety and efficiency in saving others they will have need of knowing all different strokes,— such as side-stroke, backstroke, breast-stroke, trudgeon, crawl, etc. There are three ways of using the legs, and four or five ways of using the arms; and any ingenious person can invent from these movements almost any number of combination strokes. The proper methods of floating and diving might also be demonstrated, as well as the several methods of helping out in water accidents. (See B. H., pp. 279–288.)

PROGRAM XLI

An Afternoon Hike — Signal Practice

Nature Study — Animals and Plants — Book Aids — Stalking — Observation Records — Bird Protection — Signal Practice — Geology Talk — Announcements.

The purpose of this meeting is to give ample provision for nature-study under leadership and instruction. Woods, perennial and annual plants, animals and birds should be studied for information, preferably with a few good books on trees and plants, birds, insects, and animals, afield with you. If you have such books, show the boys how to gain definite information from the books by observing the characteristics of the objects and things studied. Also instruct the Scouts in the proper stalking methods, and the manner of recording observations. Also tell them of the need of protection for birds and animals, and of the progress of such movements, so far as you know.

During part of the afternoon, signal practice by Semaphore (or code most in use) by secret code, or by whistles might be resorted to for a change.

Another good idea would be to have somebody along on this hike who could explain to the boys the main principles of geology and the reasons for the local land formation. Most of your boys, from thirteen to sixteen years, are taking the study of Physical Geography in their

SENDING A MESSAGE BY SEMAPHORE

high school courses, and are already familiar with the general knowledge of the earth history, but all will need practical instruction as to their own locality, and to the methods of applying their accumulated general knowledge along such lines to their daily observation.

Either before the start is made, or when on the way back home announcements ought to be made as to plans for the next one or two meetings. Arrive home not later than 9 o'clock.

PROGRAM XLII

Troop Business Session

Parliamentary Practice — Entertainment — Interesting Topic Talk — Contests — Scout Demonstration — Order of Business — Games — New Business — Announcements — Adjournment.

This meeting, of course, is similar to the one outlined in Program XXXIV, is suggested with the same purpose in view, and should be arranged for in the same way. The amount of parliamentary practice you plan to carry out at this meeting depends largely, of course, on the importance which you expect to give to civic instruction and practice.

Such plans as you have for other events will vary necessarily with the amount of such parliamentary practice. But the Social Entertainment Committee should always be urged to have some good stunts and games planned for.

As part of such entertainment, if the Scouts so wish, the Scout Master might arrange to give a few minutes' talk at each of these business sessions on some live topic,— as an explanation of the " Common Court System," " Messages from Other Troops," " Mosquito and Fly Crusade," " The Great World Powers," " Aviation," " Current Events," etc.

For amusement of the Scouts some sort of indoor contest might be provided for this meeting,— an award and forfeit contest on any or several of the requirements or indoor games is suggested. Also committees might be appointed at this time to make arrangements for a public Scout entertainment or for an inter-troop field day or for both,— the committees to turn in at the next indoor meeting tentative plans of such proposed demonstrations, with suggested dates for the same, etc.

1. Proceed with the meeting as outlined by your adopted " Order of Business " in your By-Laws.
   (1) Arrange for some suitable new games and stunts as proposed by the Entertainment or Sports Committee.
   (2) Under the head of " New Business " the proposed Scout Demonstrations should be introduced, talked over by all the Scouts, committees appointed, and such other necessary arrangements made.
2. Before the final adjournment, the regular announcements for the next two meetings should be outlined.
3. Adjourn in the regular way, or by Scouts' choice.

PROGRAM XLIII
Observation Scouting

Group Divisions — Assignments — Message Delivery — Map Making — Approximate Locations — Town — Approximate Locations — Country — Approximate Distances — Leaf Collection — Photography — Reports — Announcements.

This should be an afternoon or evening after school where squads of three or four or whole patrols can work together. It will be unnecessary for the Scout Masters to get out into the field, as most of this Scouting should be carried on from a central base or home rendezvous. But, if a pleasant day has been chosen and the whole afternoon is to be given to Scouting, it would probably be best to combine the observation practice with a short hike, and direct the work of patrols or squads from a field base.

1.   Divide the troop into patrols or half-patrols each under a regular leader (a patrol leader or his assistant), or else make such equal divisions into groups having common particular interests, and appoint to each group its leader for the day.

2.   Apportion one or two assignments to each group providing some definite work for each boy in the group or giving enough in the assignments to keep all members of each group busy. A suggested list of such assignments follow : —

(1)   Send out a message to someone at a distance, each Scout in the group to go and come by a different route, within a certain limit of time. And also each Scout to make map of route taken, noting all principal places passed, important buildings, tall trees, stiles, stone fences, creeks, condition of fields, woodlands, peculiarities of trees or fences or road-ways, and keep a record of tracks seen en route with approximate location on drawing.

(2)   Get a plat made of certain squares of the town or certain sections of the open land, each Scout in the group to make a certain portion of the drawing or to take down a certain proportion of the needed notes for such a map, and each Scout being given his assignment at direction of his leader while in the field.

(3)   If in town make a map of the whole or a certain proportion of its area, showing all approximate positions of public buildings, telephone booths, hydrants, fire stations, etc., giving walking distance of each from a common center, or the city or town hall.

(4)   If in the country or in the fields make a map of a certain area containing several fields, giving approximate area of each, computed upon a rectangular basis by pacing off the boundaries, etc. The map in this case should show approximate locations of wells, barns, all houses, garden patches, rocky ground, etc., and show nature and use of each field, how planted, how extensive, elevations, amount of irrigation, etc. Also a collection of soil should be made, a small amount (a handful) taken from several positions of the assigned area, or wherever the soil seems to change in formation, looks or color, approximate positions of such examples noted on map, and some filed for future analysis along with finished map.

(5)   Send out a group to determine approximate pacing distance between several well known buildings or landmarks or noticeable trees, the group to compute approximate size of building, height of tree, etc.

(6)   Send out a group to obtain leaves of a certain number of trees (25 for each boy), each tree to be of a different specie if possible, and map to be made showing approximate position of tree in respect to surrounding locality, approximate height, girth at base, distance from a certain known landmark, etc. Also 10 leaves each from ground-plants or scrubs, showing locations, distances from landmarks, size of plants.

(7)   If there is one group interested in photography send it out by wheel or on hike to make a collection of bird and animal photographs. Each Scout to make two photographs of wild birds of different species, and, if possible, a photograph of one wild animal.

3. If an afternoon is given to this observation Scouting, appoint a certain time to limit the field work, and have the Scouts gather at a certain place or local headquarters with their reports. If an evening is used, have the Scouts all report before dark, and only give short assignments.

4. Make announcements for next two meetings, and comment upon work of the day showing value thereof and the education in such observation.

PROGRAM XLIV

Evening Scout Drills

Demonstration Day Program Discussion — Drill Assignments — Address on Geology — Drill Practice — Announcements.

This should be an evening given to drill work before the day set for the Scout Demonstrations, and all such drills as can be given inside should be practiced. Games should be arranged for, or some other means of entertainment provided aside from the drill practice, as a rest period or recreative change. The program for Demonstration Day should be outlined and any changes as discussed and suggested by the Scouts should be arranged for. Since the main features of the demonstration will be wall scaling, signaling, first aid and stretcher drill, lassoing, etc., arrangements should be made previous to this meeting to see that all such material is at hand at Headquarters for such practice. A speaker should also be arranged for, preferably a Civil or Mining Engineer, or a Geologist, who will give a brief talk on land formations, soils and their origins, rocks and soil sediments, or such similar topics. Or a speech from a Scout Master from a neighboring district or the Scout Commissioner might be a drawing card at this meeting and prove of great interest and creative of enthusiasm among the boys.

1. Begin the evening by a brief talk outlining the program for Demonstration Day, and putting the subject before the boys for a general discussion. *A committee has been appointed at a previous meeting to arrange such a program and by consultation with the member of that committee the Scout Master should have a pretty definite knowledge of what the boys most want and the*

arrangements of events. But the whole troop should have a final discussion of the plan of events, with minor changes, etc.

2. Assign different drills to the different patrols each under the direction of their respective leaders. Such suggested drills should be First Aid, Stretcher, Staff, Wall Scaling, Signal Reading, etc. After a certain practice of each of these drills new assignments should be made so that each patrol will have a chance to take part in the practice.

3. If a speaker has been arranged for, he should be announced after a drill practice of forty or fifty minutes. If a Scout officer is to talk, his remarks should preferably be on the advancement of Scout work, or word of a greeting to the boys from their fellows in other parts of the districts, with announcements as to what particular troops are doing, etc. If the talk is to be technical, the address should be couched in simple language, be brief, and open to questions aroused by the interest of the boys.

4. The address should not last longer than half an hour, and the remainder of the evening should be given to drill continuation or practice of individual work, such as throwing the lariat, map reading, distance, size and weight judging, etc.

5. Make announcements for next two meetings and adjourn in the usual way — according to By-Laws, or by Scout Yells, Scout Reports, etc.

PROGRAM XLV

Scout Demonstrations

Parents and Friends — Meeting-Place — Judges — The Contest — Arrangements — Program Talk — Troop Drills — First Aid Staff — Fire Lighting — Signal Codes — Wall-Scaling — Knot-Tying — Bandaging — Scout's Pace — Compass — Lasso — Computation — Trailing — Archery — Swimming — Nature-Work — Results and Awards — Adjournment.

This meeting has been carefully prepared for and all arrangements attended to by the Scouts. For some time previous drill work in the different Scout activities has been carefully carried on in preparation for this event. It should by all means be public, and the parents and friends should be invited to come.

The meeting place should be in the open where there is plenty of room for the demonstrations, but in some locality where parents can easily attend. All paraphernalia should be on the ground, the Scout Master carefully checking up the work of the Scout Committee of Arrangements to avoid any delays or mixup.

This demonstration may have been arranged for several participating troops of the same or nearby localities, and if such is the case competent judges should be obtained who will decide as to best performance of Scout drills by troop or patrol. In such case a point system should have been previously adopted. (See Scout Master's Manual, Chapter VI.)

It is intended that these Scout demonstrations will be more for the purpose of showing to parents and friends the achievements of the boys in their Scout work, rather than to plan for a regular Scout contest, but a contest will perhaps awaken a keener spirit of rivalry between patrols of like ages, and between troops, promote the feeling of gang fellowship within the troop, and insure better results in striving for awards for best efforts.

Arrange the plan of events so that several things can be carried on at the same time, but make such arrangements so that each Scout will have a chance to enter several different events and prove his skill and efficiency in the various activities. Do not attempt too many events.

1. All Scouts having assembled, draw them up in troop formation with order "At Ease," and address those assembled in a few well-chosen words outlining the purpose of the meeting, and explaining, in case of inter-troop contest, the methods of awards and point-system in use.
2. Proceed with patrol and troop drills.
3. Show method of Stretcher Drill, and First Aid Drill. See Part IV, page 240.
4. Have a brief Staff Drill. See page 228.
5. Divide patrols into groups of two to show method and speed in building and lighting fires with or without matches, and speed in boiling water.
6. Show method of sending and receiving signals at long and short distances, by Semaphore or by

other signal code. Demonstrate by small groups, general efficiency and speed.

7. Show wall-scaling by patrol, and keep record of time made by competing patrols.

8. Show ease and ability of knot-tying of any of six or seven knots made on call.

9. Show ability in first aid work in bandaging for sprains, breaks, fainting, etc.

WALL-SCALING PRACTICE

10. Demonstrate ability to go a mile in twelve minutes at Scout's pace.

11. Demonstrate knowledge of compass points.

12. Demonstrate ability in use of the lariat.

13. Demonstrate ability in judging distance, size, weight, height, etc.

14. Show method of scouting in field for tracking and demonstrate knowledge of several tracks.

15. Demonstrate methods of archery.

16. Have a swimming contest, if facilities and weather will permit. It will always be necessary to take the usual precautions to insure health and safety.

17. Given several different leaves of different species of common trees of the locality, demonstrate knowledge of each tree by description and habits of same.

18. If awards are given for points, have the results of the decisions made before adjourning from the field.

19. Adjourn with a few brief remarks, and call for Scout yells and patrol calls.

PROGRAM XLVI

Scout Evening — Preliminary Tests

Talk — Signal   Practice — Speed — First   Aid   Quiz — Map
Reading — Computation — Nature Study — Good Turn Reports
— Scout Games — Star Study — Adjournment.

*The time is approaching for the examinations for First
Class Scouts, and an evening should be set aside as a special appointed time for preliminary tests, so that the weak
places may be discovered, and both the Scouts and the
Scout Master know the approximate results of all the previous preparation. At this stage of scouting, the Scout
should be able to give a good account of himself in almost
any emergency, and tests should be carried on with this in
view.*

*The Scout Master should know by this time what Scouts
are lacking in the first or swimming requirement, and also
all those who have fulfilled Requirement 4 and Requirement 12. It will now be necessary to determine wherein
the Scouts are proficient or lacking in the other requirements.*

1. Open the meeting by a brief talk as to the purpose
    of this meeting, the success of last meeting, and
    plans for future meetings.
2. With assistance of Patrol Leaders or Assistant
    Scout Masters, divide the patrols into groups of
    two to take and receive signal code messages.
    Give a forty or fifty word paragraph to each for
    practice, and time contestants.
3. Ask questions concerning advanced first aid, giving
    first one question to one Scout then some other
    different question to another, and so on. As —
    " What should you do in case of fire? " " What
    treatment should you give for ivy poisoning? "
    etc.
4. Have the Scouts individually show ability in reading
    different prepared maps, *which you should have on
    hand.*
5. Have a judging contest as to size, weight, height, etc.
6. Handing out different leaves, have Scouts show
    ability in describing the trees or plants from
    which they came. Also name six common wild
    birds, and ask description of same, giving form,

color, call, and habits of certain animals and the name of same.

7. Call for a few reports of " Daily Good Turn."
8. If time is left spend the remainder of evening in Scout games, or if the sky is clear in a study of the sky and constellations.
9. Make announcements for two following meetings and adjourn.

PROGRAM XLVII

Signal and Cooking Practice

Marching or Assignments — Signal Code Practice — Cooking Practice — Dinner — Observation Scouting — Reports — Adjournment.

Before the Scout examination for First Class Work, an extra practice should be given all the Scouts for signaling and cooking, and perhaps a practice of Requirements 8 and 10. Materials should be taken into the open for an afternoon or all day hike, and enough should be provided so that each Scout will have a chance under the guidance of the Scout Master to cook each of the prescribed articles of Requirement 6.

1. Having met at Scout Headquarters, get out to the selected camp site, either in patrol formation, or marching order, or by assignment by patrol on different routes, to report observations, etc.; limiting time of arrival at rendezvous.
2. All having arrived at camp site, and placed materials and paraphernalia for safe keeping, and cleaned camping site, assign positions to half-patrols each in charge of a leader or assistant, order to deploy or take positions, and give out messages for signal practice. See that each Scout of each group has a chance to send and receive messages of some length (forty or fifty words).
3. Make assignments by half-patrol or squad to gather fire-wood for camp and cooking, to make fire-places with bricks, stones or clay, to obtain fresh water, etc., and then have each Scout grouped in patrol bunches, light and make his own fire, and assign to each some different thing to prepare for cooking.

Enough time should be given to this in inspection and needed instruction to insure success, and give attention to each Scout. If there is time each Scout should be assigned three of the required articles chosen by drawing lots from printed slips of paper in the Scout Master's hat. When enough has been cooked, and such food has been kept warm as is necessary, the cooking practice should stop and the things cooked should be eaten, if properly cooked and attended to. Then clean camp.. . . . .

A PATROL PYRAMID IN SIGNAL PRACTICE

4. If there is time left in the afternoon for observation Scouting, send half-patrols into the woods to gather leaves of different trees and study the trees at first hand, observing nature of wood, bark, height of bush, method of branching, etc. Each group will stay out thirty or forty minutes, making notes of routes taken, trees observed, descriptions of same, and of all birds, animals and tracks discovered, with respective descriptions.

5. Having called all squads back to camping spot, collect or hear reports, and then adjourn, after making announcements for next meeting. Call attention to the proximity of the examination and also say a few words as to the importance of being prepared, the contemplated results, etc. State also what the general plan of Scouting will be, following the examination.

PROGRAM XLVIII
First Class Scout Examinations — Indoors

Examiner — Requirement 1 — Requirement 4 — Outdoor Examinations — Requirement 2 — Requirement 8 — Estimate Test — Requirement 5 — Requirement 10 — Requirement 11 — Requirement 12 — Evening Address — Scout Games or Scout Yarn — Adjournment.

The arrangements for this meeting have already been made and should be prepared for as in the case of the Second Class Scout examinations,— by having present as an examiner, a member or all of the Court of Honor, or a visiting Scout Master or Scout Commissioner, who will conduct the examinations.

Unless there are proper facilities and the weather permits examination in Requirement 1 will either be pre-determined or deferred until a future set date for fulfillment. Requirement 4 should have already been performed and the carrying out of this requirement will be recorded when accomplished and vouched for by the Scout Master.

This will leave for the evening examination Requirements, 2, 5, a part of 8, a part of 9, 10, 11 and 12. The bulk of this Scout examination will therefore be given outdoors, so the evening program of requirement tests should be so arranged in different sections as to provide for some means of entertainment either in scout games or in a short address of some live topic interesting to the boys by a member of the Court of Honor, the visiting Scout Master, or the Scout Master in charge.

1. Requirement 2. Proficiency can be shown by exhibition of bank book and citation of method of earning the money.

2. Those Scouts who have prepared themselves on the second section of Requirement 8, will present their article of carpentry or cabinet-making and show method of making the same.

3. An examination can be given best indoors for size, number, and weight judging. Given a certain number of things each Scout will estimate results as nearly correct as possible on same examination paper used for Requirement 5.

4. Have prepared six or seven lists of questions for requirement 5, ten or twelve to the list, and select

lists at random for the Scouts to answer by paper and pencil.

5. For Requirement 10, some will have prepared themselves specially in knowledge of trees and plants, some in knowledge of birds, and some of animals. Each will select his part of the Requirement and describe as directed, ten species of plants, six species of birds, or six species of animals. Each Scout will also be expected to show his ability to point out the North Star and three constellations if the weather will so permit the stars being seen.

6. Satisfactory evidence will be furnished for Requirement 11, if a statement signed by the teacher and parents or guardian is presented by the Scout. This statement will show whether the Scout has applied the Scout principles in his daily life, in the estimation of those who know him best.

7. Requirement 12 is examined for by a brief examination of the Tenderfoot recruit presented by each applicant for First Class rank.

8. If an address is arranged for the speaker should now be introduced (or immediately following point 2, of the suggested program). The topic selected should be of interest to all the boys.

9. If time permits the remainder of the evening should be spent in an indoor game of Scouts' choice, or in story telling by the Scout Master.

10. Make announcement for following meetings and adjourn.

PROGRAM XLIX

First Class Scout Examination — Outdoor

Requirement 3 — Requirement 8 — Requirement 7 — Requirement 9 — Requirement 6 — Adjournment.

The Scout examination outdoors should be given as soon after the evening examination as possible, preferably having the first on a Friday evening and the outdoor meeting on the Saturday afternoon following. Judges should be arranged for as before, and with the same judges as of the evening before, if at all possible.

Examination will be given in Requirements 3, 6, 7, 8, and part of 9. Those Scouts who have fulfilled Requirement 8 by producing an article of carpentry the evening before, are deemed to have taken the examination in Requirement 8, but this will not bar them trying out in first part of test. Of course where light standing timber is not available, this test will either be deferred or previously accomplished at a favorable opportunity, or else light cut trees will be furnished, the Scouts will demonstrate method of felling and trimming thereof.

Parts of Requirement 9 in judging for distance and height can best be determined in the open.

1. Divide the patrols into squads of two to take and receive a message of some twenty or thirty words. Each Scout should have a chance to both take and receive messages, and show proficiency in signaling. Any code may be used.

2. If arrangements have been made for Requirement 8, each Scout should prove his ability to show proper method of felling and trimming the timber provided.

3. Send out Scouts in different directions short distances to make notes for maps of surrounding sections of country. Upon return each Scout will make a rough sketch map from his notes fulfilling the directions of the requirement. Also each Scout will be expected to show proficiency in correctly reading already prepared maps, and in pointing out any compass direction without help of compass.

4. Examine each Scout for ability to judge distance and height from his surroundings, giving three trials to each.

5. Having prepared a place for the cooking examination, each Scout will prepare his own fire, and the judge will assign at random any of the articles of Requirement 6. Scouts will be expected to explain to the judge, or a Tenderfoot, or a new recruit, the methods followed. The same preparations are made for this examination as in the cooking practice as suggested in Program XLVI.

6. Having cleaned camp thoroughly in scout style, the meeting will be ready for adjournment. Make the usual announcements for next succeeding meetings and close with Scout yells.

PROGRAM L

Afternoon Hike — Archery

Nature-Study Hike — Soil Collection — Geology Information — Archery — Supper — Adjournment.

This afternoon should be spent in the open, preferably on a nature study hike. If a whole afternoon can be spent in scouting, materials for a Scout supper should be taken along so as to have a Scout meal in the field. In that case part of the afternoon and evening can be spent in Scout

A SCOUT HIKE IN WINTER — SCOUTS ON SNOWSHOES

field games. Also it would be an excellent idea to take bows and arrows into the field so that an archery contest can be carried on. This will serve to train both the eye and the muscle and the exercise is typically a scout activity.

1. Plan the hike for a walk through the woods and over rough ground where the trees and plants can be personally observed as to leaves, bark, method of growth, flowers, system of foliage, and where the land formation can be studied at first hand. Take something along to collect soil specimens or peculiar looking minerals for future analysis.

Have the boys ask questions freely about things observed, and open the subject to the discussion of all.

Some expert on geology or physical geography to accompany the Scouts on this hike will help out wonderfully in creating interest in the country formation, and in answering questions.

2. After the hike, a suitable spot should be chosen for an archery contest and for other Scout games.

3. If a Scout supper is planned for, the games should be followed by its preparation and having cleaned camp and told a few stories, the Scouts will adjourn for the homeward hike.

PROGRAM LI

First Class Scout Investiture

Opening Talk — Evening Address — Investiture Ceremonial — Announcements — Refreshments — Flag Salute —" America."

This meeting is important as it marks the culmination of first endeavors and opens up the field for greater activity along specialized lines and the achievement of special Scout honors. It is the goal toward which all the Scouts in the troop have constantly been striving, and toward which all the foregoing meetings have tended in their training. Achievement of First Class Scout rank should be attended with extra and as impressive ceremony as possible.

A speaker for the occasion should be obtained, and also a member representing the Court of Honor or the Local Council should be present to give out the badges of First Class Scout rank, and make a brief address on Scouting. Parents and friends might well be invited, and arrangements might likewise be made for special refreshments of ice-cream, cake, etc., in honor of the occasion.

Before the meeting it will be necessary to have ordered sufficient First Class Scout badges, so the meeting should be planned for long enough after the First Class Scout Examinations to know how many badges to order. The badges for both Scouts in file and in office are described in the Boys' Handbook, pp. 13 and 18. They are both of safety pin style; to be worn upon the sleeve. The price is 15 cents.

1. Open the meeting with a few well-chosen remarks as to importance of meeting and purpose of achievements in Scouting.
2. Have the address of the speaker for the occasion, preferably on the " National Scout Movement." *Limit this address to fifteen minutes.*
3. Proceed with the investiture ceremony as for Second Class Scouts (see Programs XXV and VII), with such additions or changes as seem best to make the ceremony more impressive. The member of the " Court of Honor " will give out the badges, and as he names the successful Scouts, each will come forward from the line to have the badge pinned on his arm.

The Officer of the Scout Council or " Court of Honor " will then address the Scouts in a brief address and the boys will then take their seats.

4. Following the investiture ceremonial the announcements will be made as to succeeding meetings, and the Scout Master will briefly outline the extent of work just covered by the First Class Scouts.
5. Refreshments are served, if provided for.
6. Scouts are called to attention in column of patrols, and salute is made to the flag. This should be followed by the singing of " America," and then the meeting is adjourned.

PROGRAM LII

Scout Reporting — Field Practice

Afternoon Observation Hike — Interesting Places — Observation Walk — Nature Study Assignments — Signal Practice — Lunch — Homeward Bound — Assignments.

This should be another meeting for the open fields or woodlands where the Scouts can spend the time in suitable games, and in scout reporting as suggested in Program XLII. If an afternoon or whole Saturday is given to this meeting, a hike should be arranged for to cover the greater part of the day, and arrangements made to have a Scout lunch on the march. Or in place of a hike through the woods, some interesting historical place could be visited, or a trip made to a zoo or museum. In the latter case the Scouts should be asked to keep their eyes open so that an observation contest as to things noticed might be later carried on.

1. Get out into the field toward a previously appointed rendezvous, or else start on the cross country hike or visit to the museum or other interesting place. Take along signal flags and note books for observation notes. Also each Scout should carry sufficient rations for a light lunch, if on a full day hike.

2. After spending a certain time on the hike make assignments for nature study work, such as bird and animal stalking, tree study, geological formations, observation, etc. After spending a certain length of time as limited by the assignment, all will gather at the rendezvous, and hand in their reports. Make these reports open for discussion.

3. Have a signal practice if not too late.

4. If the Scout lunch is arranged for prepare and eat it, while the discussion is going on. Then follow with an interesting Scout story.

5. Send each half-patrol home on different routes under direction of a patrol leader or assistant, and ask for observation reports to be turned in for future reading.

PROGRAM LIII

Business Meeting

Plan of Meeting — Evening Address — Troop Finances — New Scout Work Suggestions — Announcements.

The evening business meeting should be arranged for as on previous occasions, and carried out according to plan of meeting adopted in the troop by-laws before the real business of the meeting begins. It might be arranged to obtain a speaker to talk on some interesting subject. If this is done, it should be by the actions of the entertainment committee upon some topic agreed upon by them. This committee might also arrange for such other entertainment as seems advisable and permissible by the Scout Master.

Discussion of troop finances by the Scout Master and

troop members should be in order at this meeting, and means and plans for carrying on the scout work by interesting program suggestions, between the business meeting and the next, when a new series of program activities can be arranged for and suggested.

Before the adjournment of the meeting, announcement should be made of the plans of the next two succeeding meetings, and every Scout should be urged to attend the Inter-Patrol Contest for winning of points.

PROGRAM LIV

Inter-Patrol Contest — Point Winning

Point Systems — Award of Honor — Athletics — Scoutcraft — Competitive Events — Tardiness and Attendance — Judge — Awarding the Honors.

This meeting should be planned to create rivalry between the patrols and promote individual efficiency in the different Scout attainments. Some point system should be outlined and adopted, giving awards for each event, but all points should be accredited to the whole patrol rather than to individual Scouts of the patrols. Some award, such as a Scout banner, or especially designed patrol flag, or some other insignia, should be given to the patrol winning the highest number of points, the winners to hold the trophy for a certain length of time, when a new contest will decide the next holder of the honor, or especial banner or insignia.

Athletics should not enter into this contest, except in a minor way and only as applied in regular scouting. Proficiency in general Scoutcraft should receive highest recognition, and the patrol of younger boys should receive the same attention and same chance as patrols of older fellows.

For suggested events for winning of points see Chapter VI of the Scout Master's Manual.

Hold the meeting with such suggested order of events as given in Program XLIV, for inter-troop contest or troop demonstrations. Tardiness and attendance should also be marked down to the credit or loss of the patrol, when such award has been determined upon by the troop. There will also be any number of other points for contest, which will prove adaptable, and occur to the Scouts or Scout Master in planning for such a contest.

A Scout Master of a neighboring troop or district or some man competent to judge results of contest should be obtained for the occasion.

The Award of Honor should be on hand, and be given to the winning patrol at the end of the contest, when the decisions are announced.

CHAPTER VIII

DRILLS AND DEMONSTRATIONS

MANUAL OF MARCHING.

Preliminary note. For the proper handling of large groups of boys the requisites are: 1, A simple but definite drill manual and 2, a corps of Scout Masters who not only thoroughly understand it but can teach it and use it practically. Drills and marching are valuable, because of the qualities they develop in the individual boy such as obedience to command, mental and physical alertness and a good carriage. The boys must know how to carry out the few orders required, must be obedient to command, prompt and must maintain a good carriage.

Care must be taken, however, not to limit the operations of the boys to those movements for which these orders are given. The Scout Master should remember that the manual of drill is but a means to an end, that the temporary obedience to command required is only to enable them to do larger things in the line of their physical and mental development. The obedience is not a surrender of individuality. It should not end in suppression but expression.

Divisions. For convenience in handling, the Scouts will be grouped naturally into *patrols,* of say seven boys in

It is sometimes necessary to join with others on special occasions in drills and parades although parading for public show or self glory should in general be discouraged. Even in connection with patriotic celebrations such as Decoration Day and the Fourth of July, it might be more helpful to have troops of Scouts organize to render practical service by furnishing the marchers with water, or having the Scouts organize for First Aid work rather than to march in the parade itself. The Scouts of old rarely made a show of themselves.

charge of a patrol leader; *troops* of two or more patrols in charge of a Scout Master and *brigades* composed of two or more troops in charge of a Scout Commissioner or some other appointed or designated officer.

Commands, in this manual, usually have two parts, the first part indicates what is to be done and the second when to start doing the thing ordered. Example, " Forward, March!" on " forward " each boy should get ready to march and on " march " should step out promptly, with a

A TYPICAL SCOUT CAMP

full length step. Each command should start with the name of the group which is to execute it as " patrol, forward, march," or " Troop, halt."

On Line. On this order all the boys in each patrol should fall into line facing front, tallest boys to the right, shortest to the left.

Attention. On this order each boy should take a good position with heels together, toes somewhat spread, body erect, shoulders square and well back, arms at sides, head up and eyes to the front.

Close Up, Right (or Left). On this order each boy

except the last one on the right should turn his head to the right and step to the right until his elbow just touches the elbow of the boy on his right and he is in good line with him. He should keep his head turned until the order.

Front! On this order each boy except the one who did not turn his head should turn his head sharply back to the front.

Turns. These are always either quarter turns or half turns.

Right, Face. On this order each boy should turn on his heels one-quarter of the way round to the right. Left, turn done to the left.

Right, About, Face (or L.). On this order each boy should turn on his heels, toward the right, half way around, so that he is facing in the opposite direction.

Count Fours. On this order the boys should count off fours beginning at the right (or left if they closed up to left). Each boy when counting should turn his face to the one who is to count next and immediately turn it back to the front.

Forward, March. On the order "march," all the boys indicated should step forward promptly with the left foot about twenty-four inches, and continue marching until some other order is given.

Short Step. On this order all the boys should shorten step to about twelve inches.

Mark Time, March. On this order each boy should raise his feet, beginning with the right foot, one after the other as if marching but should not leave his place.

Halt! On this order, given on the march, when one foot strikes the ground, one step should be taken and then the boy should stop with feet together.

Backward, March. On this order all the boys indicated should march backward, while facing the front, by taking short steps with knees only slightly bent. Seldom given when in single file.

Note. In marching in single file the boys should be directly behind one another and the distance apart not more than eighteen inches. This is a lock step. In double file ("by twos") the distance apart is three feet and in fours about six feet.

Form Twos, Right Face (or L.), March. When marching single file all the boys numbered 1 and 3 shorten step a little and the boys numbered 2 and 4 lengthen step a little turning a little to the right (or left) until along side of the numbers 1 and 3, when all take full length step again.

Form Fours, Right Face (or L.), March. When marching in a double column all the boys numbered 1 and 2 shorten step a little and the boys numbered 3 and 4 lengthen step a little, turning a little to the right (or left) until along side of the numbers 1 and 2 when all take full step again.

Note. Form fours may be done directly from single file without first forming twos.

Right by Twos, March. Given on the march in column of fours. The numbers 1 and 2 lengthen step and the 3's and 4's shorten step falling in behind the 1's and 2's.

Right by File, March. Given on the march in column of twos. The numbers 1 and 3 lengthen step and the numbers 2 and 4 shorten step, falling in behind.

Note. Right by file may be given from column of fours, when 2, 3 and 4 fall into file behind number 1.

Column Right, March (or L.). When marching in single file, by twos or by fours on the order "march," the head of the column should turn to the right at right angles to the former direction, or left if so indicated. If this order is given when the men are in a column of fours, the four at the head of the column should turn to the right (or left). The boy on the right acting as a pivot and the other three turning on him until they are at right angles to the former line of march when they should march straight ahead again. When the other fours have reached the spot where the first four turned they should turn in the same way.

Fours Right, March. On this order, given from a halt or while on the march in a column of fours, the boy on the right of each four acts as a pivot while the others turn, or wheel, on him through a quarter of a circle. If the distances between the fours were correct this will bring the fours into one line, when they halt, if they started from a halt, or march forward, closing up toward the right, if they were on the march.

If fours right is given when the boys are in line, at halt or on the march, the number 1's act as pivots until the 2's, 3's and 4's have wheeled through a quarter turn to the right when they halt or march off in column of fours.

Staff Drills.

Staves. The standard size of staff in use by the Boy Scouts is 6'6½" by 1¼".

Distances. The Scouts in this drill should be 8'-6" apart from side to side and 8' apart from front to rear. Any of the ordinary methods for opening ranks may be used to get them into this arrangement.

Posture. It is important that the correct posture be taken in this drill that the desired physical effect may be produced. Done properly, i. e., correctly and with sufficient energy, the movements will develop markedly the muscles of the shoulders, waist and legs and help to " set up " the boys. They are designed also to aid digestion.

I.— EXERCISES FROM THE STAND.

Attention, as in the marching drill with staff at a " carry " in hollow of the right arm. On count 1, reach across and grasp staff with left hand and on 2 bring it in front of thighs, horizontal, arms straight. This is the starting position for this group and is always meant by the word **ATTENTION.**

Exercise 1. Raise staff to front of shoulders by bending arms on count 1, and 2 bring it back to position; continue 16 counts.

Exercise 2. Raise staff as in ex. 1 on count 1; on count 2 thrust it to the right side by extending right arm, shoulder high, count 3 same as count 1, count 4, position. On the next four counts execute the same movements, on 3 thrusting to the left side. Continue 16 counts.

Exercise 3. Raise staff to upper chest by curling hands under and raising elbows, cn count 1; on 2 thrust wand forward to front horizontal; count 3 like 1 and count 4, position. Continue 16 counts.

Exercise 4. Raise staff to front of shoulders as in exercise 1. On 2 push staff to overhead at the same time bending backward and looking up, on 3 same as 1 and on 4, position. Continue 16 counts.

Exercise 5. Bend to ground, keeping knees straight and touching staff to ground if possible, on count 1, on 2 straighten up and raise staff

to front of shoulders as in exercise 1,
on 3 push staff to overhead as in the
previous exercise, on 4, position. Continue 16 counts.

II.— CHARGES AND STAFF POINTING.

Position as in Group I.

Exercise 1. On count 1 raise staff to front horizontal,
on 2 charge straight forward with right
foot and bring end of staff to left shoulder
as in aiming a gun, count 3 like 1 and 4,
position. Repeat charging to forward
with left foot. Continue 16 counts.

Exercise 2. On count 1 raise staff to overhead, on 2
charge to right and bring staff behind
neck, extend right arm and look to right;
count three like 1 and 4, position. Repeat to left and continue 16 counts.

Exercise 3. On count 1 raise staff to right armpit parallel to ground and pointing to the front,
on 2 turn and charge back with right
foot, pointing to the rear with staff but
not bringing it to shoulder as in exercise
1, count 3 like 1, count 4, position. Continue 16 counts.

Exercise 4. On count 1 charge obliquely with the right
foot and point staff as a gun obliquely
upward in line of charge, on 2, position.
Repeat, charging to left. Continue 16
counts.

Exercise 5. On count 1 charge obliquely backward with
right foot except that weight is kept on
left foot and left knee is bent while right
leg is straight. Point staff obliquely upward in line of charge, on 2, position.
Repeat to left. Continue 16 counts.

III.— CHARGES AND STAFF PLACING.

Position as in Group 1.

Exercise 1. On count 1 charge forward with right foot,
slide hands to ends of staff and place
staff vertically on right knee, left hand
below. On 2, position. Repeat to left.

Exercise 2. On count 1, charge to right side and place

staff vertically on right knee, right hand below, face to the front, on 2, position. Repeat to left and continue 16 counts.

Exercise 3.   On count 1 charge obliquely back with right foot, otherwise like exercise 2.   Continue 16 counts.

IV.— DISLOCATES AND CHARGES.

Position as in Group 1.

Exercise 1.   On count 1 bring staff to behind neck and in a lateral plane sliding hands to ends of staff, on 2, position.   Repeat and continue 16 counts.

Exercise 2.   On count 1 bring staff to a vertical behind back, hands at ends of staff, left above, on 2 bring staff to horizontal behind back, on 3 to a vertical behind back again, right hand above and on 4, position.   Continue 16 counts and repeat in the other direction 16 counts.

Exercise 3.   On count 1 charge forward with right foot, slide hands to ends of staff and bring staff over the head and behind the back, horizontal: on 2, position.   Repeat charging to left and continue 16 counts.

Exercise 4.   On count 1 charge obliquely forward with right foot and raise staff to overhead, on 2 bend and touch staff to floor, 3 like 1 and 4, position.   Repeat to left and continue 16 counts.

ORDER OF THE STAFF.

Order Staff.
Parade Rest.
Present Staff.
Port Staff.
Shoulder Staff.
Secure Staff.
Trail Staff.
Ground Staff.
Lift Staff.

ORDER STAFF.— Position Attention. Right arm hanging naturally by the side of the body. First and second fingers in front; thumb and two other fingers behind. Staff in hollow of right shoulder. Bottom of staff on line with and just touching the little toe.

PARADE REST.— Only to be executed from the ORDER. Bottom of staff not being moved. Right foot 5 inches in rear of left, knee slightly bent. Weight of body thrown on right leg. Head, eyes, and shoulders straight to the front. Staff standing in front of the body, hands clasping the staff high.

PRESENT STAFF.— Being at PARADE REST, command PARADE ATTENTION. To Present Staff, carry the staff in front of the body with the right hand. Grasp the staff with the left hand at the balance. Steady staff naturally with right hand below the left hand. All fingers in front

Being at the PRESENT, to ORDER STAFF. Carry the staff to the right side with the left hand. Steady it with the right hand.

PORT STAFF.— Throw staff diagonally across the body, clasping firmly with both hands. Right thumb horizontal on staff; left hand clasping staff opposite junction of the neck and left shoulder.

SHOULDER STAFF.—Right and Left Shoulder.

(1) Take position of PORT STAFF.

(2) Carry and place the staff on right shoulder. Right elbow near the body. Move hand on shoulder.

(3) Drop left hand to side.

Opposite movements for Left Shoulder.

Being at SHOULDER STAFF, to come to ORDER STAFF. Clasp staff with the left hand, go to PORT and do the ORDER, as given above. In executing this command, see that heads keep steady.

SECURE STAFF.— Rest staff with right hand. Throw the butt of the staff up to the rear of the right arm. Staff sloping at an angle of 45 degrees. Right hand close to body.

TRAIL STAFF.— Grasp staff with left hand, and clasp the staff above the balance with the right hand. Drop left hand to the side. Drop butt of staff to ground at angle of 45 degrees to the rear.

To retrieve, bring staff erect at side and move to SECURE STAFF.

GROUND STAFF.—

(1) Left arm one pace to the front. Staff straight with the body.

(2) Place staff on ground, not moving butt of the staff from its original position while at Erect. Steady with left hand on knee.

(3) Release staff and resume position of Attention.

LIFT STAFF.—Take staff and replace from ground, coming to the position of Attention.

FIRST AID DRILL

POSITION TAKEN TO ASSIST A PATIENT WITH A SPRAINED ANKLE

Transportation of the Wounded.

The following drill has been found to be of great practical service in Scout patrols and troops. Instruction in the movements should first be given to individuals in the patrol, and when the positions and holds have been mastered, the drill may be given to the group as a whole. This latter method proves more interesting to the boys, and makes a good form of exhibition work in First Aid and Transportation of the Wounded.

Patient with Injured Leg.

The Scouts are formed in line, and are commanded to "count fours." The first method of transportation should be to assist a patient with a sprained ankle, or other injury to the leg. Give commands as follows: *"Number ones, Forward,* MARCH." (The first numbers called out are always the patients.) The numbers specified march forward, and when fifteen or twenty feet from their line, are commanded to *"Halt —About* FACE." (A half turn to the right brings them facing the line of Scouts.) Next order *"No. Twos, Forward, MARCH."* When about three feet from No. Ones (the patients), order No. Twos to *"Halt; Prepare to assist Patient, Right (or left) side,* POST." At "POST," No. Twos take their position by the sides of No. Ones, and to assist for sprained ankle, No. Twos place their right arms around the waists of Number Ones, grasp the wrists of the pa-

tients, and bring the arm of patient over their shoulder. In this way, material support may be given. At command "Forward, MARCH," No. 2 assists No. 1 back to the line, and without further command, they both take their positions, in alignment with the rest. Next order out other numbers, so that each boy gets an opportunity for practice; this method to be used also in all the following movements.

Fireman's Grip.

Command *"No. 1,* Forward, MARCH, *Halt. About* FACE *No. 2, Forward,* MARCH; Halt. *Prepare to assist Patient, Fireman's Grip."* No. 2 grasps the right wrist of No. 1 with his left hand, places his head under the right arm of No. 1, his right arm between the legs of No. 1 (or under both knees), gets the hips of No. 1 well on his shoulders, and at command "*Lift Patient,*" No. 2 raises No. 1.

"LIFT PATIENT, FIREMAN'S GRIP"

At command "*About FACE,*" No. 2. faces his line, and at "*Forward,* MARCH" carries his patient to the line, and without further command, deposits him, both taking their positions in line.

Note. In all the movements herein mentioned, instruct the Scouts to make no movements without command, except in depositing their patients in line.

The Firemen's Grip is generally intended for use in case of the total unconsciousness of the patient. Hence the patient is always found in the recumbent position: After the movements above have been learned, vary the commands as follows: — "*No.* 1, *Forward,* MARCH. *Halt. About* FACE. *Lie down. No.* 2, *Forward,* MARCH. *Halt. Prepare to assist Patient, Fireman's Grip.*" No. 2 kneels beside patient, rolls him over on his face, and takes his position at the head of the patient. He now grasps patient under arms and chest, and gradually raises the patient to his (the patient's) knees. Then No. 2 shifts his grip, placing his arms low around waist of patient, and raises patient to his feet. From this position, he takes the fireman's grip, as described above.

FIRST POSITION FOR FIREMAN'S GRIP

CORRECT POSITION FOR FOUR-HANDED BASKET SEAT

THE THREE-HANDED BASKET SEAT

POSITION—"HIPS, POST"

Basket Seat.

Commands: *No. 1, Forward,* MARCH. *Halt. About* FACE. *Numbers 2 and 3, Forward,* MARCH, *Halt. Prepare to assist Patient. Basket Seat; POST."* No. 2. and No. 3. each grasps his own left wrist, and then they join hands. A variation is the three handed basket seat, when it is desirable that one of the bearers have one hand free. This grip is good only for short distances. For longer distances, the following position should be taken.

Position Hips, Post.

Commands: *"No. 1, Forward,* MARCH. *Halt. About* FACE. *Lie Down. Numbers 2 and 3, Forward,* MARCH. *Halt. Hips,* POST." At the last command, Nos. 2 and 3 take their positions at the hips of patient, facing each other, having first placed the patient on his back.

POSITION —" LIFT PATIENT "

The patient is supposed to be able somewhat to help himself. At the command *"Prepare to lift,"* Nos. 2 and 3 kneel beside patient, place their arms around waist of patient, and their free arms under his thighs, grasping wrists. The patient places his arms around the necks of the bearers. Patient is lifted at command *"Lift Patient," "Forward,* MARCH."

At the command:— *" No. 1, Forward,* MARCH. *Halt. About* FACE. *Lie down. Nos. 2 and 3, Forward,*

MARCH. *Halt. Head and Feet,* POST." No. 2 takes
his position at the head of patient, No. 3 at his feet, facing
each other. At command *"Prepare to Lift,"* No. 3 spreads

POSITION FOR " HEAD AND FEET, POST " AND " PREPARE TO LIFT "

patient's feet, steps in between his knees, facing away from
patient, and kneels, getting his arms well under patient's
knees. No. 2 kneels, raises head and shoulders of patient,
places his arms under patient's arms, and around his chest,
locking his fingers in front. At command *"Lift patient,"*
they arise, and at *"Forward,* MARCH " proceed onward
with patient.

The following movements are intended for placing the
patient on a litter, or in moving him short distances in case
of serious injury.

Three Bearers.

At the command:—" No. 1, *Forward,* MARCH. *Halt.
Right Side,* POST." The three bearers take positions at the
right side of patient (or left, as commanded), *"Prepare
to lift."* Bearers kneel on knee next to patient's feet.
They get their arms well under patient's shoulders, back,

hips and thighs. "*Lift patient.*" The patient is lifted
to the knees of the bearers, who shift their grips, to get a
comfortable hold. At the further command "*Lift,*" they
arise with patient in arms. At "*Forward,* MARCH," the
patient is carried forward. To place the patient on a litter, the same movements are given, except the last; *i. e.,*
the bearers at command "*Lower Patient,*" gently lower him
from their knees; and at command "*Litter,* POST," take
their positions at the litter.

The Litter Drill.

Improvised litters, made of coats and poles may be used
in this drill; gunny sacks, through which poles have been
placed, make a good substitute. A strong and serviceable
litter may be easily made. Light poles, about six feet
long, are used, with slightly heavier and longer ones on
the outsides, the whole bound together by interweaving

CORRECT POSITION FOR THREE BEARERS IN LIFTING PATIENT AND PLACING
HIM ON A LITTER

cord or rope between the poles. Each squad is provided
with a litter, borne by No. 3 in the squad, who carries the
litter on his right shoulder, at an angle of about 45 degrees,

being at the shoulder, command *"Order Litter."* The litter is brought to the vertical position, then lowered to the ground, outside the right foot. At *"Shoulder litter,"* the litter is raised to the vertical position, then laid on the shoulder, where it is supported by the right arm, the left arm dropped by the side. At the command *"Carry Litter,"* each No. 3 brings his litter to the vertical position; then drops the litter forward and downward until it is in a horizontal position. Meanwhile, the other numbers step

ONE TYPE OF LITTER USED BY THE BOY SCOUTS OF MADISON, WISCONSIN

directly to the front; No. 2 until he is opposite the front handles, which he seizes with his left hand, and Nos. 1 and 4 until they are opposite the center of the litter. At *"Ground Litter,"* Nos. 2 and 3 gently lower the litter; at command *"Raise Litter,"* they stoop and carefully raise; and at *"Shoulder Litter"* No. 3 reaches forward with his left hand, and grasps the litter near its center; he then brings it to the vertical position, and then to the shoulder. Meanwhile, the other numbers step quickly backward, and align themselves in regular order. The litter being at the carry position, at the command *"Open Litter"* all face the litter and unfasten any straps or cords with which the improvised litter may be fastened together for drill movements. The litter being properly arranged, the original positions are taken. The litter being grounded, at command *" Change Posts "* each Scout moves around, clockwise, in order to change positions and bearers. At command *" Four Bearers,* Post," the squad moves around, clockwise, until each Scout is in position at a litter handle.

The usual general movements in marching may be given with the letters. When the squads have become proficient in the drill, they may work separately, in squads, the commands being given by Scout No. 3. Patients may be picked up, placed on the litters, and obstacles gone over, such as fences, walls, etc. The litter should always be held level. The patient is generally carried feet forward; in going upstairs, head forward, and in coming down, feet forward.

A SCOUT FIELD DAY.

Frequently during the summer months, it will be found desirable to have all of the troops of a town or city join in a one day outing. During the day a program of field events may be carried through which will prove generally interesting to the boys. Such " get together " meetings are very helpful as a means of getting boys acquainted with Scouts of other troops and giving them some idea of what other boys are doing. It broadens the boys' vision of the movement and tends to develop the fraternal spirit. Friendly rivalry in Scout activities may be judiciously used as a further incentive to proficiency in Scoutcraft.

The success of such an event will largely depend upon the amount of work done by the " Committee on Arrangements " prior to the field event in planning for it. This committee may be made up of from three to five Scout Masters.

The committee should select a site for the outing. This ought to be located near some stream, on a piece of ground well surrounded by trees and yet open enough to afford good camping and for Scout field events.

In every case where it is practicable for the Scout Master or his assistant to take his troop into camp on Friday evening, it is desirable that he do so. Where the Scout Master finds this impossible, however, he should take his troop to the camp ground on Saturday morning.

Each troop on arrival at camp should select the best available site for its tents; each patrol selecting its own location, pitching its own tent, and otherwise making all camp arrangements as though planning for a permanent camp.

In all Patrol competitions, the patrol shall be a unit consisting of eight boys including the Patrol Leader.

Regulations.

Upon reaching the grounds Scout Masters and Patrol Leaders will report at Headquarters for instructions. The following bugle calls will be used:

Assembly — Get ready for activities or contests.

Officers' Call — Scout Masters report immediately at Headquarters.

Recall — Each troop return to its own camp.

Mess — Grub.

In the contest at the call of "Assembly," all troops assemble at the edge of the parade ground. Upon one blast of the bugle each contestant takes his place for the contest; two blasts, the contest begins; three blasts, the contest ends; "Recall," the boys return to their places.

The events will be run off promptly. No Scout should be permitted, during the contests, to become separated from his patrol or troop.

In Individual Competitions in order to bring out the troop, instead of the star, each troop must enter different boys for each event, except in event Nos. 2 and 10.

The conduct of the troops will be under inspection from the time they reach the field until they break camp.

It should be needless to remind Scout Masters that, in a broader way, the conduct of each troop as it passes through the city will be under the inspection of the public.

Mess should be arranged by patrols — everything should be in readiness for the camp dinner to be served promptly at 12 o'clock Saturday noon. The day's program should be started promptly at one o'clock.

Competitions by Patrols.

1. Camp inspection.
    Credit should be given:
        (1) Upon the ability of the patrol to choose a good camp site.

(2) The way in which the tent has been erected and ditched.

(3) Neatness of arrangement of equipment both inside and outside of the tent.

(4) Original ideas shown in construction of a fireplace or other necessary features of the camp.

(5) Additional credit to be given the patrol that has made its own tent, camp hammocks, lean-tos or additional shelter.

(6) The proportion of members of the patrol present.

During the inspection the members of each patrol should be lined up in front of their tent.

At the conclusion of Camp inspection, each patrol should await the Assembly call to march to the place where the field events are to be conducted. The boys should be arranged in a square large enough to conduct the games. At the bugler's signal they may be seated upon the ground. Visitors may file in behind the Scouts.

2. First Aid Race.

Patrol Leader to supervise only. One member to act as patient. Patients are laid out fifty yards from the point where the patrols are lined up and a label is tied on them denoting the injury (English names will be used as far as possible). Staves are to be carried in hands; coats should be worn all buttoned up.

On the signal the team runs to the patient, attends to the injury, makes improvised stretcher and returns with patient to starting point.

Credit should be given for:

(1) Correct treatment.

(2) Lifting and lowering patient.

(3) Making improvised stretcher.

(4) Neatness and detail of work.

Improvised stretcher to be made of Scout uniform only. Each member to be provided with one triangular bandage, the Patrol Leader to carry splints.

3. Tent Pitching.

Tents to be provided by Committee. Two mallets furnished with each tent. Tents should be packed and placed at a distance of ten yards from the patrols.

On the signal each patrol to run and pitch tent and fall

in line outside of the tent when they have finished their work. At second signal the patrol must strike tent, pack and replace as originally found and return to their first position in line.

Time of pitching or striking to be taken from the time of giving the signal to the time when the team falls in line again.

Credit should be given for:

(1) The appearance of the tent when pitched.
(2) The security of pegs, tightness of ropes, etc., and
(3) The time of completing the work.

4. Signaling. Morse or Semaphore.

Semaphore team to consist of eight, forming two terminal stations and one transmitter.

Morse team to consist of four. No transmitting station.

One message of 100 letters will be sent by each competing team and may include any of the following: —

Alphabet and figures (Morse shortened numerals) and the following miscellaneous signs: —

| Break | Erase | Full stop |
| Oblique | Z (block) | Cypher |

Five minutes will be allowed for the Morse and four and a half minutes for the Semaphore.

Deductions further than errors in text: —

½ Minute overtime less	...... 1 point
1 " " "	...... 2 points
1½ " " "	...... 4 points
2 " " "	...... 8 points

Should two teams tie as regards accuracy, points to be allowed for speed.

No alterations may be made on the form after the message is signaled as finished.

Message forms will be supplied.

5. Staff Relay Race.

SECTION ONE. Scouts past 15th birthday.

SECTION TWO. Scouts under 15th birthday.

Patrol is distributed at intervals by Patrol Leader a distance of about 400 yards, as directed. On the signal being given No. 1 will have to hand his staff on to No. 2, who runs with both staves to No. 3, No. 3 to No. 4, and so on, the last Scout having 8 staves to carry to the winning post.

6. Message Relay Race.

The Patrol is distributed over a distance of 400 yards at the discretion of the Patrol Leader.

A verbal message is given to No. 1 who runs to No. 2, repeats it to No. 2, No. 2 to No. 3 and so on, No. 8 having to run to the winning post and deliver the message.

Credit should be given for:

   (1) Speed.

   (2) Correctness of message.

7. Spar Lashing Competition.

Task: —" Double Trestle," for support of roadway forming bridge.

Material: — Scout Staves (14 in all) and sash line, in lengths of 10 ft. for lashings (26 in all).

Team: — 8 boys and Patrol Leader in charge.

When completed to bear combined weight, upon trestle, of working party.

Time allowed, 20 minutes.

Credit should be given for:

   (1) Rigidity of trestle.

   (2) Knots.

   (3) Lashings.

8. Wall Scaling.

Material used in this event to be an " A-shaped " board wall at least 10 ft. high. Sides of the wall to be braced so as to make it rigid. The top of the sides should not come together exactly but should be at least one foot apart.

Credit should be given for:

   (1) Skill in constructing pyramids in lining up the eight members of the patrol at the side of the wall.

   (2) Speed in scaling wall. That is, in getting every member of the patrol over it.

9. Tree Reporting.

The patrol is sent out with experts over a certain limited area, and each Scout assigned to a certain part of the allotted area. The contest consists in the patrol members as a whole reporting the largest correct number of trees, shrubs, bushes, grasses, and lichens within the selected area. Experts should make verification, checking up on each Scout's report after it is made. The area allotted to each Scout must, of course, be small. Every tree, shrub and bush, and every different species of grass and lichen should be counted.

Credit should be given for:

   (1)   Number of trees, shrubs and other plants accurately named, within the appointed area.

   (2)   Speed with which the general result was obtained.

In giving credit, points should be taken off for all plants wrongly named.

This contest can, of course, be varied by substituting other forms or subjects for such observation reporting,—such as rocks, tracks, birds, grains, grasses, etc.

   10.   Tug of War.

Two events may be conducted. One between "Midget" patrols and the other between the "Giants." Three trials to be held in each event. Best two out of three to determine the winner.

   11.   Specialties.

This event to be a free-for-all competition, every patrol being given an opportunity to demonstrate some specialty in which it excels. The winning patrol to be selected by the judges.

Specialties may be suggested as follows:

   (a)   Erection of wireless apparatus.

   (b)   Bridge building.

   (c)   Construction of lean-to.

SCOUTS SENDING MESSAGES BY WIRELESS
— FIELD PRACTICE

   (d)   Signal tower.

   (e)   Demonstration of staff drill or Scout calisthenics.

   (f)   Demonstration of rescuing drowning, showing methods of release.

INDIVIDUAL COMPETITIONS.

   1.   Lasso throwing.

Lariat to be furnished by the Committee.

Credit should be given for:

(1) Form in handling the rope.

(2) Skill in roping stationary object.

(3) Ability to rope moving object.

2. Demonstration of First Aid.

(Usually three boys work together in this event.)

(a) Bandaging and stretcher work.

(b) Fireman's lift.

A PRACTICAL FIRST AID DRILL

The subject should be properly tagged showing nature of the fracture or other injury and placed at a given distance from the competing teams.

At the signal the team should rush to the aid of the subject, determine the nature of the injury and act on the case in accordance with their best judgment. When they have completed their first aid service the patient is to be placed upon a stretcher and brought back to the starting point.

Each team must carry its own first aid kit; splints, if needed, are to be improvised. Stretchers must be made on the spot.

Credit should be given for:

    (1)   Correct treatment.
    (2)   Lifting and lowering patient.
    (3)   Making improvised stretcher.
    (4)   Neatness and detail of work.

Credit in the fireman's lift should be given for:
    (1)   The method of approaching the subject in a supposedly smoky room.
    (2)   Best demonstration of the lift.
    (3)   Speed in rescuing the victim.

3. Bugling.

Judges to test competitors in two or three of the customary army calls and select the winner according to ability of the boys to execute these without hesitation.

4. Carrying Message one Mile at Scouts' Pace.

This race is not for time but to demonstrate the ability of a Scout to travel the distance in exactly twelve minutes.

First place to be awarded to the boy who crosses the tape most nearly on the twelfth minute.

5. Throwing the Life Buoy.

The regulation length of the line attached to the life buoy is 75 feet. Consequently competitions may be held for distances varying from 30 feet up to 75 feet.

When this event is conducted on land the buoy should be thrown from a six-foot circle to an object representing a drowning person to be placed at the allotted distance from the contestant.

When the event is to be held at the river's edge a float representing a drowning person may be built for the occasion. Certain known and plainly marked points, such as " A " should represent the head and " B " and " C " the hands of the individual.

The purpose of this competition is to develop accuracy in throwing a life buoy within reach of a drowning person. Therefore, credit should be given for accuracy in judging the distance in throwing the life buoy so that it may be easily grasped.

A perfect score is made when the rope crosses the head or hands and may count the total number of points for the first place in the event, say five. Three points may be given when the line crosses the arms or when the life buoy comes within the circle so as to be within reach of the hands. Nothing outside of the circle should count. Each competitor should be given three trials.

6. Laying and Lighting Fire and Boiling Water.

Only Scouts who are proficient in the use of the knife and ax should be permitted to participate in this event.

Each competitor should be furnished with a block of wood of the same size and texture. The committee should furnish tin pails of equal sizes and should carefully measure one quart of water for each boy. Only two matches are allowed. No competitor should be allowed to use any notched piece of wood previously prepared to hold his pail over the fire.

Credit should be given to the Scout who first succeeds in boiling the water.

7. Barrel Tilting.

The committee should furnish two barrels and two tilting spears made of bamboo, eight or ten feet long. These should be padded at the end with burlap.

Decision to be best two out of three rounds.

Hitting below the belt or in the face not allowed.

8. Canoe Tilting.

In this competition two boats or canoes are needed. They should each be manned with four Scouts, a spearsman who acts as Captain, a Pilot and two oarsmen.

The team winning two out of three is awarded the honors.

9. Cooking Flapjacks.

Two rows of heavy cordwood are first laid out parallel to each other, about two feet apart. Good wood fires are built between these rows of logs at intervals of five feet apart, one for each competitor.

The only material allowed will be the frying-pan of the mess-kit and the ingredients for making flapjacks. Each boy should mix his own materials. The use of prepared flour is prohibited.

When the fires are burning brightly the signal may be given for Scouts to start cooking.

The award in this contest is to be given to the Scout making the best flapjacks. Time should not enter into the competition. The judges by sampling all of the flapjacks made should decide upon the winner of the competition.

10. Signaling. Morse or Semaphore. phore.

(Two boys to a team: a sender and a receiver).

Message to be furnished the sender by the judges.

Credit to be given for:

(1) Speed in sending and receiving the message.

(2)　Accuracy.

11.　Archery.

Standard four foot target to be used at thirty yards.

Each competitor to be given a similar number of trials until by elimination the best marksmen are left for the finals. The best score with six arrows to determine the winner.

12.　Swim one hundred yards.

Points to be awarded to the first competitor crossing the line.

13.　Making Fire by Friction.

Each competitor should use a fire set made by himself. The use of artificially prepared punk or tinder not permitted nor is it allowable to have any punk previously soaked with some combustible.

Credit should be given for time actually taken in securing fire.

14.　Throwing the Assegai.

Target to be a thin sack stuffed with straw, or a canvas stretched on a frame. Assegai is made of a wand with weighted ends sharpened or with iron arrow heads on them.

15.　Life Saving Race (to be conducted on the river).

Each team should consist of a crew and a subject. The crew consists of two oarsmen and a coxswain.

The boats should be placed in a row, bottom up, on the edge of the river. Oars and oarlocks may be placed beside the boats.

At the first signal the subjects on the opposite bank are to dive into the river and swim toward the boats on the other shore.

On the second signal boats are righted, oars and oarlocks placed in position, launched. The crew rows toward the subject, hauls him aboard and brings him back safely to shore. When the boats have reached the swimmer he must give up all personal effort, allowing himself to be handled by the crew. He must not assist in his rescue.

Credit is given: For speed in effecting the rescue.

At the conclusion of this program prizes to be awarded by committee.

Supper may be had by patrols and the evening spent around the campfire. A campfire talk may be given; patrol songs may be sung, or a boys' story contest conducted.

Note: It is not presumed that it is at all possible

to carry out all of the events in this program in one day. This list is merely suggestive. Any working combination suitable to local conditions may be arranged.

CHAPTER IX

CHIVALRY AND MORALITY

Character Building.

The chief purpose of the Scout Movement is the building of character. Character is what a person really is, not what he seems to be; it is the stamp of his mental, moral and physical actions. A strong and well-fibred character embraces within it independency in thought and action, individuality, and a good mental and moral constitution. That is what the Scout Movement seeks to develop in every Scout.

The building of character in a boy depends upon his understanding and application of the principles of chivalry and morality. The true conception, then, of these two attributes of character is most essential to the Scout Master and to all other Boy Workers.

The Scout program is the practical agent through which the principles of chivalry and morality are inculcated, and the Scout life is the method of their application. But, while these principles are, for the most part, enumerated in a definite way in the tenets of the Scout Oath and Scout Law, and what is not so outlined is already inherent in cultivated and civilized manhood, the thorough understanding of chivalry and morality must include a knowledge of their origins, their definitive limitations, and their modern Scout interpretations.

Definitions and Conceptions.

Morality is characterized by practical excellence, springing from man's natural sense of what is right and proper. It conforms to or embodies righteous or just conduct. It is the quality of an intention, a character, an action, a principle, or a sentiment, when tried by the standard of right. Trustworthiness, loyalty, helpfulness, friendliness, kindness, obedience, thriftiness, cleanness, cheerfulness, courtesy, bravery, and reverence are each and all the dictates of right living and are, therefore, embodiments of a true moral standard.

Chivalry, on the other hand, is not so much a matter of conduct, governed by the conscience dictating constantly what is right and proper, as it is the voluntary choice or determination to do a certain good or a certain number of gallant acts. One has to do with the attributes of righteous manhood in daily life, the other with the attributes of gentlemanly actions and characteristics; the one is conscience-governed in all acts of daily life, the other is the will to do good deeds according to the dictates of all the best that is in a man, the opportunity, and the appeal that is made. Morality is a natural accompaniment of civilization and becomes almost a natural law as man becomes more and more governed by the dictates of conscience and the recognition of social rights and justices. Chivalry is historical in its origin, an outcome of a peculiar social development, and having become the spirit, usages, or manners of knighthood, commemorates in the qualifications or character of an ideal and altruistic manhood the dignity of manliness,— gallantry, honor, trustworthiness, cleanness, kindness to the weak and helpless, courtesy, cheerfulness, generosity to foes, loyalty, helpfulness, and bravery.

Germanic Origin of Chivalry.

To understand the conditions which gave origin to chivalry, one must delve into the realms of pre-mediæval history, and understand both the social conditions brought about by the break-up of the Roman Empire, and the characteristics of the Germanic peoples. Numerous chiefs, more or less powerful, held local sway as far as each could enforce his dominion, and often warring with one another, or banding together to repel an invasion or carry on war and pillage into surrounding territories, turmoil, robbery, pillage, rapine, and lawlessness were common characteristics of the time. In such a state of things, the rights of the humbler classes of society were at the mercy of every assailant, and it is plain, that without some check, society must have relapsed into barbarism. Such checks were found in the rivalries and jealousies of the chiefs, themselves in the influence of the Church, which, by every motive, pure or selfish, was pledged to the protection of the weak; and in the inherent characteristics of the people, who were noted for their war-like spirit, love of adventure, thirst for glory, generosity and sense of right, and devotion and esteem for women. These tribal characteristics, combined with invincible strength and valor, loyalty to superiors, courtesy to equals, compassion for weakness, and devotedness to the Church formed the chrysalis from whence issued forth the ideals of chivalry, which, if never met with in real life, was acknowledged by all as the highest model for emulation.

Ceremony of Manhood — Altruism.

Chivalry has been wholly altruistic even in its earliest conceptions. In its very origin it had in it the element of service to others. The early German performed mighty deeds of valor and strove valiantly and heroically for his leader or king and for the protection of his women. His duty of service became in time a requisite of manhood's estate, and thus grew up the Germanic custom of solemnly arming the youth in the presence of the warriors, upon his assumption of the duties of manhood. This impressive assumption of a man's obligations including the qualities of bravery, fidelity, and loyalty, was made the basis of knighthood, and the whole ceremony with all it represented became that of chivalry.

The privilege of knighthood was conferred on youths of family and fortune only, for the mass of people were not furnished with arms. The knight, then, was a mounted warrior, a man of rank, or in the maintenance or service of some man of rank, generally possessing some independent means of support, but often relying mainly on the gratitude of those whom he served or resorting to arms for the supply of his wants. In time of war the knight was in the camp of his sovereign, or commanding in the field, or acting as the governor of some castle. In times of peace he was either in attendance at his sovereign's court, taking part in banquets and tournaments and other events of court life, or he was traversing the country in quest of adventure, professedly bent on redressing wrongs and enforcing rights, sometimes in fulfilment of some vow of religion or love, sometimes for the mere love of adventure and daring.

Chivalric Duties and Privileges — Influences.

Along with the development of knighthood and feudalism, there grew up a great body of duties and privileges, essential requisites of the vassal in the service of his lord, and directly the outcome of the Germanic " man-making " ceremony. Owing their first material development to feudal usages and customs, with which chivalry had many relations, these duties and privileges were later taken over and altered by the Church to further its own control of society. Thenceforth the conception of knightly honor slowly grew up and with it the gradual union of chivalric principles with ethical ideals.

At the end of the 12th-Century, chivalry was profoundly influenced by the popular romances of Arthur, Sir Galahad, Charlemagne, and other heroes. Manners became less brutal, men strove more to attain the ideal of service in life through honor and loyalty and righteousness, and a spirit of knight-errantry grew up. This was perhaps the greatest saving element of mediæval history for from its influence arose the desire for the good, the ideal, and the altruistic spirit. This period of the " Dark Ages " was a harsh time, and chivalry with knight-errantry came to make life a little more worth the living, and form the one bright spot of truth and fidelity in all the chaos of embryonic nation-building and petty warfare.

Decline of Chivalry.

Chivalry was at its best in the 12th Century, but was rapidly declining in the 14th Century, and was thoroughly decadent in the 15th Century. Lastly the term chivalry came to be used in its present very general sense of " courtesy " and a gentlemanly service. It deteriorated from the plane of requisites of manhood qualifications to only the possibility of a man's ideals.

Chivalry gave to the world its greatest developments in early literature, its most popular romances, and hero-tales. From its effects upon mankind it gave birth to the Crusades and later to the Renaissance. Most of the greatness and the heritage of good in the middle ages must be directly traced to the influences of the ideals of chivalry. No wonder then, that its passing has left such a deep impression upon the building of civilization or the fashioning of man's inherited conceptions of fidelity, loyalty, honor and righteousness.

American Chivalry.

We trace the development of our conceptions of chivalric principles back through the vistas of European history, but we Americans have examples of greater worth and more profound impression in the tribal civilizations and of the Indians of our Continent and in the lives of our pioneer forefathers. The lives of each of these types of earlier Americans furnish us with numberless concrete examples of the practice of chivalric principles, the esteem for truth and loyalty, and the worth of right living.

The Indian has too often been deeply wronged by the false portrayal of his character. In his life as a tribesman, unsullied by the vices of the white man, his was the highest type of the primitive ideal of clean living. He was a master of woodcraft, and clean, manly, heroic, self-controlled, reverent, and truthful. Indeed we have much good to learn from his simple and healthful outdoor life and high-principled characteristics.

The daily lives of the American pioneers, the men and women who braved the dangers of unexplored forests and the hardships of an unsettled country, furnish us with still better ideals. From them directly comes the idea of " preparedness " for all things and for any emergency. They were friendly, kind, helpful, trustworthy, loyal, courteous, reverent, clean, cheerful, thrifty, and brave. We seek to typify and commemorate the principles of their character in the Scout Oath, the Scout Motto, and the Scout Law in the ideals of the Boy Scouts of America.

To Ernest Thompson Seton and Daniel Carter Beard great credit must be given for their admirable work in commemorating excellent precepts in the lives of the Indians and Pioneers by the development of their boy organizations, — the (Seton) Woodcraft Indians and the Boy Pioneers by Mr. Beard. They have given great ideals to all boys, and are ever ready to give aid from the fulness of their knowledge and experience. They have each written several books which are admirable in creating and promoting the ideals of right living,— the ideals which are personified in the development of all true Scouts. .

Recapitulation of the Feudal-Period in Boy-Life.

It is a fact generally accepted by psychologists that the child recapitulates the history of man's development in his growth from his first origin through infancy into manhood. As has been previously pointed out in a former chapter, there is one period of the boy's development which exactly coincides with this historical world-period of chivalry, and in which the boy lives over again the desires which affected his forefathers through that period of world-history. So just as we interpret the needs of the boy, and gain a better understanding of his likes and dislikes by interpreting the periods of his life according to the development of man's history, so the sooner it is recognized by the student of boyhood what the requisites of training must be during the chivalry period of the boy's development.

The Chivalry Period of Boy-Life.

The period of chivalry or early adolescence in boy-life extends generally from thirteen to sixteen years of age, immediately following and constituting a later development of the gang age, and forming an introduction to the middle adolescent or self-assertive age. This youthful period is closely parallel to the racial feudal period of history in its characteristics. In that time of knighthood, man was imbued with the desire to emulate the chosen leader, lord, or king, to seek through service of a master the path to glory and happiness,— this was an age of hero-worship. This is approximately true, as well, of this period of boy life. Gradually the boy's allegiance is turned from loyalty to his gang toward his leader, and the impulse toward hero-worship is developed. At this time the will to do or not to do is not gang-decision, but the decision of the gang leader or the teacher. The boy prefers leadership games, such as follow-the-leader, captained baseball or football, and loves pomp, display, and drill work, under his chosen captain or general; he cares to be seen doing things under the direction of Mr. (Williams), his leader, or to be known as one of " Beany's " Bunch. " The boy's will," says Mr. Fiske, " now typifies the spirit of obedience."

Personal Traits of the Leader.

This period of boy-life develops the boy who leads and the boy who follows. This boy leader of the gang may develop the personal traits of the bully, if he is attracted by the fighting qualities and animal force of some man he seeks to copy in character, or he may be the force through his selection of his own hero which will lead to the solid character building of all of his followers. The boys who follow, at first will seek to emulate the deeds of their leader, and later seek to surpass him, in the development in them of self-assertiveness. Therefore in boy training, and especially in the influence of the boy for good, the question of the boy-leadership must always be considered, and such steps adopted as will continue the natural development of boys in the life-period, under correcting and advisory influences. Fortunately the boy leader in club-life more often selects as his hero a strong-charactered older boy or an adult leader, and usually success in character building follows for the control of himself and all of his followers.

Relative Leadership.

" Relative leadership under a strongly centralized control, then, is the key to this period," says George W. Fiske, in his " Boy-Life and Self-Government." " We may count on a strong personal loyalty from the boys, if we have any sort of a personality to attract it, and we may also count on a large degree of team work and willingness to serve under the order of superiors. The difficulty is to choose officers so wisely that they will get the boys' support." When this support is gained the direction of the boys' attention may be turned toward almost any field of activity, for boy-interest will follow good leadership enthusiasm in almost any phase of development. Here then is the leader's chance to lay the foundations for best character traits, to turn the boy's attention to the good and the beautiful and the pure in life, and to direct the actions of the boy by example and leadership towards the habits of the chivalry ideal.

The Boy-Leader and Adult Group Leader.

" In boy life, the period from twelve to fifteen is a stormy period," says Dr. Winfield S. Hall. " The boy recognizes physical force and combines in cliques, gangs, clubs, ' bunches,' under leaders, who are not elected but who maintain their position by pure physical force and are leaders, by common consent, only so long as they possess the physical force to compel recognition of their domination. As soon as we recognize this race manifestation in the boy, it becomes evident that any attempt to reason the boy out of these natural instincts will be futile and time worse than wasted. Tactful leaders of boys joining in the spirit of organization of small clubs, will get them out into the woods and fields, where each boy may reënact the ancestral struggle which he in his individual development is now repeating." It is at this period of boy-life where the interests of Scouting are most instrumental in doing the boy good and giving him the gang activities he is seeking.

Importance of the Hero-Story and Folk-Tales.

The leader should encourage the boys to read of heroes of his race, or tell stories of these heroes setting forth " their

STORY-TELLING

physical attributes in glowing terms that will make every boy wish to attain as nearly as possible this heroic type of physical manhood." In the campfire and evening story-talks, " the leader has a splendid opportunity — after he has hypnotized the group — to suggest ideals of manhood which will profoundly influence the life of every boy in the group."

These hero stories, the great romance tales of the English and Germans and Northland peoples are replete with the interest-stirring, valorous deeds and fine acts of chivalry. In them is portrayed vividly the lives of strong-principled men in good service. The boy will naturally turn to stories of action in this period of his life, and will obtain much in the reading of these grand folk stories that will build habits of mind and character. The great heroes, King Arthur, Charlemagne, Alexander, Sir Galahad, Launcelot, Beowulf, and others have been so written about in story-prose, poem, and song, that there is a great mass of romance literature left as a heritage to all the ages.

Modern Conceptions and Definitions.

In the modern conception of chivalry as we seek to define its meaning to the Boy Scouts of America and the world, we use the term to include all the precepts of the Scout Law, for in reality chivalry is the ultimate and combined result of all the effects of the Scout Law. As Mr. John L. Alexander says, " to keep the law is to be chivalrous. The Scout Law may be condensed to five words,— Honesty, Courage, Kindliness, Loyalty, and Service. The awakening of these virtues in a boy is to awaken manhood." All of the great principles of life that are character building and creative of service are typified in one or the other of these twelve Scout Law principles; or in these five word-precepts.

" The Daily Good Turn."

The Boy Scout promises to obey these precepts of the Scout Law when he takes the Scout Oath, but he may not fully understand exactly the meaning of each of these different word-terms. This must be finally accomplished by the leadership of the Scout Master through explanation and demonstration, and the encouraged habit of the " Daily Good Turn." It is this latter act which will serve most to enjoin obedience to the Scout Law ideals, and make each a governing and habitual influence in the Scout's life. We therefore, in our desire to have each of the boys do one good turn daily, hope to stamp the principles of chivalry,— the Scout Law Precepts,— upon all his future life.

This " Daily Good Turn," however, should be a spontaneous action of the boy. The Scout does this good turn on his honor as a Scout and his action should always seem most natural. A practice of telling of the act should never be compulsory or encouraged, for such a practice might lead to vaingloriousness or self-conceit and would certainly belittle the value of the act. It is .far better that both the good turn itself and the boy's account of it be wholly spontaneous, and he should be taught that it is not the right thing to speak about his good act unless he is asked about it particularly by his Scout Master or Scout Commissioner.

This " Daily Good Turn," the daily doing of some special act of kindness or politeness, engenders in the boy who faithfully lives up to his Scout Laws, the growing habit of politeness and gentlemanly kindness. " To be thoughtful of others first of all," says Orison Swett Marden, " is a sacred duty which no man who pretends to gentility can afford to ignore." " There is a zest in doing good," says James M. Ludlow, " a spice to the cup you share with another, which was never tasted in a drink of selfish pleasure, not even in the intoxicating draught of secular triumph."

The Habit of Doing Good.

The habit of doing a kind deed every time there has been a chance to do so has been characteristic of many great men. Many are the anecdotes and reminiscences of such kindnesses in the lives of our great Americans. The little courtesies, little kindnesses, pleasant words, genial smiles, good wishes, and good deeds — these form the real basis of the happiness of life. " Once in a lifetime a heroic act may be performed," says George W. Childs, the great philanthropist, " but the opportunity to do one of the little things that make life beautiful comes every day and every hour. If we make the apparently trifling events of life beautiful and good, then our whole existence will be full of harmony and sweetness. Learn to think of others before thinking of yourself, and you will have friends enough, and of the best."

The Golden Rule.

As a Movement we seek to reconstruct the main principles of chivalry, and bring again to mankind the daily habits of doing good deeds which should always be inherent in the nature of a gentleman. To do unto others as you would have others do unto you, the Golden Rule, is the fairest precept ever laid down. " It breathes a spirit of unselfishness," says Orison Swett Marden. " It teaches equality, reciprocity, and self-respect." " The world loves a Lincoln, because he sacrificed self, comfort, ease, health itself, and even jeopardized his life because he loved the people. The world loves a Florence Nightingale because she gave up ease, comfort, and the luxuries of home to administer to the sick and wounded soldiers in the filth and disease of the camp. The world has no use for the man who lives only for himself. It gives its love and laurels to the chivalrous and kind. It gives them to the soldier, the fireman, the nurse, the engineer, the sailor,— every one who gives his life for others. We cannot get the world's love and esteem by paying for it in advance." " God," it is said, " has made selfishness unlovable and shaped the universal heart to despise it, and He has made unselfishness so lovable that we cannot withhold it from our admiration."

Influence of the Home, the School, and the Church.

While the Scout Movement supplies a great need in boy life and the Scout program gives to the boy the gang impetus to progress along lines of efficient training and character building, there can be no sure or important headway without the coöperation of the three greatest influences in the life of man,— the home, the church, and the school. The interested care of father and mother, the conscientious instruction and leadership of the school-master, and the encouraging and refining influence of the religious preceptor form the very bed-rock of character-shaping and man-making, and as these influences coöperate one with another so will the chance be the greater for the fulfillment of their desires and plans,— an upright, moral, conscientious, chivalrous manhood.

To the boy-environment, his home, his school, his church, his neighborhood, his societies, and his playmates has come the Scout Movement influence, not as a competition, but as an aid to all that is best in all of them. It seeks to conserve, to concentrate, and to put into character-shaping application all the corrective training and moral ideals which may be engendered by any other influence in the development of the boy and the shaping of his destiny. All this the Scout Movement does for the boy collectively, but it also comes as a boon to the boy, individually, for he finds in it the answer to his call to nature, the understanding of his adventurous and gang instincts, and the play interests and practical instruction which his continual development demands.

It is with the parents or guardians, the school-teacher, and the religious teacher, therefore, that the Scout Master should hope to find his greatest encouragement in reaching the heart-interest of his boys, and he will continue to do the greatest good for them, as he continues in perfect accord with the desires of the parent, the helpful advice of the school-teacher, and the active coöperation of the minister.

Influence by Example.

The Scout Master should go further than mere coöperation to promote the understanding of moral standards and the practice of chivalric principles. It is a stupid inconsistency to encourage boys to a certain course, and then not follow out the spirit of that same teaching, in daily life and in relations with the boys. The Scout Master will most assuredly make his greatest mistake in seeking to encourage boys to live up to a moral standard which he, himself, does not practice. The boy is direct and penetrating in his mental analysis, and will be quick to recognize the sham of pretension and condemn the method. It is necessary to be sincere and earnest as a leader, then it will not be difficult to enliven the interest of the boy and awaken the spark of aspiration in his mind. " The Scout Oath and Law are the moral ground-work of the whole Movement, and, as such, they are more important than any other branch of Scouting," says Mr. Arthur A. Carey, Chairman of the National Committee on Sea Scouting. " The problem is to make our sense of honor — supported, in the case of every particular man or boy, by his own form of personal religion — so strong and alive that it will furnish the true motive and tone for every outward activity; and, by permeating all other activities with its own spirit make our woodcraft, seamanship, athletics, sports and games, etc., *honorable activities;* that is, activities controlled by fair play and the rules of the game, whatever they may be." " We influence boys more by our example than by our teaching; and, by taking the same oath which they take themselves, we are making the fullest use of the oath in our relations to them. After the oath is once taken, the degree of our influence with the boys will depend, more than anything else, on the extent to which they feel that we practice it in our own lives. This is the real secret of the Boy Scout Movement at its best."

"A Scout is Clean."

"A Scout is clean in body and thought, stands for clean speech, clean sport, clean habits, and travels with a clean crowd." This characteristic, the summation and the result of all the other Scout standards, is, perhaps, what serves best to typify the Boy Scout among boys throughout the country, and the Scout Movement throughout the world. "Clean Sport," says Mr. Jacob A. Riis, in writing of the Boy Scouts, "puts up the bars against gambling, which goes hand in hand with all the mischief of the street and opens the door to every crime on the calendar. The very spirit of the Movement breathes loyalty to authority, to law, a lesson our boys need to learn, East and West, North and South. If this be the quality of its service to our day, what greater could anyone render?"

The Qualities of a Gentleman.

We therefore, seek to teach the boy to be honest to himself and to others; to be attentive, affectionate, benevolent and helpful; to be true, faithful and steadfast; to show courage in valor, perseverance, fortitude, and self-denial; and to at all times be altruistic in spirit in his behavior toward others.

The Important Characteristics of Manhood.

The most important characteristics that make for efficient manhood are faith, unbending rectitude, self-control, a brave, buoyant, religious manliness, and social service for the betterment of humanity. Of all these, "service," says Mr. Alexander, "is the summing up word" for all the principles and ideals of Chivalry. "It is service which speaks the 'daily good turn,' and adjusts the boy to the interest of the community. To be chivalrous in mind and habit is to be a man. A man's job is service. Therefore service is the Scout Master's objective."

The Results of Scoutcraft through Chivalry.

The teachings and principles of Scoutcraft seek to give all this to the boy through leadership and an awakening knowledge and want in him for a truer conception of life and efficient manhood. Faith, rectitude, self-control, service,— these are the attributes by which the Scout Master and efficient leader should seek to inculcate by example in his relations with the boys, in the true spirit of Scouting, true manhood and efficiency.

Chapter X

SUGGESTIVE COURSES OF STUDY

It is stated in Chapter I and also in the special Information Bulletin of the Boy Scouts of America, that a Scout Master need not be an expert in Scoutcraft but that he should at least, by personal study and effort, seek to keep himself enough in advance of his boys to be prepared on the different topics of study as they are considered in the Scout program. It is suggested and expected that, unless the Scout Master is familiar with the activities which have developed in the Scout work, he will obtain the aid of men known to be expert in these various activities. It is expected that he will keep in advance of his boys, so that he may become their actual adviser and teacher, as well as their leader, in all of the things which they do as Scouts. Because of his adult mind and the greater ability, therefore, to grasp and understand ideas, it should be easy for the Scout Master to do this. Because of his mature comprehension of the Scout work and by his own initiative he will easily progress and become conversant with the essentials of the Scout Movement and the Scout program.

It is, however, undeniable that much more can be accomplished along all lines of Scouting if the Scout Master is familiar with or even expert in the various Scout activities. He may have gained this knowledge in previous experience in an out-of-door life, or he may have acquired a great part of it in actual study or through reading. In either case the fact that he has a fair knowledge of the scope of any particular Scout activity will tend, through his leadership, to make the Scouts more proficient along that particular line, and through his initiative, made greater by his familiarity with the subject, it will undoubtedly make all his knowledge a source of greater interest along that line for his boys.

The Boy Scouts of America since its foundation as a Movement in America in 1910, has been gradually developing and expanding in its scope of Scout activities, and little by little it is acquiring a larger field of work; therefore, there is a steadily increasing demand for a greater number of experts or authorities to aid the Scout Master in carrying on his work and giving the necessary instruction to his boys.

It is very true that Scout Masters, as a rule, have not the time to give to this previous preparation as much as they would probably like to do or as the needs seem to demand, so that this expert aid from men familiar with the different kinds of work is almost a necessity. But it is being recognized more and more that for a Scout Master to accomplish his best work, he should have a pretty fair knowledge of the essentials in all the different Scouting activities, such as First Aid, Cooking, Camping, Hiking, Bird Study, Star Study, Animal Study, Signalling, Knot Tying, Physical Geography, Swimming, Tracking, etc.

Because it is being so generally recognized that Scout Masters really need help along this line, a number of cities and districts hold frequent conferences for general discussion of Scout problems and progress, and provide some sort of a lecture course of instruction in the different Scouting activities. This is admirable in its trend and should be most enthusiastically encouraged.

Moreover, because of the growing prominence of Scout work as a means of helping and developing the American boy, and also because of the growing demand for instruction for Scout Masters, a number of the larger schools and universities of the country have been seriously considering the establishing of special courses for Scout Masters, or else providing such work in their curricula for those of their graduates who wish to take up Scout work after leaving college. Also, several of the large schools during the summer of 1913 provided special summer school courses for Scout Masters, which were planned to give the Scout worker a basic idea of all the needful information which he should have to enlarge his knowledge of the Scouting activities, and to enliven thereby the interest of the Scouts along these different lines.

There has also been another phase of this desire for special preparation, which is centered in specially planned summer schools for Scout Masters, giving from two to three weeks in a training course in boy work, camping and Scout activities. There were a number of such camps established during the summers of 1912 and 1913, and it is to be hoped that such training school camps will become more or less permanent institutions and will be productive of the very best results.

The creation of special summer school courses for Scout Masters in colleges and universities will undoubtedly do a great deal of good in supplying the demands for a knowledge of the elements of Scouting and the psychology of boyhood. Certainly, the establishment of such courses either in the summer schools or throughout the year should be most actively encouraged throughout all parts of the country, so that both those men who desire to take up Scout work after their graduation and those Scout workers who may have the chance to take a special course during the summer, may obtain the training they desire and which will help them so greatly in the development of their Scout work.

As a suggestion of what these courses might include, we desire to call attention to the suggestive courses which have been given in several of the summer schools and special training camp schools for Scout Masters.

At the University of Virginia Summer School, at Charlottesville, Va., a two weeks' course was given in a series of lectures covering all the special subjects in Scoutcraft. These were prepared specially for Scout Masters and were delivered from time to time during the course. The members of the faculty were strong men who had been instructing in the subjects they offered for a number of years. There was a tuition of $5.00 for the two weeks' course and this included all special courses, attendance at the lectures on psychology and pedagogy and such other subjects as were of interest and value to Scout workers. It also included all visiting privileges to places of interest. Text books were not used other than copies of the official Scout Handbooks. A pair of good field glasses for observation work in Bird Study and note-books for all lecture-work were also required. The course consisted of lectures on the following subjects:

(1) Scout Law; Principles of the Movement; Organization and Leadership.

(2) Scoutcraft and Scout Mastery; Principles of Pedagogy as applied Leadership; Playground Direction.

(3) Woodcraft; Campcraft; Practical Field Work and Honor Test.
(4) Signalling.
(5) Physical Training; Organization of First Aid Teams, etc.
(6) Hygiene; Physiology; Woodcraft; First Aid; Sports.
(7) Manual Training.
(8) Bird Study; Field Work.
(9) Special lectures on Psychology and other subjects of vital interest to all men interested in work with boys.

At the Summer School at the University of Wisconsin, a session which lasted six weeks, the following course for Scout Masters and other workers interested in the development of boys and girls was given under the Department of Physical Education and Play. This included (1) a course on Scoutcraft and the Camp Fire Girls of America, which in turn included: the Consideration of the Objects and History of the Movement; Woodcraft and Camp Instruction; Signalling and Code Telegraphy; Nature Study; Photography; Life Saving and Scout Games and Sports; Indian Signs; Cookery; Organization and Management of Patrols; and (2) a course on First Aid to the Injured which included: The Treatment of Emergencies and Accidents in the Homes, on the Streets, in Vocational Pursuits and on the Athletic Field; Lectures and Demonstrations; Practical Work in Bandaging; Application of Splints and Tourniquets, and Transportation of the Wounded; Demonstration and Practice of the U. S. and B. S. O. A. Stretcher Drill.

At Cornell University, Ithaca, New York, in a session which lasted from June 24th to July 4th, the following course of lectures was given in the School for Leadership in Country Life:

(1) The Psychology of Leadership.
(2) The Study of Human Nature.
(3) The Pedagogy of Leadership.
(4) Group Organization.
(5) The Development of Rural Character.
(6) The Coôperation and Federation of Rural Social Agencies.
(7) The Farm Boy.

(8)   Rural Play and Demonstrations in the Naming, Explaining and Playing of Games with a Group.

At the University of California, the Summer School offered the following courses which were valuable to Scout Masters and workers with boys:

(1)   First Aid.
(2)   Home Care of Sick.
(3)   Practical Conduct of Play and Athletics.
(4)   Organized Playground Games.
(5)   Recreation Course in Swimming.
(6)   Value of Training for Scout Masters and Boy Workers.
(7)   Social and Recreation Centers.
(8)   Dancing and Its Relation to Physical Education.
(9)   Nature and Function of Play; General Demonstration of Play.
(10)   Physical Georgraphy.
(11)   Applied Psychology.
(12)   Applied Pedagogy.
(13)   Special Course in Agriculture.
(14)   Special Course in Manual Training.

At the Scout Masters Training School, Cos Cob, during the summer of 1912, lectures were given on the following subjects: Scoutcraft; Snakes; Signalling and Map Making and Knot Tying; Sex Education and Hygiene; Character Culture; Camp Sanitation and Hygiene; Boy Life and Leadership; Life Saving; Scout Requirements; Camp Management and Camp Construction; First Aid; Camp Cooking.

At the Summer School at Silver Bay during the summer of 1912, a number of excellent talks were given to Scout Masters and other Boy Workers on the following subjects: Present Social Problems; Eugenics; Approved Methods of Sex Education; Indian Signs; Bird Study and Field Work; Cultivation of the Personal Religious Life of Boys; Community Work and Community Problems; Woodcraft and Scoutcraft activities including Fire Making, Cooking, Knot Tying, Camp Construction, etc.

During the winter of 1911-1912, the Greater Boston Council provided a training course for Scout Masters in the form of series of lectures comprising three different groups. These courses included lectures on the following subjects: Organization; Chivalry and Discipline; Campcraft; First Aid and Public Health; Signalling; Woodcraft;

Hunting with Canoe and Camera; Study of Animal Life; Fire Drill; Fire Fighting; Personal Touch and its Possibilities; Mental Traits of the Boy Scout; Knot Tying and Seamanship; Bird Study and the Protection of Birds; Forestry and Conservation; Play and its Influence on the Development of Character.

The Association Institute of the Y. M. C. A., in Buffalo during 1912, gave a special course for the training and development of Scout Masters and Patrol Leaders. This outline of instruction included the following:

(1) The Object and History of the Boy Scout Movement.
(2) Fundamental Principles of Scoutcraft.
(3) Boy Scout Games.
(4) Camping for Boys.
(5) Camp Leadership, Demonstration, Discipline.
(6) First Aid and Sexological Instruction.
(7) The Scout Oath and the Scout Law.
(8) Scout Regulations.
(9) Scout Organization.
(10) Methods of Coöperation.
(11) Instruction in Signalling and Sign-making.
(12) Leadership Qualifications.
(13) Psychology of the Adolescent.
(14) Play Life and Leisure-time of Boys.
(15) Camping and Out-door Activities.
(16) Physical Development — Periods of Growth and Development of Functions.
(17) The Normal Home Life.
(18) The Religious Life of the Boy.
(19) Juvenile Delinquency.
(20) Principles of Organization for Boys.
(21) Coöperative Work of Boy Workers with Social and Religious Agencies.

In connection with and as a part of the course of education, almost every University and College gives instruction in playground activities and club work for children, as well as classes in child psychology, physiology, and the sciences of the out-doors,— botany, zoology, geology, entomology, surveying, etc. With this already established work in each school, and the foregoing lecture subjects, as suggestions, any college man by arranging his course can prepare himself admirably for taking up the Scout Work.

From these suggestions of what can be obtained as preparatory information in Scout Work, and from what has already been accomplished in the several big schools interested in providing special courses for Scout Masters and other boy workers, it should be easy to draw up and arrange for such a good course in every University or School becoming interested in the development of Scout Work in education.

As a matter of further interest and because we believe that much valuable information can be obtained from special reading and because, too, some Scout Masters may be helped thereby who will not have the opportunity to attend a special training school, we desire to recommend the following books for reading. We believe that the reading of some of these books will do a great deal to give just the information that is needed and that they will help very materially in the progressive development of the Scout Work. We have tried in the compilation of this book list to recommend only such books as can be easily obtainable at the public libraries, or the several books which treat each subject in the clearest and fullest manner and which are at the same time popular in price.

HELPFUL BOOKS FOR SCOUT MASTERS

It will be observed that the books in the following list are arranged in two general groups, one as suggestions for special reading in different phases of Boys Work, and the other as a selected list of several good books for each Merit Badge and kindred subject. This grouping is for the convenience of Scout Masters and other Scout workers, who desire a more thorough knowledge of child-training and the boy problem, or who wish to read up on the Merit Badge subjects. As far as possible, both elementary and advanced books are included for each subject.

These books are not specially recommended as the best books available for the different subjects, but they are all very good and will certainly prove helpful to the Scout Master in his understanding of boy nature, and in his Scout work.

All books listed should be readily obtainable at the public libraries or local book-stores. If the books can not be obtained at home, they can be purchased through the Book Department at National Headquarters. When books are ordered sent by mail, five or ten cents should be added to the price for postage, as only net prices are listed.

1. BOOKS ON BOYS WORK

MORAL EDUCATION

Title	Author	Price
The Boy and the Sunday School	Alexander	$ 1.00
Sunday School and the Teens	Alexander	1.00
Boy Training	Alexander et al.	.75
Adolescent Boyhood	Burr	.75
Applied Ideals in Work with Boys	Crampton, et al.	1.00
Moral Principles in Education	Dewey	.35
Boy Life and Self Government	Fiske	1.00
The Boy Problem	Forbush	1.00
The Coming Generation	Forbush	1.50
Moral Education	Griggs	1.60
A Boy's Religion	Jones	.75
Farm Boys and Girls	McKeever	1.50
Parenthood and Race Culture	Saleeby	2.50
Character Shaping and Character Working	Trumbull	.50

GENERAL EDUCATION

Title	Author	Price
Youth	Hall	1.50
The Boy and His Gang	Puffer	1.00
Habit Formation	Rowe	1.50
Youth and the Race	Swift	1.50
Education	Thorndyke	1.25

SEXOLOGY

From Youth into Manhood	Hall	.50
Reproduction and Sexual Hygiene	Hall	.90
Talks with Young Men	Sperry	.75
The American Boy and the Social Evil	Willson	1.00

PHYSIOLOGY AND HYGIENE

Making Life Worth While	Fisher	1.20
Power and Health Through Progressive Exercise	Flint	1.50
High School Physiology	Hewes	1.00
Exercise and Health	Hutchinson	.70
Preventable Diseases	Hutchinson	1.50
The Body and Its Defences	Jewett	.65
Man—A History of the Human Body	Keith	.50
Health, Strength and Power	Sargent	1.75
Diet in Relation to Age and Activity	Thompson	1.00
Growth and Education	Tyler	1.50
Personal Hygiene	Woodhull	1.00
Care of the Body	Woodworth	1.50

PSYCHOLOGY

Story of the Mind	Baldwin	.35
The Child	Chamberlain	1.50
Psychology—Briefer Course	James	1.60
Psychology (2 Volumes)	James	5.00
Primer of Psychology	Ladd	1.00
The Power of Self-Suggestion	McComb	.50
Psychology	McDougall	.50
Child Problems	Mangold	1.25
Principles of Psychology (2 Volumes)	Spencer	4.00
Mind in the Making	Swift	1.50
Brain and Personality	Thomson	1.20
Psychology of Childhood	Tracy & Stimpfl	1.20

SOCIOLOGY

The Spirit of Youth and the City Streets	Addams	.60
Misery and Its Causes	Devine	.60
The Spirit of Social Work	Devine	1.00
Principles of Sociology	Giddings	3.00
Poverty	Hunter	1.50
Crime and its Causes	Morrison	1.00
How the Other Half Lives	Riis	1.25
Changing America	Ross	1.25
Study of Sociology	Spencer	1.50
Laws of Imitation	Tarde	3.00
The Young Malefactor	Travis	1.50
The New Democracy	Weyl	2.00
Punishment and Reformation	Wines	1.75

PHILOSOPHY

Title	Author	Price
Mystery of Sleep	Bigelow	1.50
Studies of Good and Evil	Royce	1.50
First Principles	Spencer	.60
Introduction of the Study of Philosophy	Stuckenberg	1.50

MANNERS AND CONDUCT

Lessons on Manners	Dewey	.60
Book of Good Manners	Kingsland	1.50
Manners and Social Usages	Sherwood	1.25

II. BOOKS ON MERIT BADGE AND KINDRED SUBJECTS

AGRICULTURE

Principles of Agriculture	Bailey	1.25
Intensive Farming	Corbett	.70
First Principles of Agriculture	Goff & Mayne	.80
Fundamentals of Agriculture	Halligan	1.25
Manual of Farm Animals	Harper	2.00
Soils	Lyon & Fippin	1.75
Farm Grasses of the United States	Spillman	1.00
Elements of Agriculture	Warren	1.10
School Agriculture	Wood	.90

ANGLING

Fishing Kits and Equipment	Camp	.70
Bait Angling for Common Fishes	Rhead	1.25
Book of Fish and Fishing	Rhead	1.50
Fly Rods and Fly Tackle	Wells	1.75

ANIMAL STUDY

Introduction to Zoology	Davenport	1.10
The Animal World	Gamble	.50
Life of Animals—The Mammals	Ingersoll	2.00
Nature's Craftsmen	McCook	2.00
Familiar Animals and Their Field Kindred	Montieth	.50
Evolution	Thomson & Geddes	.50

ARCHITECTURE

History of Architecture (3 Volumes)	Sturgis	15.00
Successful Houses and How to Build Them	White	2.00

ART

How to Draw	Barritt	2.00
History of Art	Goodyear	2.80
Elements of Drawing	Ruskin	.35
History of Greek Art	Tarbell	1.00

ART OF PAINTING

Water Color Painting	Allen	1.25
Manual of Oil Paintings	Collier	.75
Pictorial Composition	Poore	1.50
Text-book of the History of Painting	Van Dyke	1.50

ASTRONOMY

Astronomy for Amateurs	Flammarion	1.50
Popular Astronomy	Flammarion	4.50
An Easy Guide to the Constellations	Gall	.75
A Beginner's Star Book	McKready	2.50

ASTRONOMY—CONTINUED

Title	Author	Price
Astronomy for Everybody	Newcomb	2.00
A Field Book of the Stars	Olcott	1.00
Astronomy with the Naked Eye	Serviss	1.40
Steele's Popular Astronomy	Steele	1.00
Star Atlas	Upton	2.00

ATHLETICS

Rowing and Track Athletics	Crowther & Ruhl	2.00
Exercise and Health	Hutchinson	.70
Track Athletics	Lee	1.25

AUTOMOBILING

Automobile Troubles and How to Remedy Them	Root	1.00
The Gasoline Motor	Slauson	.70
The Automobile—Its Selection, Care and Use	Sloss	.70
Automobiling—Motor Car Principles	Whitman	1.50

AVIATION

Vehicles and the Air	Lougheed	2.50
Aviation Pocket Book	Matthews	1.00
Harper's Aircraft Book	Verrill	1.00
Aerial Navigation	Zahm	3.00

BASKET MAKING

Basket Work	Hasluck	.50
How to Make Baskets	Talbot	1.00
How to Make Baskets	White	1.00

BEE KEEPING

How to Keep Bees	Comstock	1.00
ABC and XYZ of Bee Keeping	Root & Root	1.50

BIRD STUDY

Birds of the United States	Apgar	2.00
Bird Neighbors	Blanchan	2.00
Birds that Hunt and Are Hunted	Blanchan	2.00
Bird-Life	Chapman	2.00
Bird Houses	Dugmore	2.00
How to Study Birds	Job	1.50
The Sport of Bird Study	Job	1.50
Field Book of Wild Birds and Their Music	Mathews	2.00
Birdcraft	Wright	2.00

BLACKSMITHING

(See any good authority on Sloyd-work, Forging, Pattern Making, etc.)

BOOK BINDING

Book-binding and Care of Books	Cockerell	1.25
Book Binding	Hasluck	.50

BOTANY

Practical Course in Botany	Andrews	1.25
Lessons with Plants	Bailey	1.10
Practical Botany	Bergen & Caldwell	1.30
New Manual of Botany	Gray	1.50
Field Botany	Manton	.50

BUGLING

Title	Author	Price
Infantry Drill Regulations, U. S. A.		.50

(See Article on "Bugling" in Boys' Life
  Magazine for January, 1913.)

BUSINESS

Business Letters	Althouse	.50
Principles of Book Keeping and Farm Accounts	Bexell & Nichols	.65
Commercial Geography	Bishop & Keller	1.00
Economics of Business	Brisco	1.50
Essentials of Business Law	Burdick	1.10
Goodwin's Improved Book-keeping and Business Manual	Goodwin	3.00

CAMPING

Camping and Camp Cooking	Bates	.75
Camping for Boys	Gibson	1.00
Camping in the Woods	Gibson	1.00
Harper's Camping and Scouting	Grinnell & Swan	1.75
Book of Camping and Woodcraft	Kephart	1.50

CANOEING AND BOATING

Boat-Building and Boating	Beard	1.00
Harper's Boating Book for Boys	Davis	1.50
Harper's Motor Boating	Davis	.50
Boat Sailing ....:.............	Kenealy	1.00
Canoe and Boat Building	Stephens	2.00

CARVING AND WHITTLING

Woodcarving, Design and Workmanship	Jack ..:..............	2.00
Wood-carving	Jackson	1.20
Elementary Woodwork	Kilbon	.75

CHEMISTRY

Chemistry	Morgan & Lyman	1.25
Elementary Modern Chemistry	Ostwold & Morse	1.00
Inorganic Chemistry	Remsen	3.00
Chemistry of Animal and Plant Life	Snyder	1.50
History of Chemistry	Thorpe	1.50

CIVICS

The Government—What It Is and What it Does	Clark	.75
The American Government	Haskin	1.00
The Government of the U. S.	Moses	1.05
Elements of Civil Government	Peterman	.60
Civil Government	Reinsch	.60
Good Citizenship	Richman & Wallach	.45
Civics	Sherman	.90
The State	Wilson	2.00

CLOTH MAKING

Tailoring	Hasluck	.50
Dyeing and Cleaning of Textile Fabrics	Owen	2.00
Textiles	Woolman & McGowan ..	2.00

CONSERVATION

The Land We Live In	Price	1.50
The Conservation of Natural Resources of the U. S.	Van Hise	2.00

(See also the U. S. Dept. of Agriculture
  Publications.)

COOKING

Title	Author	Price
Camping and Camp Cooking	Bates	.75
The Nutrition of Man	Chittenden	3.00
Camp Cookery	Kephart	.70
Theory and Practice of Cookery	William & Fisher	1.00

CRAFTSMANSHIP

Box Furniture	Brigham	1.60
Art Craft and Cabinet Making	Denning	1.50
Elementary Metal Work	Godfrey	1.50
Bent Iron Work	Hasluck	.50
Glass Writing, Embossing and Fascia Work	Hasluck	.50
Upholstery	Hasluck	.50
Manual for China Painting	Monachesi	1.25
Art Crafts for Beginners	Sanford	1.20
Stained Glass Work	Whall	1.50
Silver-work and Jewelry	Wilson	2.00

DAIRYING

Dairy Cattle and Milk Production	Eckles	1.60
The Feeding of Animals	Jordan	1.50
Diseases of Animals	Mayo	1.30
Dairy Chemistry	Snyder	1.00
Milk and Its Products	Wing	1.50

DEBATING

Argumentation and Debating	Foster	1.25
Parlimentary Usage	Fox	.65
Handbook of Debate	Knowles	.50
Argumentation and Debate	Laycock & Scales	1.10

DRAWING

Elements of Mechanical Drawing	Anthony	1.50
How to Draw	Barritt	2.00
Design in Theory and Practice	Batchelder	1.75
Free-hand Drawing	Cross	.80
Elements of Design	Rimmer	2.00

DRILLS AND MARCHING

School Gymnastics	Bancroft	1.75
Manual of Physical Drill	Butts	1.25
A Manual of Marching	Cornell	.50
Physical Education	Sargent	1.50

ELECTRICITY

Electricity for Everybody	Atkinson	1.50
Electrical Experiments	Bonney	.75
Electrical Engineer's Pocket Book	Foster	5.00
Electric Bells	McKay	.50
Electricity and Locomotion	Whyte	.40
Electricity—What Is It?	Verschoyle	1.00

EXPLORING

Tracks and Tracking	Brunner	.70
Winter Camping	Carpenter	.70
New Rivers of the North	Footner	1.75
Saddle and Camp in the Rockies	Wallace	1.75

FIREMANSHIP

Title	Author	Price
Fighting a Fire	Hill	1.50

FIRST AID

First Aid to the Injured	Doty	1.00
Emergencies	Gulick	.40
American Red Cross Abridged Textbook and First Aid	Lynch	.30
Backwoods Surgery and Medicine	Moody	.70
First Aid in Illness and Injury	Pilcher	2.00

FIRST AID TO ANIMALS

Manual of Farm Animals	Harper	2.00
Diseases of Animals	Mayo	1.50
The Horse	Roberts	1.25

FISH STUDY

Story of Fishes	Baskett	.75
American Fishes	Goode	3.50
West Coast Shells	Keep	2.00
Familiar Fish	McCarthy	1.50
The Book of Fish and Fishing	Rhead	1.50
The Shell Book	Rogers	4.00
Home Aquarium and How to Care for It	Smith	1.20

FORESTRY

Ornamental Shrubs of the U. S.	Apgar	1.50
Trees of the Northern U. S.	Apgar	1.00
North American Forests and Forestry	Bruncken	2.00
Practical Forestry for Beginners in Forestry	Clifford	1.20
Practical Forestry	Fuller	1.50
The Tree Book	Rogers	4.00
The Forester's Manual	Seton	1.00
(See also U. S. Dept of Agriculture Publications.)		

GARDENING

Farm and Garden Rule Book	Bailey	2.00
Manual of Gardening	Bailey	2.00
Practical Flower Garden	Ely	2.00
How to Grow Vegetables and Garden Herbs	French	.50
Gardening for Profit	Henderson	1.50
Our Garden Flowers	Keeler	2.00
Home and School Gardens	Meier	.80
Greenhouse Construction	Taft	1.50
Vegetable Gardening	Watts	1.75

GEOGRAPHY

Commercial Geography	Brigham	1.30
Methods and Aids in Geography	King	1.00
Advanced Geography	Redway & Hinman	1.25
Complete Geography	Tarbell	1.00

GEOLOGY

Geological Story Briefly Told	Dana	1.15
Treatise on Rocks	Merrill	4.00
The Earth	Poynting	.40
Elementary Meteorology	Waldo	1.50
Ice Age in North America	Wright	5.00

GLASS WORKING

Title	Author	Price
Glass	Dillon	7.50
Glass Writing, Embossing and Fascia Work	Hasluck	.50
Stained Glass Work	Whall	1.50

HANDICRAFT

Harper's Indoor Book for Boys	Adams	1.75
American Boys' Handybook	Beard	2.00
Indoor and Outdoor Handicraft	Beard	2.00
Scientific American Boy	Bond	2.00
Handy Farm Devices and How to Make Them	Cobleigh	1.50
Educational Wood Working for Home and School	Park	1.00

HORSEMANSHIP

Riding and Driving	Anderson & Collier	2.00
The Horse—Its Selection, Care and Use	Buffum	.70
The Training and Breaking of Horses	Harper	1.75
The Horse	Roberts	1.25

INSECTS, STUDY OF

Moths and Butterflies	Ballard	1.50
Manual for the Study of Insects	Comstock	3.75
Our Insect Friends and Foes	Crisgin	1.75
Butterfly Book	Holland	3.00
Insect Book	Howard	3.00
American Insects	Kellogg	5.00
Injurious Insects	O'Kane	2.00
Romance of Insect Life	Selous	1.50
Injurious Insects of the Farm and Garden	Treat	1.50
Insects and Insecticides	Weed	1.50

(See also Publications of U. S. Dept. of Agriculture.)

INVENTION

Boys' Book of Inventions	Baker	2.00
Historic Inventions	Holland	1.50
American Inventions and Inventors	Mowry & Mowry	.65
Romance of Modern Invention	Williams	1.50

KEEPING OF PETS

The Airedale	Haynes	.70
The Bull Terrier	Haynes	.70
The Fox Terrier	Haynes	.70
Practical Dog Keeping	Haynes	.70
Taming the Bird Dog	Whitford	1.25

LEATHER WORKING

Leather Working	Hasluck	.50

LUMBERING

Among the Loggers	Burleigh	1.50
Timber Cruising Manual and Record	Chase	1.00
The Tree Book	Rogers	4.00
The Forester's Manual	Seton	1.00

MACHINERY

Harper's Machinery Book for Boys	Adams	1.50
Tools and Machines	Barnard	.60
Home Mechanics for Amateurs	Hopkins	1.50
Mechanical Engineer's Pocket Book	Kent	5.00
Spon's Mechanics' Own Book	Spon	2.50

MAN, STUDY OF

Title	Author	Price
Races of Man	Deniker	1.50
Man's Place in Nature	Huxley	1.25
Physiognomy	Lomax	.50
Phrenology	Olin	.50
Mental Growth and Control	Oppenheim	1.00
History of the Races of Man	Pickering	1.50
The Structure of Man	Wiedersheim	2.60

MAP MAKING

Freehand Lettering	Daniels	1.00
Topographical Drawing	Daniels	1.50
Grammar of Lettering	Lyons	2.50
Manual of Topographical Drawing	McMillan & Smith	2.50
Topographical Drawing and Sketching	Reed	5.00

MASONRY

Stones for Building and Decoration	Merrill	5.00
Concrete Block Manufacture	Rice	2.00
Building Mechanics' Ready Reference Series— Stone and Brick Masons' Edition	Richey	1.50
Modern Stone-Cutting and Masonry	Siebert & Biggin	1.50

METAL WORKING

Minerals and Metals	Goessel	3.00
Bent Iron Work	Hasluck	.50
The Decoration of Metal, Wood, Glass, etc.	Standage	2.00
Silver Work and Jewelry	Wilson	2.00

MINERALOGY

A Catalogue of Minerals	Chester	1.25
Common Minerals and Rocks	Crosby	.60
Minerals and How to Study Them	Dana	1.50
Minerals and Metals	Goessel	3.00
Practical Metallurgy and Assaying	Hiorns	1.50
Mineralogy	Phillips	3.75

MINING

Ore Mining Methods	Crane	3.00
Handbook for Field Geologists	Hayes	1.50
A Manual of Mining	Ihlsend & Wilson	5.00
Hydraulic and Placer Mining	Wilson	2.50

(See also Metal Working, Geology and Mineralogy.)

MISCELLANEOUS

Webster's New International Dictionary		12.00
World Almanac and Encyclopedia		.50
Young Folks' Cyclopedia of Common Things	Champlin	3.00
Proverbs, Maxims and Phrases	Christy	2.50
Chivalry	Cornish	1.25
Manual of Mythology	Murray	1.25
New Imperial Atlas of the World	Rand, McNally	2.50

MUSIC

Encyclopedia of Music and Musicians	DeBekker	3.00
History of American Music	Elson	5.00
What is Good Music	Henderson	1.00
Orchestral Instruments	Mason	1.25

NATURE STUDY

Title	Author	Price
A Short History of Natural Science	Fisher	2.00
Nature's Miracles (3 Volumes)	Gray	1.80
Nature Study and Life	Hodge	1.50
Nature Study	Holtz	1.50
Natural History	Hooker	.90
American Natural History	Hornaday	3.50

ORCHARD GROWING

The Nursery Book	Bailey	1.50
Principles of Fruit Growing	Bailey	1.50
The Pruning Book	Bailey	1.50
American Horticultural Manual (2 Volumes)	Budd & Hansen	3.00
Apple Growing	Burritt	.70
(See also Publications of U. S. Dept. of Agriculture.)		

PATHFINDING

Tracks and Tracking	Brunner	.70
Winter Camping	Carpenter	.70
Book of Camping and Woodcraft	Kephart	1.50
Packing and Portaging	Wallace	.70

PERSONAL HEALTH

(See List I, Physiology and Hygiene.)

PHOTOGRAPHY

The Complete Photographer	Bayley	3.50
Photography for the Sportsman Naturalist	Brownell	2.00
Outdoor Photography	Dimock	.70
Photography	Hasluck	.50
Photography for Young People	Jenks	1.50
Animal Snapshots and How Made	Lottridge	2.00
Practical Pocket-Book of Photography	Vogel & Conrad	1.00

PHYSICAL CULTURE

The Posture of School Children	Bancroft	1.60
School Gymnastics	Bancroft	1.50
Power and Health through Progressive Exercise	Flint	1.50
Exercise and Health	Hutchinson	.70

PHYSICAL GEOGRAPHY

Introduction to Physical Geography	Gilbert & Brigham	1.25
Physical Geography	Gilbert & Brigham	1.25
Glaciers	Hobbs	3.25
Elements of Physical Geography	Hopkins	1.50
Elementary Physical Geography	Tarr	1.40

PHYSICS

Text-Book of Physics	Anthony, Brackett & Magie	3.00
Elementary Book on Electricity and Magnetism	Jackson & Jackson	1.40
Heat	Tait	2.00
Sound	Tyndall	2.00

PHYSIOLOGY

Anatomy of the Human Body	Cleland & McKay	6.50
High School Physiology	Hewes	1.00
Man—A History of the Human Body	Keith	.50

PLAY AND GAMES

Title	Author	Price
Games	Bancroft	1.50
Fencing	Breck	.70
Young Folks' Cyclopedia of Games and Sports	Champlin	3.00
How to Ski	Hack	.50
The Strategy of Tennis	Little	.70
American Playgrounds	Mero	2.00
Golf for Beginners and Others	Whitlock	2.00

PLUMBING

Care of the House	Clarke	1.50
Plumbing	Helyer	1.25
Sanitary Fittings and Plumbing	Sutcliffe	1.60

POTTERY

Pottery and Porcelain	Bohn	1.50
How to Make Pottery	White	1.00

POULTRY KEEPING

Our Domestic Birds	Robinson	1.35
American Poultry Culture	Sando	1.50
Practical Poultry Keeping	Sands	.70
How to Keep Hens for Profit	Valentine	.50
Farm Poultry	Watson	1.50
Profitable Breeds of Poultry	Wheeler	.70

PROTECTION OF BIRDS AND ANIMALS

Farm Friends and Farm Foes	Weed	.90

(See also Publications of U. S. Dept. of Agriculture, and State Publications of Game Wardens' Reports, etc.)

PUBLIC HEALTH

Water and Public Health	Fuertes	1.50
Consumption and Civilization	Huber	3.00
Food Inspection and Analysis	Leach	7.50
Home Care of the Sick	Pope	1.50
Handbook of Sanitation	Price	1.50
Principles of Sanitary Science	Sedgwick	3.00

ROAD BUILDING

Treatise on Roads and Pavements	Baker	5.00
Ravenel's Road Primer	Ravenel	1.00
Highway Construction	Byrne	5.00
Text-Book on Roads and Pavements	Spalding	2.00

SAFETY

Safety	Tolman	3.00
Social Engineering	Tolman	3.00

SCULPTURE

Clay Modelling and Plaster Casting	Hasluck	.50
Clay Modelling	Holland	.75
Text-Book of the History of Sculpture	Marquand & Frothingham	1.50
The Appreciation of Sculpture	Sturgis	1.50

SEAMANSHIP

The Life Boat	Ballantyne	.60
American Yachting	Cautley	2.00

SEAMANSHIP—CONTINUED

Title	Author	Price
Elements of Navigation	Henderson	1.00
Boat Sailing	Kenealy	1.00
Navigation for the Amateur	Morton	.70
The Yachtman's Handbook	Stone	.70

SIGNALLING

Signal Book of the U. S. A. Circular No. 7		.25
Outdoor Signaling	Wells	.70

STALKING

Tracks and Tracking	Brunner	.70
The Deer Family	Roosevelt *et al.*	2.00
The Still Hunter	Van Dyke	1.75

STOCK RAISING

The Horse—Its Selection, Care and Use	Buffum	.70
Manual of Farm Animals	Harper	2.00
The Feeding of Animals	Jordan	1.50
Diseases of Animals	Mayo	1.50

STUDY OF FLOWERS, FERNS, WEEDS, ETC.

Who's Who Among the Ferns	Beecroft	1.00
Field, Forest, and Wayside Flowers	Going	1.50
Moulds, Mildews, and Mushrooms	Underwood	1.50
Practical Guide to Wild Flowers and Fruits	Walton	1.50
Flowers and Ferns in Their Haunts	Wright	2.00

SURVEYING

Engineers' Surveying Instruments	Baker	3.00
The Principles and Practice of Surveying— Elementary	Breed & Hosmer	3.00
Description of Lands	Cautley	1.00
Surveying and Surveying Instruments	Middleton	1.25
The Civil Engineer's Pocket-Book	Trautwine	5.00

SWIMMING

Swimming	Brewster	1.00
At Home in the Wate	Corsan	.75
How to Swim	Dalton	1.00

TAXIDERMY

Taxidermy Without a Teacher	Manton	.50
Taxidermy	Pray	.70
Art of Taxidermy	Rowley	2.00
Amateur Taxidermist	Scorso	.50

TELEGRAPHY

Telegraphy	Herbert	1.50
Elementary Telegraphy	Pendry	1.00
The Storage Battery	Treadwell	1.75

TIMBER CRUISING

Timber Cruising Maunal and Record	Chase	1.00
The Important Timber Trees of the United States	Elliott	2.50

TREE STUDY

Title	Author	Price
Trees of the Northern United States	Apgar	1.00
Trees in Winter	Blakeslee & Jarvis	2.00
Study of Trees in Winter	Huntington	2.50
Our Native Trees	Keeler	2.00
Getting Acquainted with the Trees	McFarland	1.50
The Tree Book	Rogers	4.00

TYPEWRITING

Correspondent's Manual	Hickox	.50
A Manual of Typewriting	Humphrey	1.50

WIRELESS TELEGRAPHY

Wireless Telegraphy	Bottone	1.00
Manual of Wireless Telegraphy and Telephony	Collins	1.50
Electric Waves	Hertz	3.00
Wireless Telegraphy and Telephony	White	1.00

WOODCRAFT

The Book of Camping and Woodcraft	Kephart	1.50
The Book of Woodcraft	Seton	1.75
The Forester's Manual	Seton	1.00
Camp and Trail	White	1.25

CARPENTRY

Constructive Carpentry	King	.70
Elements of Wood-work and Construction	King	.90
Wood-Working for Beginners	Wheeler	2.50
A Shorter Course in Wood-Working	Wheeler	1.50
How to Use Wood-Working Tools	Whitaker	.60

INDEX

339